T0301796

The Crossroads of Globalization

A Latin American View

The Crossroads of Globalization

A Latin American View

Alfredo Toro Hardy

Venezuelan Scholar and Diplomat

 **World Scientific**

NEW JERSEY · LONDON · SINGAPORE · BEIJING · SHANGHAI · HONG KONG · TAIPEI · CHENNAI · TOKYO

Published by

World Scientific Publishing Co. Pte. Ltd.

5 Toh Tuck Link, Singapore 596224

USA office: 27 Warren Street, Suite 401-402, Hackensack, NJ 07601

UK office: 57 Shelton Street, Covent Garden, London WC2H 9HE

British Library Cataloguing-in-Publication Data
A catalogue record for this book is available from the British Library.

THE CROSSROADS OF GLOBALIZATION
A Latin American View

ISBN 978-981-3277-30-4

For any available supplementary material, please visit
https://www.worldscientific.com/worldscibooks/10.1142/11185#t=suppl

Desk Editor: Sandhya Venkatesh

Typeset by Stallion Press
Email: enquiries@stallionpress.com

Printed in Singapore

To the joyful arrival of my new grandson and namesake
Alfredo Daniel.

To my sister-in-law Marcela, with deep affection.

FOREWORD

As so often in the history of mankind, the fate of globalization is currently at stake. It appears, once again, the world is at a crossroad between development and contraction. The economic and political polarizations within or among countries, the rise of populism and the number of unstable democracies, the tensions resulting from migration, inequality, robotization and the demands of emerging economies like China, India and (perhaps) Brazil, require attention. Protectionism, EU-skepticism, nationalism, racism, and rejections of economic multilateralism and multicultural approaches are becoming increasingly important. Only few critical observers are not concerned about the strength and the little understood direction of the world's driving forces.

Globalization is much more than the persistent global integration of the flow of goods, capital and labor. It also merges cultures and enforces permanent and immediate exchange of knowledge and sentiments. Latin America was once forced to accept globalization. The region was unprepared and stumbled, as it accepted globalization. However, the region survived by adapting itself to the inevitable and unavoidable force of globalization. Latin America is an export-based economy. Exiting from globalization may prove to be costly in economic terms for the region. Is this unavoidable or are there alternatives?

Globalization, as it is widely perceived, mainly benefits liberal democracies. But is this really true? The Chinese pro-globalization strategy certainly questions this position. And if globalization collapses in parts of the world, does it make sense to follow like lemmings. Or is it not better to move forward as much as possible, making use of the potentials of globalization? In other words, if the United Kingdom wants Brexit, why should the remaining European Union give up its ambitions?

Globalization will not end, since economic advantages and constraints will enforce its rise, as it materialized over the entire history of mankind. The rise of *homo sapiens* over thousands of years has taken place due to a superior brain, excellent language abilities and a *tremendous talent to collaborate*. But, of course, mistakes of humans and that of political and social organizations can interrupt further globalization for a short period of time. In many ways, the current world is not much more open than it was before World War I. In any case, nations and continents ignoring historical lessons will eventually fall behind.

Alfredo Toro Hardy, a top diplomat and a global scholar, makes use of his deep knowledge and the experience acquired over a long and successful career, to tackle some of the most pressing issues of our time.

I have had the privilege to learn from him during a joint tenure as Rockefeller Foundation Bellagio Center Resident Scholars in 2017. During this period, we had many inspiring and fruitful exchanges about the future of our world and the challenges of life. I was impressed by his deep insights in complex issues and his balanced views on controversial or even explosive topics.

In his own unique way, Alfredo Toro Hardy expresses the perspectives of the Latin American region at the crossroads, by becoming the *Voice of Latin America*. He looks at the current and future challenges faced by the region and the forces that the region is able to mobilize to move along the path of globalization. What is the right path for the Latin American region? As the author states : "Fast moving nations, indeed, appeared to be the better prepared to take advantage from a rapidly moving global market-place." It is 'flexibility' that makes the difference. Investing in technological advances in the fields of knowledge transfer, communications and transportations still make sense. And the region needs to embrace, not fight, these advances.

Alfredo Toro Hardy suggests that "pragmatism, resilience, creativity, imagination, and the joining together of Latin American forces, will guide the region's actions in the foreseeable future." This implies the further strengthening of integration of the Latin American markets, while being open to the global economy. Certainly, institutions like the Inter-American Development Bank or the Economic Commission for Latin America and the Caribbean can serve as instruments that foster this process.

Klaus F. Zimmermann
President of the Global Labor Organization
Professor Emeritus at Bonn University
Co-Director, Population, Development and Labor Economics at the
United Nations University & Maastricht University
Former President of the German Institute
for Economic Research

ABOUT THE AUTHOR

Alfredo Toro Hardy is a Venezuelan retired diplomat, scholar and author. He graduated in Law from the Central University of Venezuela and has master degrees from the University of Pennsylvania and the Central University of Venezuela, postgraduate degrees from the University of Paris II and the Ecole Nationale d´Administration, ENA, and has also completed a course on International Negotiations from Harvard University.

He was one of his country's most senior career diplomats, having served as Ambassador to Washington, London, Madrid, Brasilia, Singapore, Santiago de Chile and Dublin.

As a scholar, he was Director of the Pedro Gual Diplomatic Academy of the Venezuelan Ministry of Foreign Affairs and Associate Professor at the Simón Bolívar University in Caracas, where he was Director of the Center for North American Studies and Coordinator of the Institute for Higher Latin American Studies. He was elected as "Simón Bolívar Chair Professor for Latin American Studies" by the Council of Faculties of the University of Cambridge, but had to decline election due to diplomatic constrains. A Visiting Professor at Princeton University, he also taught at the universities of Brasilia and Barcelona, while lecturing extensively at universities and think tanks from the Americas, Europe and Asia. He has been a member of the Advising Committee of the Diplomatic Academy of London, a Fulbright Scholar and a two-times Rockefeller Foundation Bellagio Center Resident Scholar. He has also been a member of the Bellagio Center Nominations Committee.

He has authored 19 books and co-authored 13 more on international affairs and history. He has received the "Latino Book Award" (best book by an author whose original language is in Spanish or Portuguese) twice at the ExpoBook America fairs celebrated in Chicago and Los Angeles in 2003 and 2008, respectively. His two previous books were published by World Scientific: *The World Turned Upside Down: The Complex Partnership between China and Latin America* (2013) and *Understanding Latin America: A Decoding Guide* (2017). The online cataloguing application LibraryThing chose the first of them as one of the nine basic readings on South America.

He has authored 30 papers in peer-reviewed journals from the Americas, Europe and Asia, including the *Cambridge Review of International Affairs*. He is also a weekly senior columnist at Venezuela's leading newspaper *El Universal* and a frequent contributor to several Latin American and Spanish written media.

He has been a member of the Global Labor Organization, the Iberian-American Network of Sinologists, Chatham House, Canning House and the Windsor Energy Group, among other similar institutions.

ACKNOWLEDGMENTS

I would like to express my deep gratitude to the following persons and institutions whose support has been fundamental in relation to this book.

The Rockefeller Foundation Bellagio Center hosted me for several weeks in the fall of 2017. It was the second time that this institution honored me with one of its prestigious residencies for scholars. The occasion allowed for the conceptualization of the book, and for the preparation of its first draft. The combination of a contemplative atmosphere within the beautiful surrounding of Lake Como, and the interaction with some of the most brilliant minds of the day, was a magical formula for creativeness. Pilar Palacia, Director of the Center, was the perfect hostess and provided its residents with all the necessary support for their work.

The group of people that supported this book by writing its foreword and back cover comments are an outstanding cohort of scholars whose common denominator is their generosity. I feel great pride in having obtained their endorsement.

Gloria Carnevali-Hawthorn, a very solid Cambridge-based author, generously assumed the tedious revision of the manuscript, correcting my English deficiencies while enriching the text with many highly relevant suggestions.

Mary Forero, a respected Venezuelan journalist and diplomat, provided me with invaluable technical support.

Finally, but in a very particular way, I would like to mention World Scientific which, for a third time, shelters a book of mine under its highly prestigious editorial label. Special reference and acknowledgment has to go to Ms. Sandhya Venkatesh of World Scientific, who supported the project of this book since its inception, becoming instrumental in bringing it to the readers.

To all of them, my most sincere thanks.

CONTENTS

INTRODUCTION

The Economist defines globalization as the "global integration of the movement of goods, capital and jobs".[1] Nowadays, two powerful forces measure their strength by acting upon globalization. One of them pushes globalization forward. The other hinders its advance and promotes its decline. At this point in time, it is not clear which of them will end up prevailing.

In which of those directions should Latin America move? Uncertainty hinders the region's strategic vision. If the future entailed a relaunching of globalization, it seems obvious that Latin America should follow along its lines. The most logical move would be to position itself in the best possible terms so as to increase any potential benefits. Even though the region was forced to open itself to globalization, Latin America has fitted well into its rules. The easiest solution would be, then, that this trend prevails.

However, if globalization were to go into a declining phase and an endangered future, Latin America would need to look for other options. To go back to the economic autarky, which prevailed during the many decades that preceded its entrance into the globalized economy, seems highly unrealistic. A certain degree of economic introspection, though, is called for. Whatever the alternatives, a retreating globalization would force a traumatic economic reconversion, and may bring with it the frustrations associated with a lost period. Nonetheless, if international trade

---

[1] "Turning their backs on the world", *The Economist*, 19 February 2009.

were to falter and put the region's opportunities in jeopardy, there would be no option but to change.

Latin America faces, therefore, not only a dramatic uncertainty as a result of forces beyond its control, but also needs to anticipate unforeseen events to the best of its abilities, and react to or act upon them. Strategic reflection becomes imperative in order to manage both uncertainty and the possibility of rapid change. To leave the flux of events in the hands of the market would hamper Latin American countries' ability to deal with them, and, equally crucial, it would limit the possibility of converging actions.

This exercise in strategic reflection implies an immersion in fraught international surroundings, analyzing the forces that push for and against globalization, and trying to measure their respective strength, convergence capacity and potential impact. At the same time, it requires looking into the flaws, weaknesses and contradictions of such forces. With these elements in hand, it might be easier to envisage where the trends are leading to and, by extension, where Latin America might end up standing. Moreover, suggesting initiatives and policies to better protect the interests of the region, while helping to identify which goals to follow, would be part of the reflection.

In short, this book tries to make sense of events amid the current conundrum, while searching a path for Latin America. Written with Latin American decision makers, scholars and public intellectuals in mind — for many of whom English is a familiar second language — this book is equally useful to a much wider audience. Readers interested in subjects like globalization, the converging and diverging forces that surround it, the future of China and India, the South China Sea controversies, Asia's expanding middle classes and the Western world declining ones, the economic polarization in the United States, populism and the political rage that feeds it, Putin and Trump, the return of the European extreme left or the incoming disruptive impact of the Fourth Industrial Revolution will also find fresh analysis and information on these topics. Moreover, they will be able to look at these subjects from an interrelated perspective, thus acquiring a better understanding of them.

CHAPTER ONE

LATIN AMERICA: A BACKGROUND

Since the beginning of their independent life, Latin American countries opted for free trade and access to international capital markets. As the new states began to stabilize, the ruling elites decided that the future development of the region was to be linked to the export of natural resources and the import of needed capital goods. From the mid-nineteenth century onwards, Latin American exports began to expand, bringing with them economic growth. Between the 1860s and the 1910s, Latin American grew more than other peripheral regions and kept pace with European growth, even though at a lesser pace than the United States or Germany.

Raw Materials Bonanza

According to Victor Bulmer-Thomas *et al.*: "The integration of the Latin American economies between 1850 and World War I was unprecedented in scale and complexity. The fall in transportation costs attributable to technological innovations was the key factor in Latin American exports reaching the European and North American markets ... This became possible through the dramatic fall in ocean freight rates and land transportation costs from the interior to the ports made possible by the construction of a very wide railway network."[1]

---

[1] Victor Bulmer-Thomas, John, H Coastworth and Roberto Cortes Conde, *The Cambridge Economic History of Latin America, Volume II: The Long Twentieth Century* (Cambridge: Cambridge University Press, 2006), p. 4.

Not surprisingly, some of the countries of the region were among the richest of the world at the time. Between 1870 and 1913, Latin American GDP grew 3.5 percent while the world GDP grew 2.1 percent.[2] Brazil generated 70 percent of the planet's coffee exports, while in terms of meat, cereal and wool, Argentinean exports had very few competitors worldwide. Uruguay, a much smaller country than Argentina, was also booming with the same export commodities.

With the introduction of cold storage, during the first decade of the century, profits from meat exports multiplied by fourfold. On the other hand, silver export booms in Mexico, Peru and Bolivia had their equivalent in copper export booms in Chile and Peru. But there was also saltpeter in Chile and Peru. The latter also exported sugar and guano. Sugar was also prevalent in the tropical countries in the northern part of the region, as was also the case of bananas.[3]

World War I, though, interrupted the bonanza brought up by this first era of globalization, both in Latin America and elsewhere. However, at the end of the 1920s, Latin American countries had been able to reestablish the primacy of their export sector. Capital streams began flowing again into Latin America, but this time not so much from Great Britain, as had been the case since Independence, but mainly from the United States.

And then, unexpectedly, the Great Depression of the 1930s hit the region. The fragility of the economic world order to which Latin America had pledged itself, not only as a reliable commodities supplier but also as a relevant importer of manufactured goods, was becoming too evident. Indebted and in bad economic situation as a result of the global crisis, the primary productive sector had to be subsidized by the State. Predictably, industrialization began to be seen as the appropriate medicine to provide more stability and a firmer economic ground. A light industry thus began to take shape in the region, in order to compensate for the import needs left uncovered by the international crisis.

---

[2] Claudio Loser, *The Impact of Globalization on Latin America Task Force* (Miami: University of Miami Center for Hemispheric Policy, 2012), p. 4.
[3] Tulio Halperin Donghi, *História Contemporánea de América Latina* (Buenos Aires: Alianza Editorial, 1997).

The Import-Substituting Industrialization

World War II gave new impetus to this industrialization process, which, even if relevant for Latin American standards, was still modest for international ones. Especially so in view of the limitations for importing capital goods. The aim was to manufacture goods that could no longer be imported. Compensating for the shortcomings of its primary industry was no longer necessary as, due to the war, the export of commodities began to boom again.

Argentina, which took the lead in this area, attained impressive results. In 1947, its industrial sector showed a bigger percentage of the country's GDP than its primary sector. At the end of the war, what was already a fact — the import-substituting industrialization process — began to be conceptualized. In 1948, indeed, the theoretical framework for this process began to take shape. Two economists and one organization were ultimately responsible for it. Raul Prebisch and Sir Hans Wolfang Singer were the economists. The organization entrusted with this endeavor was the Economic Commission for Latin America (ECLA), an institution born in 1948 under the umbrella of the United Nations.

Prebisch, a well-known Argentinean economist, had been the first General Director of the Argentinean Central Bank. In 1949, while working for ECLA, the Secretary General of this organization asked him to write an analysis on the deterioration of the terms of trade of raw materials. Soon after he had written the first draft of a long text, he came to read Singer's recent paper "Post-war relations between under-developed and industrialized countries". This paper complemented his own ideas.

As a result, Prebisch changed his first version and introduced fresh material in which he extensively quoted Singer in his conclusions. The latter, a German, had been a protégé and a pupil of both Schumpeter and Keynes and was one of the first economists at the new Economics Department of the United Nations. The result was a 1949 book entitled *The Economic Development of Latin America and Some of its Main Problems*. Without collaborating directly, and having arrived to similar conclusions separately, both economists gave birth to what was to be called the Prebisch–Singer hypothesis.

The above proposal was to be extensively spread throughout the region by ECLA. Not surprisingly, given that between 1950 and 1963 its Secretary General would be Prebisch himself. Under the auspices of this institution, a group of outstanding Latin American economists would follow suit, elaborating on the need of developing a substitutive manufacturing base for the region.

The so-called "hypothesis" was made up of two sub-hypotheses. The first had to do with the fact that the prices of primary products had a declining tendency in time. Countries specialized in their production were thus condemned to lag behind the industrial ones, and the terms of trade between them would be detrimental to raw material producers. As for the second one, as Daniel Yergin and Joseph Stanislaw point out: "They argued that the world economy was divided into the industrial 'center' — the United States and Western Europe — and the commodity producing 'periphery'. The terms of trade would always work against the periphery".[4]

In order to face this double-negative situation ECLA's economists, with Prebisch at their helm, argued that the answer was to create a substitutive manufacturing base. In Daniel Yergin and Joseph Stanislaw words: "So instead, the periphery would go its own way. Rather than exporting commodities and importing finished goods, these countries would move as rapidly as possible towards what was called 'import-substituting' industrialization. This would be achieved by breaking the links to world trade through high tariffs and other forms of protectionism...Currencies were overvalued, which cheapened equipment imports needed for industrialization; all other imports were tightly rationed through permits and licenses".[5]

Unlike Asia, where an "outward-oriented industrial growth" would be emphasized since the 1960s, Latin America visualized industrialization as an "inward-oriented process". The region would manufacture products domestically instead of importing them. "By 1955 the contribution of manufacturing to real GDP had overtaken agriculture".[6]

---

[4] Daniel Yergin and Joseph Stainslaw, *The Commanding Heights* (New York: Simon & Schuster, 1998), p. 234.

[5] *Ibid.*

[6] Victor Bulmer-Thomas, *The Economic History of Latin America since Independence,* Chapter 1 (Cambridge: Cambridge University Press, 2003), p. 204.

Two Big Flaws

The import-substituting industrialization presented two important flaws, which in time would prove to be very costly to the region. The first was to visualize this process as permanent in nature. In doing so, they did not proceed like all major developed economies have done, that is, using its interventionist economic policies to promote industrialization and protect national companies until they were prepared to compete internationally.

Thus, domestic industries were indefinitely isolated from international competition. The "industries in their infancy" — a protectionist thesis developed by Alexander Hamilton at the end of the eighteenth century — assumed a permanent character in the Latin America of the twentieth century. This implied creating a gap between highly competitive companies abroad and highly protected ones inside. As long as domestic companies were cut off from the outside world by thick walls, there was no problem. Nonetheless, if those walls were ever to suddenly fall, industrial massacre would follow.

The second flaw was that the dependency on commodities continued to be fundamental, as they were the ones generating the currency that nurtured this whole process. Indeed, while local manufactures were sold inside the protected trade area, commodities were sold abroad, thus becoming the fundamental source of currency. In this way, the whole import-substituting industrialization structure became dependent on the same commodities from which it wanted to gain independence.

Notwithstanding these flaws, the system provided important results. Some qualified opinions can attest to it. According to Kevin Gallager and Roberto Porzecanski, "It will be easy and tempting to look backward to the period roughly between 1940 and 1970. During that period Latin America was indeed able to build innovation and industrial capabilities. Indeed, that period was certainly the 'golden age' of economic growth in Latin America that is yet to be matched".[7]

Joseph Stiglitz's opinion goes in the same direction: "In earlier decades, Latin America had had notable success with strong government interventionist policies...focused more on the restriction of imports than

---

[7] Kevin P Gallager and Roberto Porzecanski, *The Dragon in the Room* (Stanford: Stanford University Press, 2010), p. 140.

on the expansion of exports. High tariffs were placed on certain imports, to encourage the development of local industries — a strategy often referred to as import substitution".[8] Greg Grandin, on his part, adds: "If we take Latin America in its entirety we find that between 1947 and 1973 (the state-dominance stage) the per capita income grew by 73% in real terms".[9]

The success of the model, based on the Keynesian doctrine, mirrored the unprecedented prosperity that these policies brought to the Western World between 1945 and 1975. However, between 1950 and 1973 Latin America grew even faster than the world average: 5.4 percent versus 4.9 percent. Moreover, in 1981, shortly before the system began to crumble, Latin America's share of the world´s GDP was 11 percent, while its GDP per capita exceeded the world's average by 10 percent during the third quarter of that year.[10]

Collapse

The collapse of the import-substituting industrialization model would be closely linked to the end of Keynesianism in Western economies, where a combination of inflation and stagnation, known as stagflation, would lift von Hayek's neoliberal ideas from the dusted bookshelf.

The inherent vulnerabilities within the import-substituting industrialization model were ready to concatenate when the right set of international conditions appeared. And they did as a result of the debt crisis. It all began during the 1970s, when an international banking system, overflowed with petrodollars resulting from the sudden hike of oil prices, devoted itself to grant plentiful loans.

This easy access to international credits, actively promoted by lenders themselves, was seen by Latin American governments as an excellent opportunity to invest in infrastructure and the modernization of its State industries. As a consequence of these policies, the region got greatly indebted. Nonetheless, this did not seem to be a problem as the conventional wisdom

---

[8] Joseph Stiglitz, *Making Globalization Work* (London: Allen Lane, 2006), p. 35.
[9] Greg Grandin, *Empire's Workshop: Latin America, the United States and the Rise of the New Imperialism* (New York: Metropolitan Books, 2006), p. 198.
[10] Claudio Loser, *op. cit.*, p. 2.

of the day assured that the interest rates would remain low for the foreseeable future.

But they did not. As Joseph Stiglitz points out: "In 1980, fighting its own problem of inflation, the United States initiated interest rate increases that climbed to over 20 percent. These rates spilled over to loans to Latin America, triggering the Latin American debt crisis of the early 1980s, when Mexico, Argentina, Brazil, Costa Rica, and a host of other countries defaulted on their debt".[11]

The debt crisis hit Latin America very hard, and between 1975 and 1982 the regional debt increased from US$45.2 billion to US$333 billion.[12] Needless to say, this increase had much to do with the snowball effect derived from the combination of interest rates over 20 percent and short-term loans and credits needed to pay the old debt.

But at the same time that interest rates were hiking, the price of primary products was going down. The reasons behind these two phenomena were very much the same. Faced with the hike in the oil prices in 1979, the new governments of Ronald Reagan and Margaret Thatcher decided to fight inflation not only through monetary tools (such as interest rate increases) but also by reducing fiscal expenditure.

These policies resulted in a recession that increased unemployment and precipitated the fall in the demand, and by extension in the prices, of commodities. Such an unexpected downturn in the prices of primary products gravely affected the capacity of Latin American governments to meet their debts. While the sources of currency income were dropping significantly, the external debt was growing exponentially as a result of the interest rates hike.

This situation of extreme weakness was compounded by the appearance of a new economic paradigm brought in, again, by the duo Reagan–Thatcher: neoliberalism. Just when Latin American governments were in need of renegotiating their debts and acquiring fresh loans to pay for the old ones, they were confronted with this all-powerful ideology. With its negotiating leverage collapsed, the region had no other option but to bow to the so-called Washington Consensus and to the directives of its executive arm, the International Monetary Fund (IMF).

---

[11] Claudio Loser, *op. cit.*, p. 36.
[12] Daniel Yergin and Joseph Stanislaw, *op. cit.*, p. 234.

Falling off a Cliff

The Washington Consensus was the result of the converging positions of a group of institutions based in Washington D.C., chiefly the U.S. Treasury Department, the World Bank and the IMF. Its agenda included structural reforms such as trade liberalization, privatization of public assets, economic deregulation, fiscal discipline, fiscal reform, etc.

The acceptance of this agenda became unavoidable given the confluence of several factors. First: "As part of the rescue packages, the International Monetary Fund became…a sort of international bankruptcy receiver".[13] As such, indebted countries willing to renegotiate their debts had to accept the IMF conditions. Second, because international credibility or ostracism parameters were tied to the acceptance or rejection of the neoliberal credo. Third, because of the influence of the so-called "Chicago boys" (a term broadly applied to Ivy League graduates imbued with market economy ideas) in leading economic positions within Latin American governments.

All of the above led to the sudden and widespread opening of Latin American trade barriers. According to Richard Baldwin: "In Latin America, especially South America, the tariff cuts look like a river falling off a cliff in the late 1980s or early 1990s".[14] This forced a totally unprepared industrial sector to compete with the most efficient companies of the world.

The impact that this measure had on employment was clearly described by Joseph Stiglitz: "It is easy to destroy jobs, and this is often the immediate impact of trade liberalization, as inefficient industries close down under pressure from international competition. IMF ideology holds that new, more productive jobs will be created as the old inefficient jobs that have been created behind protectionist walls are eliminated. But that is simply not the case".[15] As for the industries themselves, Rubens Ricupero, Secretary General of the United Nations Commission for Trade and Development (UNCTAD), pointed out that this sudden opening of

---

[13] Daniel Yergin and Joseph Stanislaw, *op. cit.*, p 132.
[14] Richard Baldwin, *The Great Convergence: Information Technology and the New Globalization* (Cambridge: The Belknap Press of Harvard University Press, 2016), p. 101.
[15] Joseph Stiglitz, *Globalization and its Discontents* (London: W.W. Norton & Company, 2002), p. 59.

protective barriers resulted in an accelerated and premature disappearance of an important part of the Latin American industrial base.[16] Transforming the infant-industry logic into a mature-industry logic that indefinitely isolated local industries from outside competition had indeed been a huge mistake. But the corrective medicine should never have been the sudden opening of trade barriers. As Joseph Stiglitz remarks: "The most successful developing countries, those in East Asia, opened themselves to the outside world but did it slowly and in a sequenced way. These countries…dropped protective barriers carefully and systematically".[17]

No one doubts that Latin America had an important catch up process ahead. However, the reform process should have been guided by common sense and not by ideology. If there was much to be dismantled, there was much to be preserved as well. What happened instead was equivalent to suddenly throwing down the protective walls of the citadel to let Attila's Huns in. Companies that had thrived under the old system began to be slaughtered in mass.

The Ideological Juggernaut

On the other hand, and also under the ideological commands of the Washington Consensus, an irrational privatization process of state-owned companies took place. Again in Joseph Stiglitz words: "Unfortunately, the IMF and the World Bank have approached the issues from a narrow ideological perspective — privatization was to be pursued rapidly…those who privatized faster were given the high marks".[18] As a result of this fast paced logic, the very same State companies and public utilities whose expansion had indebted the governments of the region started to be sold at laughable prices. Usually, the beneficiaries of this process were transnational corporations.

Hence, while Latin American governments were facing a foreign debt that had grown all out of proportion in relation to the original loans, the assets that had been developed with them were being bargained to the

---

[16] Alfredo Toro Hardy, Foreword, in *¿Tiene Futuro América Latina?* (Bogotá: Villegas Editores, 2004).

[17] Joseph Stiglitz, 2002, *op. cit.*, p. 60.

[18] *Ibid.*, p. 54.

transnational capital. This involved a net and massive transfer of wealth overseas.

An additional part of the problem had to do with the fact that privatized companies were disconnected from their traditional domestic suppliers and reconnected to intra-corporative supply chains. As a result, national productive chains were totally disrupted and supplanted by foreign supply chains. Big local companies, precisely those bought by foreign corporations, ceased to be the turbines of industrial development that they had been so far and became disconnected islands within their domestic economies. Amid these islands, numerous medium- and small-sized enterprises hitherto linked to them began to disappear.

Not surprisingly, the effects of the neoliberal policies were devastating for the Latin America industrial base, which between 1980 and 2002 suffered a significant contraction. In Argentina, the industrial participation in the country's GDP went down from 29 percent to 15 percent, in Brazil from 31 percent to 19.9 percent, in Uruguay from 28.6 percent to 17 percent, in Peru from 29.3 percent to 14.4 percent, in Colombia from 21.5 percent to 13.5 percent and in Ecuador from 20 percent to 7 percent.[19]

But not only was the industrial base shrinking, the technological capabilities that had been associated with those industries dramatically contracted as well. During the import-substituting industrialization phase, great effort in Research and Development had taken place. The industrial development strategy had indeed required the build-up of endogenous technological capacities. Through the implementation of the Washington Consensus, not only were regional R&D efforts abandoned but the whole idea of generating local technology was begun to be seen as outmoded.

Henceforward, imported technology became the aim, as it was assumed that this would naturally come by way of trade or foreign direct investments. According to the neoliberal set of beliefs, the market would automatically allocate such capabilities. But, as it happened in Mexico, the most extreme showcase in this matter, more than 40 years of sustained technological efforts were swept away and supplanted by an "enclave" assembly sector.

---

[19] Emir Sader, Ivana Jinkings, *et al.*, coord., *Latinoamérica: Enciclopedia Contemporánea de América Latina y El Caribe* (Madrid: Clacso-Ediciones AKAL, S.A., 2009), p. 471.

It must be added that the most serious impact of these reforms was felt in the social area. In Greg Grandin's terms: "If we take Latin America in its entirety we find that between 1947 and 1973 (the state-dominance stage) the per capita income grew by 73% in real terms. By contrast, during the era of the free market fundamentalism, the average per capita income stagnated at 0%. By the late seventies, 11% of Latin Americans could be considered as poverty-stricken...By 1996, the number of indigents rose to a third of its total population. That is, 165 million people. And by 2005, 221 million people lived below the poverty line, an increase of 20 million in just a decade".[20]

Although positive in macroeconomic terms, neoliberal policies had a profoundly regressive effect for Latin America's industrial and technological sectors (not to speak of its huge social costs). Had Latin America followed a common-sense approach to reform, as was the case in China during the same period, the history of the region would have evolved in a very different direction.

If instead of applying a shock therapy to change the system, they had adopted the famous economic reform dictum by Deng Xiaoping, of "crossing the river by feeling the stones", many good things could have been preserved. At the same time, inefficiencies could have been purged in a rational way. However, to do that became impossible as neoliberals, with their "level playing field" notion, rejected as unfair competition the natural tools of industrial policies.

The Chinese Avalanche

While Latin America witnessed during those years an accelerated downward tendency, China showed a spectacular climbing one. These reverse tendencies would become evident when China and Latin America's roads crossed each other at the beginning of the millennium. When Latin America's industries were beginning to redress from the impact caused to them by the neoliberal tsunami, the avalanche of the Chinese low-cost products came along. It was a second shock that pushed to the corner those Latin American industries that had been able to survive.

---

[20] Greg Grandin, *op. cit.*, p. 198.

China, though, had a redeeming virtue that the Washington Consensus never did: it was a voracious consumer of commodities. Thanks to this voraciousness, the price of natural resources began booming everywhere. According to the IMF, between 2002 and 2006 the general index of commodities worldwide, excluding oil, was increased by 60 percent in real terms. Moreover, in the areas of oil and metals, such an increase reached 150 percent and 180 percent, respectively. Conversely, before the China-led boom and for the five previous decades the price of commodities had been falling at an annual rate of 1.6 percent in relation to manufactured goods.[21]

While the regional industrial base got hammered, the commodities sector began thus to blossom in an unexpected way. For this sector, a gigantic market suddenly appeared out of the blue. In Kevin Gallager and Roberto Porzecanski words: "Indeed, 70 percent of the growth in Latin American countries exports was due to growth in commodities exports, and commodities exports comprised 74 percent of all Latin American countries growth. China had both indirect and direct effects in this trend. Directly, Latin American countries exports to China have increased 370 percent since 2000...Indirectly, Chinese consumption of global commodities was making them scarcer and boosting global prices and leading somewhat to more Latin American countries exports".[22]

Unfortunately, there was a price tag attached to this bonanza. The countries of the region that benefited from the Chinese market region had to redefine their role within a new international division of labor. This meant that a substantial part of Latin America, essentially all of South America, had to go back in time to the beginning of the twentieth century, when it shone as a producer of commodities. With the exception of Brazil, and to a smaller extend Argentina, which still retained a respectable manufacturing base, manufactures almost disappeared from South America's export offer. And even in Brazil and Argentina, commodities assumed a clear lead within their export offer.

But commodities exporters, within the region, were not the only ones who had to redefine their role in this new international division of labor. Mexico, the Dominican Republic and Central America also had to find a

---

[21] Bernardo Kosacoff and Sebastián Campanario, *La Revalorizacion de las Materias Primas y sus Efectos en América Latina* (Santiago de Chile: CEPAL, mayo 2007), p. 11.
[22] Kevin P Gallager and Robert Porzecanski, *op. cit.*, p. 37.

new one. They specialized in labor-intensive assembly lines, transforming their economies in what Ian Bremmer categorized as "shadow states". By this he meant countries that have tied their economic possibilities almost entirely to a single powerful partner.[23] For these Latin American countries, the dominant partner is the United States.

Latin America's Dichotomy

The Inter-American Development Bank refers to this dichotomy as Mexican-type countries and Brazilian-type ones. As mentioned, Central America and the Dominican Republic joined Mexico within the first group, whereas South America plus Cuba conformed to the second one.[24] It has to be added that this categorization, although didactic, is not entirely accurate. Mexico is also a relevant exporter of oil, in the same manner in which an important percentage of Brazil's exports is represented by manufactures (including airplanes). However, the distribution of their respective exports does indeed reflect the predominance of manufactures or commodities.

For both groups, nonetheless, economic subsidiarity to others became a matter of survival. However, even if highly dependent on China and always subjected to the volatility in the price of commodities, the Brazilian-type economies have wider economic options than the Mexican-type ones. Natural resources can sell everywhere, whereas the shadow nature of the Mexican-type countries in relation to the United States leaves them with lesser room for maneuver. A sneeze in Washington can cause them pneumonia.

Both Brazilian-type and Mexican-type economies have had to adapt to these new realities. How satisfactory or unsatisfactory have they been? Let us begin with the Brazilian group. The complexity or the value added of the commodity business sector should not be downplayed. To be globally competitive in the commodities sector is by no means an easy or elemental task. According to the World Bank: "Latin American countries

---

[23] Ian Bremmer, *Every Nation for Itself: Winners and losers in a G-Zero World*, (New York: Portfolio, 2012).

[24] Alejandro Izquierdo and Ernesto Talvi, coord., *One Region, Two Speeds?* (Washington D.C.: Inter-American Development Bank, March 2011).

have been not only moving towards the production of more sophisticated and higher-value-added products within its natural resource based industries but clustering and production chains are being developed".[25]

On the other hand, it could be argued that dependence on commodities just reflects a classical comparative advantage situation. In pure David Ricardo's terms, every country or region has to emphasize those productive sectors where they can be more competitive, letting their own consumers benefit from imports coming from lower-cost producers. If as a result of this work specialization the economy grows, positive trade balances are obtained, strong accumulation of reserves takes place and domestic consumers have access to more affordable goods, then the benefits would seem to exceed the costs of deindustrialization.

This is the line of argument of the World Bank, for which regional dependence on commodities should not be seen as a "curse" but, much to the contrary, as a development opportunity. For this institution, there is not much evidence to support the idea that commodities represent an area of slow growth in productivity or that they have a lower potential for generating a positive economic outcome. What matters, in the long run, is being able to administer well the periods of bonanza. In other words, to invest the resulting incomes in human development, infrastructure and innovation, so as to guaranty a sustainable growth.[26] Australia, Canada or Norway, which are also commodities producers, have done precisely that with very good results.

Conversely, though, it can be argued that commodity prices are by definition highly volatile, which places natural resource producers at the mercy of economic cycles and international shocks beyond their control. Not surprisingly, since 2013 the commodities boom ceased, thoroughly affecting Latin American producers. In Francisco Rojas Aravena's words: "The export value of the region's products shows an important contraction which, according the Inter-American Development Bank, reached 14%. The most affected countries by such export contraction have been those from South America, whose basic products, oil and mining products have

[25] World Bank, *Latin America and the Caribbean's Long Term Growth: Made in China?* (Washington D.C.: The World Bank, 2011), p. 37.
[26] Emily Sinnot, John Nash and Augusto de la Torre, *Natural Resources in Latin America and the Caribbean: Beyond Booms and Busts?* (Washington D.C.: The World Bank, 2010).

fallen as a result of Asia's lower demand. In 2015 South American exports reached minus 21%, a rate that doubles that of world trade".[27]

As Guadalupe Paz expresses: "Although the China-driven commodity boom clearly helped the region weather the global financial crisis that erupted in 2008–2009, Latin America's policymakers are increasingly preoccupied with the unbalanced nature of their trade relationship with China, particularly as the Asian giant faces an economic slowdown and global commodity prices are on a downward trend".[28]

But not all commodities have been equally affected by the downturn of global prices since the boom ended. According to Anthony Spanakos, the downturn percentage has been the following: energy products −31%; base metals and minerals −18%; agricultural products −4%.[29] Hence, not all Latin American commodity exporters have been equally affected. Venezuela tops the list of the most affected as the overwhelming majority of its exports come from oil, while Argentina and Uruguay are on the safer side with a majority of their exports coming from the food sector. Brazil is punished more in energy, metals and minerals than in agricultural products, but is in a better position than Venezuela thanks to its wider offer of commodities. Hence, a larger diversification within the commodities sector becomes an additional hedge against the volatility in prices.

Even if far from ideal, the position of commodities producers can be enhanced if a group of commonsensical measures are taken. These would include administering well their periods of bonanza as mentioned earlier; creating sovereign wealth funds during their fat cow periods, so as to have a secure source of income during their lean cow ones; and diversifying their natural resources export offer so as to mitigate the impact of downturn in prices, as not all commodities are equally affected by them.

---

[27] "América Latina en un ciclo de baja, pero con señales esperanzadoras", *Pensamiento Iberoamericano* (Tercera Época, enero, 2016), p. 58.

[28] Guadalupe Paz (eds.), "Assessing Latin America's relations with the Asian giants" in, *Latin America and the Asian Giants: Evolving Ties with China and India* (Washington D.C.: Brookings Institution Press, 2016), p. 1.

[29] Anthony Spanakos, *"One Tightening Belt, One Bumpy Road: Chinese Extension to Latin America at a Time of Increased Political and Market Risk,"* Lecture delivered at the East Asian Institute, National University of Singapore, 9 June, 2017.

The position in which Mexican-type economies find themselves could be less promising. Having gone into the manufacturing sector, they entered into direct competition with China, which turned out to be a true nightmare. Not even China's current contraction in the labor-intensive manufacturing sector represents a solution for them. Other Asian economies, such as Vietnam, Indonesia or the Philippines, are firmly taking control in this area. Asia's supply chain of production is simply unbeatable. Not even geographical proximity and free trade agreements with the United States, have proven to be sufficient to overcome the challenges faced.

Their options are limited by the fact that they are not able to compete at the top, through domestically generated high-tech manufactures, but at the same time they have to retain competitiveness in the crowded labor-intensive one. Under continuous pressure by Asia's lower wage economies, their position is always stressed.

Mexico exhibits a whole array of high-tech export products, but this is still a foreign-generated technology. But still, Mexico is in a totally different league from Central American countries and the Dominican Republic. The country not only has an impressive number of engineers graduating every year but has also been able to create five important technological clusters in the State Queretaro.

The country's positioning in the aeronautical sector, as represented by the fact that both U.S.'s Boeing and Canada's Bombardier manufacture there, is very significant. The same can be said in relation to the thriving auto sector. This has been helped by transport costs from Asia and by NAFTA rules of origin. As Kevin Gallager and Roberto Porzecanski point out: "Mexico is losing out in sectors abundant in unskilled labor where value-to-transport costs are cheap. It is holding steady, instead, in assembly sectors where transport costs are more significant and NAFTA's rules of origin serve as local content rules mandating that production stay in North America".[30]

However, it cannot be forgotten that these are but foreign assembly plants dependent on foreign-generated technology. At the end of the day, as Jose Luis de la Cruz, Director of the Mexican Institute for Industrial

---

[30] Kevin P Gallager and Roberto Porzecanski, *op. cit.,* p. 93.

Development and Economic Growth, expresses: industrial development in his country is based on labor-intensive manufacturing with limited value added and massive imports of intermediary supplies.[31]

Window of Opportunity and Closing Doors

For both Mexican-type economies and Brazilian-type economies, stepping into the international tradable services sector looks like a very good option. Indeed, this could become a window of opportunity to overcome many of region's current limitations. This is a sector particularly relevant within the global chains of value. Several developing economies, mainly India, have proven the relevance of this area as an instrument of economic growth. Latin America seems well positioned to play an important role in this area for the following reasons.

First, Latin America is part of Western civilization and, for all its particularities, shares the same heritage and background. If cultural affinity is a relevant consideration, Latin America enjoys a comparative advantage for companies from the Western world.

Second, Latin America has a strong online culture. According to Basil Puglisi, a digital brand marketing consultant formerly with AOL: "Although Latin America makes up only 8.2% of the world's population, they are the second largest consumer of social media. The online behavior of Latin Americans is evolving right along with the rest of the world, but in many cases, a bit faster".[32]

Third, Latin America has a special know-how and experience in productive sectors associated with commodities. That specialized knowledge could be projected internationally through the so-called Information Technology-Enabled Services. Among those productive sectors are agro-industry in Brazil or Argentina; hydrocarbons in Venezuela, Mexico, Brazil and Colombia; mining in Brazil, Chile and Peru; cattle management in Brazil, Argentina or Uruguay; and so on.

---

[31] *Expansión*, 15 de marzo, 2018.

[32] "Social Networking Statistics in Latin America", Digital Doughnut. Available at: http:// digitaldoughnut.com/social-networking-statistics-in-latin-america. Accessed 15 February 2013.

Fourth, Latin America is within the Western Hemisphere time zones. As a result, the region shares the same or a not to dissimilar time frame with United States and Canada. This allows for a direct follow-up of operations.

Fifth, as a result of the closeness to the United States, English is widely spoken as a second language in the region.

Notwithstanding potential opportunities to expand Latin America's options, it becomes highly frustrating for the region to witness how former ardent proponents of the Washington Consensus have now become prominent critics of globalization. For countries that took on the burden of immense social, political and economic costs, in order to reconvert their economies in accordance to the imperatives of said Consensus, this switch of convictions is damaging. Protectionism leads to the closing up Latin American export markets. Chiefly among these figures, we find Larry Summers.

According to Nikil Saval: "Perhaps the most surprising such transformation has been that of Larry Summers. Possessed of a panoply of elite titles — former chief economist of the World Bank, former Treasury secretary, president emeritus of Harvard, former economic adviser to President Barack Obama — Summers was renowned in the 1990s and 2000s for being a blustery proponent of globalisation. For Summers, it seemed, market logic was so inexorable that its dictates prevailed over social concerns… "The laws of economics, it's often forgotten, are like the laws of engineering" he said in a 1991 speech at a World Bank-IMF meeting in Bangkok. "There's only one set of laws and they work everywhere. One of the things I've learnt in my short time at the World Bank is that whenever anybody says, but economics works differently here, they're about to say something dumb". Over the last two years a different, in some ways unrecognizable Larry Summers has been appearing in newspaper editorial pages…In Summer's recent writings, this somber conclusion has often been paired with a surprising political goal: advocating for a 'responsible nationalism'. Now he argues that politicians must recognize 'that the basic responsibility for government is to maximize the welfare of citizens, not to pursue some abstract concept of global good'".[33]

---

[33] Nikil Saval, "Globalisation: The Rise and Fall of an Idea that Swept the World", *The Guardian*, 14 July 2017.

According to Pankaj Ghemawat: "Fifteen years ago, British economist John Kay wrote, 'Few components of globalization are inevitable if there is a genuine popular will to stop them. But mostly there is not'. The last bit is what has changed in the last few years".[34]

The Trump–Brexit duo, which expresses a genuine popular will to stop globalization, might trigger a process of transformation similar to the one put in motion by the Reagan–Thatcher duo three decades ago. More to the point, the curious equation formed by protectionism, populism, political rage, robots, algorithms, 3D printing machines and deep learning, among many other elements, may end up suctioning the oxygen of globalization. Needless to say that Summers's "responsible nationalism" is part of this equation.

However, while there are forces that suction globalization's oxygen, there are countervailing forces giving it fresh air, as we shall see next.

---

[34] Pankaj Ghemawat, "People are angry about globalization. Here's what to do", *Harvard Business Review*, Nov. 4, 2016, p. 9.

CHAPTER TWO

THE PRO-GLOBALIZATION COALITION

In favor of globalization is the conviction that this phenomenon has still a very important role to play. This conviction is supported by a complex combination of ideological beliefs, pragmatic considerations, economic processes, interests and institutional frameworks. This is associated with market economy, supply chains, the international fragmentation of production, global value chains, the New Division of Labor, China's emergence, East Asian economies, India, global cities, international maritime routes, newly industrialized economies, beneficiaries of the commodities super cycle, big retailers, freight movers, and all the institutional and financial structure that revolves around international trade.

At the Beginning It was the Ideology

Matters were straightforward at the beginning. The original stance was an ideological choice between shareholder capitalism and stakeholder capitalism. This goes back to the collapse of the Soviet system, which resulted not from military defeat but because of its own economic shortcomings and its incapacity to sustain the economic challenge posed by the West. While the capitalist model emerged as the big winner, there were several kinds of capitalism models to choose from, among these the Anglo-Saxon model, the East Asian one and the several varieties prevailing in Continental Europe.[1]

Germany and East Asia highlighted the search for social consensus and work stability within a stakeholder mentality, while in France and East Asia free market and State planning complemented each other. In all of them, there was a common denominator: companies were guided by a long-term approach to business.

The Anglo-Saxon version excluded the State and had a much more flexible attitude towards employment and social benefits, while it combined an economic shareholder mentality with a short-term vision for profits. In sum, market-oriented capitalism plus the subordination of manufacture to finance focuses the attention of companies on profit maximization and immediate returns, at the expense of their long-term strengths.

Anglo-Saxon capitalism reached commanding heights. The combination of inflation and stagnation, known as stagflation, had brought down Keynesianism and boosted von Hayek's market economy ideas, which were being propelled by Washington and London. The post-war years, up to the early 1970s, had been very good. In France, this era was called *les trente glorieuses*, i.e., the 30 glorious years. However, several causes brought a downturn.

Overcapacity in key post-war industries such as textiles and steel combined with the excesses of militant labor movements contributed to the downturn. In Europe, this was aggravated by the abandonment of capital controls and in, the US by the abandonment of a fixed and overvalued currency, which had given Europeans a price advantage. The oil price hike that began in 1973 compounded all of this. As a result, the economy slowed, government revenues declined, while in Europe social welfare expenditure kept rising sharply.[2]

Under these conditions, when Ronald Reagan and Margaret Thatcher decided to join forces behind market economy ideas, the capacity for resistance of Continental Europe was at a very low point. Moreover, Washington not only presented itself as the epicenter of global political power, after the collapse of communism, but headquartered several

---

[1] Michel Albert, *Capitalisme contre Capitalisme* (París: Editions de Seuil, 1991).

[2] John B Judis, *The Populist Explosion: How the Great Recession Transformed American and European Politics* (New York: Columbia Global Reports, 2016).

financial multilateral organizations and think tanks, whose economic views converged with that of the Reagan Administration. Neither Europe nor Asia seemed strong enough to oppose the tsunami of the emerging ideas.

Not surprisingly, according to Will Hutton and Anthony Giddens: "Globalisation favours shareholder-value-driven capitalism, and is being driven by it, so it is hardly surprising that other variants of capitalism that try to balance the other interests in the enterprise, like those of the workers, and to behave more ethically — stakeholders capitalism — are under pressure".[3] The Anglo-Saxon version thus became the dominant economic paradigm in the initial stages and, as such, the one in charge of putting in motion and guiding globalization.

Two Converging Pincers

The Anglo-Saxon model was to be instrumented at the global level by two powerful mechanisms: the General Agreement on Tariffs and Trade (GATT) and the International Monetary Fund (IMF). The former dated back to 1947, while the latter was created in 1944. Together with the World Bank, they were part of the Bretton Woods system, born under the auspices of the United States with the aim of regulating the world economy. Both GATT and IMF became fundamental forces in the launching of globalization. As a matter of fact, they acted as two huge converging pincers, generating the conditions for the developing economies to submit to market economy.

Between 1974 and the first years of the 1980s, the developing world had shown both ambition and cohesion in its quest for a more equitable economic order. During that period, its fight for what was called the New International Economic Order (NIEO), was channeled through the United Nations Commission for Trade and Development (UNCTAD). As a result, a North–South dialogue was institutionalized, covering a wide range of trade, financial and debt-related issues.

Within such negotiations, the developing countries managed to present a common front via the so-called G-77. They aimed at obtaining

---

[3] Will Hutton and Anthony Giddens (eds.), *Global Capitalism* (New York: New York Press, 2000), p. 31.

greater participation and voice in world economic matters. This implied a revision of the prevailing economic order, with the intention of replacing the collapsing Bretton Woods system, which in their opinion had benefited the richer countries at their expense.[4]

The conjunction of the external debt and the collapse in the price of commodities, including the loss of negotiating power by the Organization of Petroleum Exporting Countries (OPEC), seriously shattered the strength and the cohesion of the G-77. As a result, these countries were forced to take a much more flexible position. According to Joan E. Spero and Jeffrey A. Hart: "The new realities of the 1980s altered the trade strategy of the developing countries. The South's demand for a new international economic order was undermined by the collapse of commodity power, including the OPEC threat...and by the weakened economic position of the South, especially the debt crisis".[5]

The rapid build-up of debt reached its peak at a bad time: just when, as mentioned earlier, owing to the recession in industrial countries, demand was weakening for commodities that made up the livelihood of most developing countries. This translated into lower prices for their goods, and thus lower income for them. At the same time, the high interest rates of the early 1980s, which aimed at counteracting inflation in developed economies, raised the cost of the floating debt in the developing countries, thus increasing their repayment burden.[6]

Bending the Knee

The weakened position of developing economies became evident after the so-called UNCTAD VI, celebrated in Belgrade in 1983. As reported by the Spanish newspaper *El País*, at the conclusion of these negotiations: "Mexico, Argentina and Brazil, a trio that owes more than 200,000 million

---

[4] Robert L Rohthstein, *Global Bargaining: UNCTAD and the Quest for a New International Economic Order* (Princeton: Princeton University Press, 1979); Robert Looney, *Routledge Encyclopaedia of International Political Economy* (London: Routledge, 1999).

[5] Joan E Spero and Jeffrey A Hart, *The Politics of International Economic Relations* (Belmont, CA: Thompson/Wadswoth, 2003), p. 249.

[6] David Held and Anthony McGrew (eds.), "Order, globalization and inequality", in *The Global Transformations Reader* (Cambridge: Polity Press, 2000), p. 392.

dollars, induced restrain in the table of debtor countries...The three main indebted nations of the world recommended not to irritate the international financial markets in order to avoid being included in black lists."[7]

As a result of such impaired position, negotiations with the industrialized economies returned to the GATT. The implications of this were clear: the Bretton Wood spirit was back in place. In Joan E. Spero and Jeffrey A. Hart words: "The new forces of the 1980s also called into question the effectiveness of the South's preferred forums for governance, especially UNCTAD...As the strategy of confrontation and the NIEO collapsed, developing countries shifted their focus to the GATT".[8]

For developed nations, this meant opening a new round of trade negotiations within a friendlier and familiar institutional framework. Moreover, according to Ngaire Woods, one that they could also control: "Until 1993 international trade was regulated globally under the auspices of the GATT, a very loose institution whose rules and procedures were developed in an *ad hoc* way. Within this arrangement there was a clear inequality of power, with the 'Quad' (the US, the European Union, Japan, and Canada) being able to work behind the scenes to shape most decisions".[9]

For Joseph Stiglitz, hypocrisy and abuse of a dominant position were part of this game as well: "The United States and Europe have perfected the art of arguing for free trade while simultaneously working for trade agreements that protect themselves against imports from developing countries. Much of the success of the advanced industrial countries has to do with shaping the agenda — they set the agenda so that markets were opened up for the goods and services that represented their comparative advantage. Western negotiators almost take for granted that they can control what gets discussed, and determines the outcome".[10]

Again, in Ngaire Woods' words: "The results were trading rules which had a very uneven impact on countries...Importantly, these results reflected a process which magnified inequalities among members. The

---

[7] 29 September 1983.

[8] Joan E Spero and Jeffrey A Hart, *op. cit.*, p. 249.

[9] Ngaire Woods, *op. cit.*, pp. 78–79.

[10] Joseph Stiglitz, *Globalization and its Discontents* (London: W.W. Norton & Company, 2002), p. 392.

GATT operated as a club with a core membership empowered to decide who to admit and on what conditions".[11]

Such negotiations within the GATT, known as the Uruguay Round, were called to cover the "new trade areas" — that is to say, services, intellectual property and investments. Agriculture would also be included. In contrast to the confrontational attitude that prevailed within the framework of the North–South Dialogue, developing countries approached the Uruguay Round willing to make multiple concessions.

These concessions materialized in areas such as foreign investment liberalization, reduction of tariffs and export subsidies, extension of international trade law to the service sector, reduction of limits to imports of foreign goods, acceptance of the intellectual property guidelines from the North, etc. The decisive reason for this complacent attitude before the demands of the developed world, responded to what may be labeled as the "credibility syndrome".

The debt crisis collapsed commodity prices and neoliberalism, and put the developing economies under such pressure that they were left with no other option but to give in to the prevailing order. Again, according to Joan E. Spero and Jeffrey A. Hart, "Although many developing countries were reluctant to mar the appearance of Southern unity in international forums, these countries frequently chose to pursue a more pragmatic strategy...believing that only those who played the game had any chance of winning concessions".[12]

But there was more to it than the mere "credibility syndrome". Developing economies were told that compliance would translate into reciprocity. As Joseph Stiglitz explains: "The Uruguay Round had been based on what became known as the 'Grand Bargain', in which the developed countries promised to liberalize trade in agriculture and textiles (that is, labour-intensive goods of interest to exporters in developing countries) and, in return, developing countries agreed to reduce tariffs and accept a range of new rules and obligations on intellectual property rights, investments and services. Afterward, many developing countries felt that they

---

[11] Ngaire Woods, *op. cit.*, p. 77.
[12] Joan E Spero and Jeffrey A Hart, *op. cit.*, p. 253.

had been misled into agreeing to the Great Bargain: the developed countries did not keep their side of the deal".[13]

Enforcing the Washington Consensus

But while the GATT pincer was pushing in direction of the "new trade areas", the IMF pincer was enforcing the Washington Consensus. Again, going back in time can provide the proper perspective.

The IMF's initial aim was to promote international monetary cooperation, clearing the obstacles for the convertibility of the different currencies. It was the time when, according to Stephen D. King: "Stable monetary conditions in the US left central bank managers around the world confident that US dollars could be swapped for gold at the prevailing exchange rate of $35 per ounce".[14]

This stability was put in jeopardy by the escalating costs of the war in Vietnam, Johnson's "Great Society" and the Space Program, all of which set inflation in motion. As foreign holders of dollars were becoming increasingly doubtful of the convertibility of the dollar into gold, President Nixon decided in 1971 to decree the flotation of the dollar. This seriously affected the objectives of the IMF, taking away its role in monetary affairs and threatening it with irrelevance. Not surprisingly, the organization entered into a lethargic period. In 1982, however, Mexico provided the occasion for an institutional rebirth when it defaulted on its sovereign debt.

A second chance to become a relevant player in the international economy was thus given to this organization. As developing countries whose debts were becoming unmanageable were in serious trouble, and the embattled former communist countries transitioning into capitalism were in need of economic help, someone had to be put in charge of managing the required relief. The IMF was officially entrusted with that role and became, indeed, the custodian of the gate that gave access to the creditors' funds. Without its blessing, debtor countries were not able to accede

---

[13] Joseph Stiglitz, *op. cit.*, p. 77.
[14] Stephen D King, *Grave New World: The End of Globalization and the Return to History* (New Haven: Yale University Press, 2017), p. 49.

to the loans of the World Bank, other multilateral financial bodies, the G-7 countries or the private banks. Compliance with the Washington Consensus rules, as implemented by the IMF, became the only way through which indebted economies could borrow fresh money.

The IMF executed this role with proverbial inflexibility. This was closely related to the new economic paradigm, which permeated all corners of the institution. The comeback to life of a set of ideas on the virtues of the market, relegated as they had been to the dusted bookshelves during a good part of the twentieth century, was an ideal prescription for dogmatism.

A whole set of new economic icons emerged: Von Hayek, Von Mises, Friedman, Stigler, Becker, Lucas, Joseph, the Faculty of Economics of the University of Chicago, the Mont Pelerin Society, London's Institute of Economic Affairs.[15] Once victorious, the fundamentalist style that had allowed them to keep faith alive during the wilderness years, became their trademark. IMF's technocrats were to become the best expression of this fundamentalism. Keynes could have told them, what he once wrote to Hayek: "You greatly under-estimate the practicability of the middle course".

Like sorcerer's apprentices, though, GATT and IMF put in motion a process that had a force of its own. Especially so, because technology allowed for a new kind of fluidity in international trade that defied all intents of control. Supply chains became the first step in tying off the winds of change.

The Disassembly Line

Shareholder mentality, profit maximization and the compulsion for imme-diate returns, fundamental pieces of the Anglo-Saxon capitalism, naturally led to a search for the lowest production costs. The gigantic advancements · in information and communication technology (ITC) and transports, allowed for this search to take place at a global scale. Supply chains would soon appear as a result.

In Robyn Meredith's words: "But during the 1990s, companies began searching for the lowest-cost place to make each component of their

---

[15] *Ibid.*

products. At the same time, sophisticated technology made reality of what had once been a logistical pipe dream: creating a seamless connection between multiple factories, sometimes in multiple countries. Cost-cutting efforts combined with powerful new technologies allowed companies to change the way they built most consumer products. The last time a manufacturing revolution of this magnitude occurred was in the early twentieth century, when Henry Ford revolutionized the business world by popularizing the assembly line...In the twenty-first century, everything has changed...The new system — call it a disassembly line — is the result of companies rushing to break up their products into specialized subassemblies to drive down costs...The manufacturing process is so different from the last century that the term 'assembly line' has been replaced by the phrase 'supply chain'". [16]

The last time, indeed, that a manufacturing revolution of this magnitude took place was at the beginning of the twentieth century, when in 1911 Frederick W. Taylor conceptualized standardized principles of industrial efficiency in his book *The Principles of Scientific Management*. Henry Ford subsequently applied these principles in the manufacturing of his vehicles, giving rise to the assembly line. According to it, each worker was called to fulfill a repetitive and specific function, within an immense mechanized line. Henceforward, the assembly line became synonymous of modern industrial production. Charles Chaplin's "Modern Times", epitomized, early in time, the assembly line and the cruelty of turning humans into machines.

The supply chain, on its side, responded to the principle that every product that reaches an end user represents the cumulative effort of multiple organizations. These organizations are referred to, collectively, as the supply chain. Supply chains, which include the fragmentation of production, aim at the manufacturing of each piece or component of a final product, wherever the cheapest cost of production can be found.

As Robyn Meredith puts it: "The disassembly line has let companies become extremely efficient, by building each piece of a finished good in the country where it is cheapest, then moving the part on to the next

---

[16] Robyn Meredith, *The Elephant and the Dragon* (New York, W.W. Norton & Company, 2007), p. 99.

factory in line".[17] So, with parts and components passing from factories in Vietnam to factories in Indonesia, to factories in the Philippines, always in the search for the cheapest cost, profit maximization became king, hence the cumulative effort involved.

The result of supply chains is a puzzle raised to the *n*th power, which can only be solved thanks to the impressive advancements in the technologies of information, communication and transport. The monitoring, control and mobilization of endless pieces, parts and components, moving in the most diverse directions, are indeed complex tasks. They require among other things highly sophisticated software, giant freighters that have taken Malcolm MacLean's revolution on containerization to a maximum degree of efficiency and exceptional port logistics. The estimated number of containers moving around the word in 2012 was thought to be in excess of 32 million.[18]

Each of the countries involved has to provide the necessary infrastructure, both physical and digital, so that this dizzying dance of pieces, parts and components can move with ease. As a result, the network of stakeholders within this process keeps increasing with each link of the chain involved, multiplying thus the number of supporters of globalization.

The Smile Curve

Global value chains represent a natural extension to the supply chain, which aims at adding value to the product in every step. While the supply chain activities are essentially concerned with the transfer of materials from one place to another, the value chain is primarily concerned in providing greater value for price product. The latter leads to a larger integration of both manufactures and services. Herein involved is the full range of activities required to bring a product from its conception and design to its final marketing, distribution and attached services to the buyer.

According to Richard Baldwin, a typical value chain is made up of three stages: prefabrication activities (such as design, finance and organizational activities), fabrication activities (things done in factories) and

---

[17] *Ibid*, p. 101.

[18] Finbarr Livesey, *From Global to Local: The Making of Things and the End of Globalization* (New York: Pantheon Books, 2017), p. 82.

post-fabrication activities (such as marketing, post-sales services and the like). Of these activities, he adds, those related to the trend called "servicification" of manufactures are the ones that add more value to the product.

In his words: "The main changes can be organized around a handy intellectual construct known as the 'smile curve'. Introduced by Acer founder and CEO Stan Shih in the early 1990s, the smile-curve logic asserts that the distribution of value added in manufacturing is shifting. More and more of the value is being added by services that are related to manufacturing; less and less is being added by simple manufacturing itself".[19]

Finbarr Livesey, explains the smile-curve in the following terms: "... something referred to as the 'smile curve'...that the valuable activities are at the start (R&D) and the end (sales and brand control)...production in the middle is thought of as low value...hence the 'smile' with a curve high at the start, dropping in the middle, and back up again at the end".[20]

A very important part of such services remains in the developed economies. However, as the dematerialization of companies keeps advancing, corporations tend to stick to their core areas, while the bulk of their activities is being outsourced and offshored. In the process, assembly lines and services are being scattered in the search for the lowest manpower costs. As Thomas L. Friedman argues, with the global economy transformed in a level playing field of sorts, there is little impediment to having not only production, but also design, research and services broken up and placed around the world. Distance does not matter.[21]

In the area of services, several reasons have facilitated this leveled playing field: (a) the strong diffusion in the technologies of information and communications; (b) the globalization of competences, which allows to look for the best available talents at the lower possible costs and (c) the homogenization of practices of consumption, production and management induced by globalization.

---

[19] Richard Baldwin, *op. cit.*, p. 153.
[20] Finbarr Livesey, *op. cit.*, p. 37.
[21] Thomas L Friedman, *The World is Flat: A Brief History of the Twenty-First Century* (London: Penguin Books, 2006).

The cost of communications alone speaks for itself. Between 1950 and 1997, the cost of a three-minute phone call between the US and the UK or between Japan and Germany fell by around two-thirds, dropping from US$12 to just US$3 in each case. The introduction of dense optic-fiber communications and the arrival of Skype, FaceTime or WhatsApp have made costs negligible or inexistent for the average user.[22]

According to *Bloomberg/Business Week*: "Some observers even believe Big Business is on the cusp of a new burst of productivity growth, ignited in part by offshore outsourcing as a catalyst...As executives shed more operations, they also are spurring new debate about how the future of corporations will look. Some management pundits theorize about the 'totally disaggregated corporation', wherein every function not regarded as crucial is stripped away...The rise of the offshore option is dramatically changing the economics of reengineering. With millions of low-cost engineers, financial analysts, consumer marketers, and architects now readily available via the Web, CEOs can see a quicker payoff. 'It used to be that companies struggled for a few years to show a 5% or 10% increase in productivity from outsourcing', says Pramod Bhasin, CEO of Genpact, the 19,000-employee back-office-processing unit spun off by GE last year. 'But by offshoring work, they can see savings of 30% to 40% in the first year' in labor costs...Professor Mohanbir Sawhney of Northwestern University's Kellogg School of Management, a self-proclaimed 'big believer in total disaggregation', says: 'One of our tasks in business schools is to train people to manage the virtual, globally distributed corporation.'"[23]

In other words, the company not only searches for the lowest blue-collar worker cost, for each manufacturing step, but also for the better qualified designer, engineer, financial analyst or accountant, at the best available costs. Hence, Indian white-collar work may be actively interacting with Chinese or Indonesian blue-collar work, within an integrated global process. While high-technology capabilities are normally found in developed economies and thus remain within the company's core areas, most of the manufacturing and service processes can be offshored.

---

[22] Finbarr Livesey, *op. cit.*, p. 94.

[23] Joel P. Engardio, "The future of outsourcing", *Bloomberg/Business Week*, 30 January 2006.

The network of globalization stakeholders thus keeps increasing and, with it, its level of support.

East Asia's emerging economies and India play a fundamental role within the global value chains, the first in manufactures, the second in services.

Asia's Blue-Collar and White-Collar Jobs

According to Robyn Meredith: "Twenty years ago, developing countries provided just 14 percent of rich countries' manufacturing imports, but by 2006 that figure had increased to 40 percent, and by 2030 it would rise to more than 65 percent, according to the World Bank".[24] East Asia has been the greatest beneficiary of this manufacturing offshoring process.

Needless to say, China represented the zenith of this process, being the greatest beneficiary of the supply chain. Thanks to it, this country was able to attain the fastest economic growth of a major economy in the documented history of humanity: an average 9 percent for 30 years. Between 1980 and 1990, the country's GDP doubled, and between 1990 and 2000, it doubled again. According to the IMF, China's GDP rose from US$309 billion in 1980 to US$1.2 trillion in 2000.[25] As a result, 600 million human beings were lifted out of poverty.

But not only were countless factories interconnected within supply chains inside China, but China itself was just a part, although the most relevant one, of the East Asia supply chain. As China's manpower costs are now rising, Vietnam, Indonesia, the Philippines and other East Asian countries have taken its place at the bottom of the cost production equation. Not surprisingly, some analysts say that China is reaching the so-called Lewis turning point. That is, the stage in the development of an emerging economy when labor shortages bring up inflation and slower economic growth. However, with 40 percent of the Chinese labor force remaining in agriculture, where its productivity is about one-sixth less than the industrial worker, and with a working-age population that in 2015

---

[24] Robyn Meredith, *op. cit.*, p. 107.
[25] John Naisbitt and Doris Naisbitt, *China's Megatrends* (New York: Harper Business, 2010).

was close to a billion human beings, it makes no sense to talk about labor shortages in China.[26]

Much more significant as a reason is the rebalancing of China's economy towards domestic consumption and the service sector. In order to widen the number of its domestic consumers and allow the migration into the more valuable service sector, Beijing is no longer interested in retaining a leadership position as a labor-intensive manufacturer. Much to the contrary, the country is climbing the technological ladder at great speed.

Hence, although China has not reached the Lewis turning point, its labor costs are increasing and this leads to the search of new destinations for cheaper blue-collar jobs. The East Asian supply chain juggernaut is well up and ready to provide alternatives.

But while East Asian emerging economies play a leading role within the manufacturing sector, India plays an equally important one within the service sector. This results from their different economic strategies. East Asian economies relied in their early stages on low-skilled export-oriented manufacturing, as the proper way to motor economic growth. India followed a different route. The country has tried to escape underdevelopment by using relatively skill-intensive activities as the launching pad for sustained economic growth. No other developing economy has tried to leapfrog into progress this way.

Instead of adopting the classic East Asian strategy of labor-intensive export-oriented economies, India relied more on its domestic market. It has also emphasized services over industry and knowledge-intensive manufacturing over low-skill manufacturing. More importantly in what relates to globalization, they approached international markets by way of skill-intensive export-oriented services.

A World Bank paper argues that the "Indian experience has led researchers to challenge the conventional notion that industrialization is the only plausible route to rapid economic development".[27] According to this perspective, services have to be seen under a different light as they

---

[26] "Is China's labour market at a turning point?", *The Economist*, 12 June 2010.

[27] Saurabh Mishrah, Susanna Lundstrom and Rahul Anand, "Service sophistication and economic growth", The World Bank South Asia Region Policy Research, Working Paper 5606 (March 2011), p. 2.

have become international tradable elements in themselves. That is, "final exports" for direct consumption. Hence, India's bet was not a pipe dream but a reasonable option. As Richard Baldwin says: "India is a unique case in that its export boom was driven by its service sector rather than its manufacturing or primary goods".[28]

According to Anil K. Gupta and Haiyan Wang: "India is far ahead of China in software services as well as most other services that can be delivered remotely by information technology. Examples of the latter range from low-end commodity services (such as call centres) to high-end knowledge-intensive services (such as software development, chip design, market research, marketing analytics, legal research, securities analysis, drug discovery services and so forth)".[29]

As they explain: "India's lead in IT services rest on multiple factors: a very strong service orientation, extensive experience at remote delivery of IT services to global clients, highly developed process rigor, in depth knowledge of specific industries, and fluency in the English language".[30]

As Nida Najar says: "India's information technology industry grew at a breakneck speed over the past two decades thanks to the trend commonly called offshoring. The industry and related business generate more than $150 billion in annual revenue and employ about four million people to build and test software, to enter and analyze data and to provide customer support for American and European companies looking for relatively inexpensive labor".[31] As a result, India is equally supportive of globalization as their East Asian counterparts are, but for different reasons.

Both China and India, as well as several of the newly industrialized economies of South East Asia such as Vietnam, Indonesia and so on, have seen a staggering growth of their middle classes since the fall of the Berlin Wall, which signaled the beginning of the globalization era. The so-called Elephant Chart graph, devised by Branko Milanovich, shows that these emerging middle classes enjoyed of an income growth of more than

---

[28] Richard Baldwin, *op. cit.,* p. 95.
[29] Anil K Gupta and Haiyan Wang, *Getting China and India Right* (San Francisco: Jossey-Bass, 2009), p. 42.
[30] *Ibid*, p. 53.
[31] Nida Najar, "Indian technology workers worry about a job threat: Technology", *The New York Times*, 25 June 2017.

80 percent during that period.[32] Moreover, as Edward Luce, reminds us: "The original chart ended in 2008. In that short period since the 'global' recession, China's urban income had already doubled".[33]

But the group of countries whose interests are associated with the globalization process is wider than those which have benefited from global value chains and supply chains. Commodities producers are also included within this list.

Commodity Chains

Raw materials participate in the global economy as the "basic building blocks of our manufactured world".[34] However, they retain their own specificity within the so-called commodity chains. "A commodity chain refers to a 'network of labor and production processes whose end results is a finished commodity'".[35] Each production site in the chain involves organizing the acquisition of necessary raw materials plus semi-finished inputs, the recruitment of labor power and its provisioning, transportation to the next site and the construction of distribution and consumption.

Each year, 60 billion tons of raw materials are extracted or collected, representing not only the bloodline of manufacturing processes, but providing the base for infrastructural and urbanization developments and, ultimately, feeding the world. And, even if substantial advances have been made at generating economic value using less raw materials — a dollar of GDP uses a third less material than it did at the beginning of the 1980s — global population increase and the rise into middle classes of hundreds of millions of Asians keeps adding new demand.[36]

Raw materials producers profited from this super cycle of commodities, which was directly linked to the extraordinary emergence of China.

---

[32] Edward Luce, *The Retreat of Western Liberalism* (Electronic book, London: Little, Brown, 2017), p. 352/4115.

[33] *Ibid*, p. 354/4115.

[34] Finbarr Livesey, *op. cit.*, p. 101.

[35] Joonkoo Lee, "Global commodity chains and global value chains", Oxford Encyclopedia of International Studies, http://internationalstudies.oxfordre.com/view/10.1093/acrefore/9780190846626.001.0001/acrefore-9780190846626-e-201. Accessed 10 February 2018.

[36] *Ibid*, p. 101.

According to the IMF, between 2002 and 2006, the general index of commodities worldwide, excluding oil, was increased by 60 percent in real terms. Moreover, in the areas of oil and metals, such increase reached 150 percent and 180 percent, respectively. Contrariwise, for the five previous decades, before the boom led by China, the price of commodities had been falling at an annual rate of 1.6 percent in relation to manufactured goods.[37] This super cycle, though, ended in 2013.

However, new bullish commodity price periods could certainly emerge in the future under the right set of circumstances. The example provided by the One Belt, One Road Initiative comes to mind. If this project materializes, it would certainly boost the prices of natural resources worldwide.

But more than the One Belt, One Road initiative, China has ahead of it an ambitious infrastructure and urbanization process. While the coastal areas of the country have already attained their maturity, there are immense inland areas yet to be properly developed. More than 300 million people currently living in the countryside are expected to be moving into them, as hundreds of new cities and infrastructural projects will be built in the next two decades. India, on its side, still has to go a long way in infrastructural development.

Moreover, if the population of the world's middle sectors reaches 5 billion people by 2030, as it has been forecast by the Organization of Economic Cooperation and Development (OECD), there would be an increase of 3 billion people.[38] Demand for natural resources would skyrocket as a result. On its side, the Food and Agriculture Organization (FAO) estimates that the world's population will reach 9 billion by 2050, and demand for food may increase by 70 percent.[39] As may well be imagined, commodities producers are firmly within the camp of the globalization supporters.

---

[37] Bernardo Kosacoff y Sebastián Campanario, *La Revalorizacion de las Materias Primas y sus Efectos en América Latina* (Santiago de Chile: CEPAL, 2007)., p. 11.

[38] Homi Kharas, "The emerging middle class in developing countries", OECD, February 2010, http://www.oecd.org/dev/44457738.pdf. Accessed 3 January 2017.

[39] Food and Agriculture Organization, "How to feed the world in 2050", Presentation at the World Summit of Food Security in Rome, 16–19 November 2009, http://www.fao.org/fileadmin/templates/wsfs/docs/expert_paper/How_to_Feed_the_World_in_2050.pdf. Accessed 18 October 2012.

The Many Labels of the Emerging World

Low-cost manufacturers and long-distance service providers, together with commodities producers, are all part of the emerging economies. This mixed group has received many labels. In 2003, Goldman Sachs coined the acronym BRIC, which included Brazil, Russia, India and China. In 2005 Goldman Sachs mooted the BRIC successors, calling them the NEXT 11 (N11). Among its ranks were Vietnam, Mexico, Turkey, Indonesia, the Philippines, Egypt and Bangladesh. In 2006, PricewaterhouseCoopers published a report entitled *The World in 2050*, where it listed its own emerging luminaires under the name of E7: China, India, Brazil, Mexico, Indonesia, Turkey and Russia.

In 2010, the BRIC, already established as a formal group, decided to incorporate South Africa as one of them, thus giving rise to the BRICS. A year before, the OECD had coined the term BRIICS, including not only South Africa but also Indonesia. In 2006, the BRIC Economic Institute of Japan created the acronym VISTA, to present its own list: Vietnam Indonesia, South Africa, Turkey and Argentina. In 2009, the Economist Intelligence Unit produced the acronym CIVETS to list its favorite emerging economies: Colombia, Indonesia, Vietnam, Egypt, Turkey and South Africa.[40]

Richard Baldwin refers that between 1990 and 2016, the G7's share percentage of the global GDP declined from two-thirds to under one half. And he asks himself: "…the G7's share losses must correspond to share gains for others. Who were the GDP share winners?".[41] According to his answer, the G7's share loss basically benefited 11 nations: "Together, these Rising Eleven, or R11 for short — China, India, Brazil, Indonesia, Nigeria, Korea, Australia, Mexico, Venezuela, Poland and Turkey — accounted for fourteen of the seventeen percentage points lost by the G7. The whole rest of the world — almost 200 nations — accounted for the remaining three percentage points".[42] The list is in itself surprising, as it does not include countries such as Saudi Arabia. On the other hand, the inclusion of Venezuela is a painful reminder of how, notwithstanding the

---

[40]Toro Hardy Alfredo, *The World Turned Upside Down: The Complex Partnership between China and Latin America* (New Jersey: World Scientific, 2013), p. 144.
[41]Richard Baldwin, *op. cit.*, p. 92.
[42]*Ibid.*

gains accrued, the country decided to take these last few years a time machine into the Neolithic.

Besides the economic benefits derived from globalization, there is an important reason that explains the support given to this movement by so many emerging economies. Indeed, globalization was able to move away from the ideologically rigid boundaries of its beginnings, into much more open spaces. Even if its initial expansion was driven by Anglo-Saxon market-oriented rules, its subsequent evolution became more plural in nature. Before going further with the list of supporters of globalization, a parenthesis must be opened to explain this evolution.

Washington Consensus: A Damaged Brand

This takes us back to an enlightening exercise of scenarios realized by Shell in 2002. When envisaging year 2020, the exercise defined two alternative routes: the first was represented by the "Executive Class" scenario, the second by the "Prism" scenario. The first of them envisaged a continuation of the market economy rules — a world characterized by a single modernity — where an all-powerful and cohesive international elite supported those rules. The "Prism", as its name suggests, dispersed different colors. This symbolized a multicultural world economy in which a plural sense of modernity prevailed. This implied a major emphasis on cultural, national or regional diversities.[43]

A group of successive circumstances played against the "Executive Class" scenario: the economic emergence of two powerful civilization-states: China and India; the spectacular success of the economic opening process in China; the contrast between the flexibility of the Chinese model and the rigidities of the Washington Consensus (the Beijing Consensus vs. the Washington Consensus); the relative decline of the West, in particular after the 2008 financial crisis; the strong disappointment of several East Asian states with market economy, after the Asian Crisis of 1997; the social and political disruptions brought up by the implementation of the Washington Consensus in different parts of the world (Mexico, Russia, Brazil, Argentina, etc.).

---

[43] Shell Group of Companies, *Peoples and Connections: Global Scenarios for 2020* (London: Shell Editions, 2002).

In Edward Luce's words: "At some point during the 2008 global financial crisis, the Washington Consensus died. In truth, that economic model had been declared a 'damaged brand' back in 2003 by John Williamson, the man who coined the term in the late 1980s...Countries that swallowed the prescriptions suffered terribly during the 1995 Mexican peso crisis, the 1997 Asian flu crisis and in Russia, Brazil and elsewhere during the later 1990s (…) Most of the world has since chosen China's more pragmatic path of opening slowly and in its own terms. China's unorthodox route to development exposed the limits of the Washington Consensus".[44]

Globalization, it should be outlined, is both fact and content. The fact derives from the information, communication and transport revolutions, which have led to what has been labeled as the "death of distance".[45] The result has been a mobile economy where goods are conceived, designed, produced and assembled in different countries, and where manufactures and services are integrated within the same production processes.

Behind the factual side of globalization, or rather coexisting with it, a group of ideas gave it substance. Such ideas not only entered into the realm of ideology, but also within the notion of hegemony as defined by Antonio Gramsci. For him, the capacity to define the agenda, through ideological and cultural persuasion and consensual acceptance, was the most stable and effective form of predominance.[46]

In its beginning, as previously mentioned, globalization was firmly identified with market economy ideas. However, when the cracks of the model began appearing and the faltering of its consensual acceptance became obvious, the whole notion of a single modernity lost ground. As a consequence, globalization as content evolved into something much more multicultural in nature. The "Prism" replaced the "Executive Class".

Between the No One's World and the Davos Man

This is what Charles Kupchan means when stating: "We are heading towards no-one's world, a world with multiple modernities, interdependent

---

[44] Edward Luce, *op. cit.*, p. 332/4115.

[45] Frances Cairncross, *The Death of Distance* (Cambridge, Mass.: Harvard Business School Press, 1997).

[46] David Forgacs, *Antonio Gramsci Reader* (London: Lawrence & Wishart, 2001); Alfredo Toro Hardy, *Hegemonía e Imperio* (Bogotá: Villegas Editores, 2007).

and globalized without a political center or model".[47] Martin Jacques agrees: "In the future, then, instead of there being one dominant Western modernity, they will be many distinct modernities. It is clear that we have already entered this era of multiple modernities...Hitherto, we have lived in a Western-made and Western-dominated world, in which the economic, political and cultural traffic has been overwhelmingly one-directional, from the West to the others".[48]

And he adds: "The emergence of new modernities not only mean that the West no longer enjoys a virtual monopoly of modernity, but that the histories, cultures and values of those societies will be affirmed in a new way and can no longer be equated with backwardness or, worse, failure. On the contrary, they will experience a new sense of legitimacy".[49] Martin Wolf, on his part, wrote: "We are, in short, at the end of both an economic period — that of western-led globalization — and a geopolitical one — the post-cold war 'unipolar moment' of a U.S.-led global order".[50]

This evolution from a market economy western-led-globalization, into a much more plural globalization, has great significance. The process can no longer be hijacked by a hegemonic ideology, and consequently be tied to its fate. Moreover, its base of support has greatly expanded, as the different colors of the prism find accommodation within it. An important number of emerging economies can now comfortably identify themselves with globalization. Even if the Western world turns its back on it, the process has sufficient strength to keep moving ahead. Globalization represents today different things for different people, while pragmatic considerations and not ideology becomes the glue that holds the movement together.

But, notwithstanding the fact that the "business class" option has been superseded, a market-oriented business elite still plays an important role in the support of globalization. Its most emblematic expression is the Davos group. The neologism "Davos man", attributed to Samuel P. Huntington, was coined to describe a very particular typology. According

---

[47] Charles Kupchan, "Refunding good governance", *The New York Times,* 19 December 2011.
[48] Martin Jacques, *When China Rules the World* (London: Allen Lane, 2009), p. 142.
[49] *Ibid,* p. 144.
[50] Martin Wolf, "The long and painful journey to world disorder", *Financial Times,* 5 January 2017.

to him, the members of this global elite "have little need for national loyalty, view national boundaries as obstacles that thankfully are vanishing, and see national governments as residues from the past whose only useful function is to facilitate the elite's operations".[51]

Since the term "Davos man" was coined, the World Economic Forum has evolved from its clearly Western origins to become a much more multinational gathering. Lawrence Summers calls them "stateless elite", and as such they are perceived.[52] An elite detached from its surrounding national realities. Edward Luce defines them as follows: "The gulf between the view from the Swiss Alps and realities on the ground continually widens (...) Davos has become the emblem of a global elite that has lost the ability to listen".[53]

Under the current circumstances, though, they are just part of the prevailing plurality, but in no way the guardians of globalization that they still pretend to be. As such, they add weight to this movement, but are far from representing its core. Theirs, is just one of the many colors irradiated by the prism. Perhaps this explains why leaders holding different visions of the world economy no longer feel reluctant to attend their meetings. However, in the same manner in which they add weight to globalization, they are one of the most visible targets of the anti-globalizer movement.

Global Cities

Also, within the line of support we find the so-called global cities. They have been identified as centers of management and control of the global economy. The term was coined by sociologist Saskia Sassen of the University of Chicago, for whom globalization contains parallel dynamics of dispersion and centralization. The massive spatial dispersion of economic activities generates the need of new forms of territorial centralization for the management and control of such activities.[54]

---

[51] Timothy Garton Ash, "Davos man's death wish", *The Guardian*, 3 February 2005.
[52] Lawrence Summers, "America needs to make a new case of trade", *Financial Times*, 20 June 2013.
[53] Edward Luce, *op. cit.*, pp. 839/4115 and 849/4115.
[54] Saskia Sassen, "The global city: Introducing a concept", *Brown Journal of World Affairs*, 2005, Volume XI, Issue 2, pp. 27–43.

Global cities have been also called alpha cities. In the words of Alec Ross: "The most important cities from an economic standpoint are so-called alpha cities, for example, Shanghai, London, New York or Tokyo... I am much more likely to run into an American who is a leading innovator in an alpha city like Shanghai or Dubai than I am to see her or him in St. Louis, Missouri or Manchester, England. They visit the same 20 cities around the world in a circuit of sorts...".[55]

These cities concentrate in themselves decision, coordination and servicing functions of global projection. According to Brookings: "The concentration of economic growth and prosperity in large metro areas defines the modern global economy".[56] Their importance is measured by elements such as the number of corporate headquarters that they exhibit, their innovation capacity, the range of business activities under their coverage, the volume of Foreign Direct Investment that they can muster or attract, the interconnectivity of areas under their control, the strength of their service sectors, the volume of their international communications, etc. Moreover, global cities are skill-clusters or, as Enrico Moretti calls them, "brain hubs".[57]

The hierarchical classification of these cities is clear in relation to its first two spots. London and New York top the list. However, the place of others within the ranking is open to discussion. The cities entitled to be included in the list admit no doubt, but its rank does. Amid such cities we could mention Paris, Singapore, Hong Kong, San Francisco, Dubai, Beijing, Shanghai or Tokyo.

Singapore is the perfect example of a global city, exhibiting numerous hubs of global projection, in addition to being a major Foreign Direct Investment outflow and inflow center. Among such hubs, the city-state has the world's third largest financial center; the second busiest port in the world by cargo tonnage; has been ranked as the second best place to do business in the world; is among the top global biotechnology centers; is the pricing center and the major oil hub in Asia, being amid the three

---

[55] Alec Ross, *The Industries of the Future* (Electronic book, New York: Simon & Schuster, 2017) p. 2930/5911.
[56] Max Bouchet, Sifan Liu, Joseph Parilla and Nader Kabbani, "Global metro monitor 2018", https://www.brookings.edu/research/global-metro-monitor-2018. Accessed 14 June 2018.
[57] Richard Baldwin, *op. cit.,* p. 234.

largest global export refining centers, and so on. In addition to that, Singapore is the largest foreign direct investor in such major economies as China and India, while it has been ranked as the world's fifth largest Foreign Direct Investment inflow economy.

These cities conform a sort of modern Hanseatic League. The latter was a commercial and defensive confederation of merchant guilds and their market towns, that stretched from the Baltic Sea to the North Sea, and which from the thirteenth century onwards, controlled for three centuries the economy of that part of the world. The combined economic power of these urban centers allowed them to confront successfully the big empires of the time. The global cities of our day share much of the interaction that characterized those Hanseatic cities, but this time at a global level.

The members of the Hanseatic League were city-states, whereas the members of this contemporary informal club show different variables. Within them, we find a city-state like Singapore, a city-emirate as Dubai, or an autonomous city as Hong Kong. But, at the same time, most of these cities are located within important countries. Some of them, like London, control a third of their country's GDP and are global economic dynamos within states that no longer exhibit such condition.[58] Others, as New York, have to share primacy within its national boundaries, in this case with a global political and multilateral financial center as Washington.

However, when a global city is part of a larger country, there tends to be a gulf between the two of them. For inland United States, New York is a totally alien place, in the same manner in which London's multiculturalism goes against the United Kingdom's national mood.

Not surprisingly, while a majority of UK citizens voted for Brexit, almost two-thirds of Londoners voted to stay in the European Union.[59] As Edward Luce says: "Britain's left-behinds vetoed London's economic interests in the Brexit referendum".[60] And he adds: "As the more educated people move to global cities, those with fewer qualifications find

---

[58] Edward Luce, *op. cit.*, p. 558/4115.

[59] *Ibid*, p. 558/4115.

[60] *Ibid*, p. 573/4115.

themselves shut out".[61] Indeed, when the rich and the brightest are attracted by the global city, cost of living goes up making of it an unwelcoming place for the less well off.

Hence, while global cities are natural supporters of globalization, their national environments may frequently go in the opposite direction. Maritime routes, or more exactly, the countries that control them are also in the list of supporters.

Maritime Routes

Maritime transport represents the fundamental bloodstream of the globalized economy. It carries more than 90 percent of the world's goods and around 50 percent of global oil, playing a fundamental role within the global supply chains.[62] Such transport tends to concentrate itself around the so-called maritime routes.

These routes represent compulsory crossing points between oceans, between seas or between oceans and seas. They can be man-made or natural. Among the first, we find the Panama or the Suez canals. Among the second, the Malacca or the Gibraltar straits. In both cases, they represent funnels of high strategic significance. Some more than others, of course.

The main four maritime routes are the Malacca Strait, the Suez Canal, the Panama Canal and the Ormuz Strait. The first of them connects the Indian Ocean with the South China Sea. It is the path through which around 50 thousand ships, representing 30 percent of the global maritime trade and around 80 percent of the oil that feeds China, Japan and South Korea, pass every year. The Suez Canal links the Mediterranean Sea and the Gulf of Suez, which leads to the Indian Ocean. Twenty thousand ships, representing 15 percent of the world's maritime trade, use it on yearly basis.

The Panama Canal connects the Pacific and the Atlantic oceans, and until 2014 it allowed for the crossing of 13,000 ships a year, representing 5 percent of the total maritime trade. Moreover, while Suez allows the

---

[61] *Ibid*, p. 570/4115.
[62] Robert D Kaplan, *Asia's Cauldron: The South China Sea and the End of a Stable Pacific* (New York: Random House: 2014), p. 11.

transit of supertankers of up to 200,000 tons, Panama was limited to 65,000 tons and to a configuration adapted to its particular standards, the so-called Panamax. Since 2014, as a result of the expansion of the Panama Canal, a New Panamax standard applies, substantially increasing its capacity and doubling the allowed tonnage per ship.

The Ormuz Strait, finally, is the compulsory crossing between the Persian Gulf and the Indian Ocean, being the path for 88 percent of the oil exported by the countries of the Gulf. It covers, as well, an important merchandise transit, as the gigantic containers port of Dubai make obvious.

In addition to the aforementioned big maritime routes, we can add the Cape of Good Hope which connects the Atlantic and the Indian Ocean at the South of the African continent, and the Magallanes Strait that links the Pacific and the Atlantic oceans in the Southern seas of South America. The first of them has a much bigger strategic significance, as the latter lost much of its own as a result of the construction in the 1980s of the North American Continental Bridge. This "bridge" is a railroad track dedicated to the massive transport of containers between New York and Los Angeles, by way of Chicago.

Of much importance, as well, are the straits of Gibraltar, Bosporus and Denmark (more than one in this last case). They link, respectively, the Atlantic Ocean and the Mediterranean Sea, the Mediterranean and the Death Sea, and the Baltic Sea and the North Sea. As a result of global warming, two additional routes are being opened in the Artic: the North East one, bordering Canada and the North West one, bordering Russia. While they are considered to be interior waters by such states, United States rejects that position, seeing them as international routes.

The geopolitical and economic significance of the Artic routes may be enormous, as they could end up representing an active new passage between the Atlantic and the Pacific oceans, skirting round the Indian Ocean and the Malacca Strait. The latter would substantially diminish the geostrategic importance of a place like Singapore.

Needless to say is that in addition to their economic relevance, or precisely because of it, maritime routes are highly sensitive geopolitical spots. A blockade of the Malacca Strait, for instance, could deprive China of 80 percent of its oil imports.

Each of these maritime routes remains fundamental not only for the states that control their passage, some of which have invested heavily in upgrading available infrastructures, but also for the bordering countries. In many cases, important ports have been built in order to take advantage of the strategic nature of these maritime routes. In every one of these cases, stakeholders of globalization have emerged.

Companies: Their Many Hats

A very important addition to this list of supporters comes from the companies that benefit from globalization. Naturally, they represent a diverse group. Among them, we find Western corporations involved in global value chains; Asian corporations that have blossomed as a result of international trade; Asian corporations involved in offshored manufacturing and big retailers and freighters.

In Zachary Karabell terms: "A substantial portion of China's trade with the world since the beginning of the millennium has been generated by foreign firms sourcing products in China in order to sell them somewhere else, and not because Chinese factory owners figured out what foreigners wanted and decided to produce low-cost versions...In addition, it's been estimated that more than 50 percent of China's exports were paid by foreign firms and were the result of foreign investments in China that led to the constructions of the factories that produced those goods. Those same foreign firms are also responsible for more than half of China's imports".[63]

Edward Luce expectedly points out: "Xi Jinping and his peers can bank on the support of their largest foreign investors, the multinational companies that have located large chunks of their production supply chains in China and other parts of the Asia Pacific".[64] The list of these foreign firms is huge. They include, among many others, illustrious names such as Apple, General Electric, Caterpillar, John

---

[63]Zachary Karabell, *Superfusion: How China and America Became One Economy and Why the World's Prosperity Depends on It* (New York: Simon & Schuster, 2009), pp. 156–157.
[64]Edward Luce, *op. cit.*, p. 294/4115.

Deere, Motorola, Nike, Intel, Procter & Gamble or General Motors. And, of course, their presence is far from limited to China. IBM has offshored a substantial part of its white-collar jobs to its subsidiary in India. In 2003, the company had 6,000 employees in India and 135,000 in the United States. In 2012, the situation had reversed: 110,000 Indian employees had substantially overtaken the company's US workforce.[65]

As for Asian companies that have extensively profited from international trade, we could begin by referring to China's "national champions". They represent the tip of the iceberg of China's well-defined technological strategy of concentrating efforts and synergies in 17 specific productive sectors and in a group of key state companies. Among them, we could name companies such as Lenovo, Huawei, Sunzone, Haier, Chery, PetroChina, Legend, TCL, China Mobile, etc. But beyond them, we find the four Chinese home-grown high-tech giants: Tencent, Alibaba, Baidu and Xiaomi.

India, as well, has its own giant companies. The most globalized of them are those involved in the international IT sector. Among a long list, we find Tata Consultancy Services, Infosys, Wipro, HCL Technologies, Tech Mahindra, Mphasis, Mindtree and Hexaware Technologies.

Other Asian companies as well have concentrated in offshored manufacturing, playing an important role within the global value chains. The most visible of these is Taiwan's Foxconn, the world's largest electronics manufacturer with 1.2 million workers just in its Chinese factories. Besides manufacturing Apple's iPhone, its most important product, Foxconn produces Sony's PlayStation 3, the Nintendo Wii and Amazon's Kindle Fire. It is also a major assembler of TVs for Sony, Sharp and Toshiba, of networking equipment for CISCO, of PCs for Hewlett-Packard, Dell and ACER, and of consoles for Microsoft, Nintendo and Sony. It is obvious that Foxconn and its customers are involved in a mutually dependent relationship.

Within these stakeholders of globalization, we find as well the large Western retailers. Chiefly among them is Walmart. In Zachary Karabell's

---

[65] Edward Luce, *Time to Start Thinking: America and the Spectre of Decline* (London: Little, Brown, 2012).

words: "It's been estimated that in the first years of the twenty-first century, as much as 15 percent of all U.S. imports from China were goods for sale at Walmart stores, worth a total of $ 18 billion in 2004 alone. If Walmart were a country, it would have been China's sixth largest export market".[66]

As a result, Walmart has not only disrupted small businesses all around the United States, but has offered to tens of millions of economically displaced or stressed Americans access to middle class goods that, otherwise, would have been beyond their reach. Besides this emblematic company, but never to the same extent, many other large retailers in the US or Europe benefited from China's low-cost products.

Also, within the group of beneficiaries of globalization, reference must be made to the global freighters. Maritime freighters top the list. Two main modes of shipping are herein involved: the tramp and the liner. The tramp market is for the movement of bulk commodities like oil, grain or coal, and is essentially based on charter. Tramp ships trade on the spot market, with no fixed schedule, itinerary or ports of call. Moreover, the volatility in the price of commodities, with particular reference to oil, creates a lot of uncertainty in tramp shipping costs. Chartering is done chiefly at London, New York or Singapore ship broking's exchanges. Amid the larger tramp ship companies, we find Japan's Mitsuy OSK Lines, US's United Maritime Group and Seabulk Tankers or Denmark's D/S Norden and Dampskibsselkabet Torm.

The liner shipping, on the other hand, is for general cargo, with the large majority of it being containerized and based on a fixed set of routes and a fixed timetable of movements. Transport costs, by contrast to tramp shipping, are much more predictable, although as spaces come and go on board, prices also move. Many of these behemoths carry over 19,000 standard-size containers per trip.[67]

The largest of them, the so-called Triple E class, can carry 30 times as many containers as the original container ships dating back to 1950, with their building costs being in the order of US$200 million.[68] In 2016, 20 of

---

[66] Zachary Karabell, *op. cit.*, p. 223.
[67] Finbarr Livesey, *op. cit.*, p. 83.
[68] *Ibid*, pp. 84–90.

the largest shipping companies sold US$200 billion in transport services.[69]

Denmark's Moller–Maersk Group is the largest of the liner shipping companies. With subsidiaries and offices in more than 135 countries, 89,000 employees and 585 ships, it has a tonnage capacity of 301,172. Closely following Maersk is the Swiss company Mediterranean Shipping Company (MSC) with 496 ships and a tonnage capacity of 2,659,489. In the group, as well, are the French CMA CGM S.A., the Chinese Cosco Shipping Corporation, the Taiwanese Evergreen Marine, the Germans Hapag-Lloyd and Hamburg Sud, the South Korean Hanjin Shipping, Hong Kong's OOCL, Dubai's United Arab Shipping Company, the Japanese Mitsuy O.S.K. Lines, the Singaporean American President Lines and Taiwan's Yang Mig Marine.

The air freighters play a less relevant role than the maritime ones, although still important. Among them, we could mention America's FedEx and UPS Airlines, the German DHL, Luxembourg's Cargolux or the Chinese Sinotrans. The main commercial airlines have also freighter's subsidiaries. The efforts made by these companies, in order to capture a part of the gigantic market of documents and industrial parts, is exemplified by FedEx. In Zachary Karabell's words: "In the 1990s alone, FedEx purchase of a local air carrier, its construction of new airports, and its spending on logistic capabilities through Asia in order to serve the China market, amounted to billions of dollars".[70] These, like any many other similar companies, have been active helping services and manufacturing.

The Entrusted Ones

Finally, we have to add to this long list the names of two multilateral institutions who have been entrusted with the promotion and stability of international trade: the World Trade Organization (WTO) and the IMF.

---

[69] Jaime Malet, "International trade is slowing. What does this mean for globalization?", *World Economic Forum*, 17 November 2017. https://www.weforum.org/agenda/2017/11/international-trade-is-slowing-what-does-this-mean-for-globalization/. Accessed 3 March 2018.

[70] Zachary Karabell, *op. cit.*, p. 107.

WTO is an international body of 164 members, including all major trading economies. It deals with the rules of trade between nations. It aims at helping a smooth international trade, while providing a constructive outlet for dealing with disputes over trade issues. The WTO succeeded the famous GATT.

The IMF, of which much has been said, is an international organization of 189 member countries that works to ensure the stability of the international monetary and financial system. However, its mandate includes facilitating the expansion and balance growth of international trade. The work of the WTO and the IMF becomes, thus, complementary and a good deal of cooperation exists between them.

Since the overwhelming influence that the IMF and the WTO's predecessor GATT, held during the launching years of globalization, much water has passed under bridge. Let us retake their history at the point where we left it, in order to understand where they stand today.

WTO originated in 1995 as the appointed heir to GATT, which had disappeared the year before at the completion of the Uruguay Round. It was in this new forum that subsequent international negotiations in trade and investments were to take place. However, at the WTO summit in Seattle in November–December 1999, a turning point took place.

In Seattle, developing economies, faced with the fact that their costly sacrifices in the areas of services, intellectual property and trade liberalization had not been met with due reciprocity, began to assume a much more assertive position. In Joan E. Spero and Jeffrey A. Hart words: "Significant differences existed between the North and the South. The developed countries pressed for the inclusion of new issues such as labor and environmental standards, while the developing countries demanded a focus on dismantling existing barriers to trade in agricultural goods and apparel and on tempering antidumping measures in developed economies".[71]

At the time of this summit, the United States was not only passing stricter trade regulations and raising its non-tariff barriers, but most of the developed countries had not reduced agricultural subsidies as offered during the Uruguay Round. According to Joseph Stiglitz: "Western countries

---

[71] Joan E Spero and Jeffrey A Hart, *op. cit.*, p. 106.

pushed trade liberalization for the products that they exported, but at the same time continued to protect those sectors in which competition from developing countries might have threatened their economies. This was one of the bases of the opposition to the new round of trade negotiations that was supposed to be launched in Seattle".[72]

A New Feeling of Empowerment

China's entry into the WTO in 2001 and the combined leverage of this nation with the other three big emerging economies, India, Brazil and South Africa, provided the developing world with a new platform. The weakness and prostration that had prevailed among these countries during the Uruguay Round, were definitively left behind. A new feeling of empowerment was in the air.

The developing countries would consolidate this new attitude during the three subsequent WTO summits at Doha, Cancun and Hong Kong, and at related negotiations in Paris, Potsdam and Geneva (the Doha Development Round). As Joan E. Spero and Jeffrey A. Hart explained: "In Seattle in 1999 and Doha in 2001, the developing countries argued that they have achieved little in the Uruguay Round and had made important and costly concessions to the developed countries in services and intellectual property...The South was strongly opposed to including new issues in the next round until old issues were satisfactorily resolved".[73]

In Kishore Mahbubani words, "The Doha Round is not making progress ostensibly because both the EU and the US refuse to adhere to their previous commitment and end the massive subsidies to their agricultural sectors. Each year, the EU spends an average of 49 billion euros (US$ 67.5) and the US more than US$ 20 billion on agricultural subsidies".[74]

The Doha Development Round showcased the confrontation between developed and developing economies. Within it, developing economies forged common positions around matters such as elimination of

---

[72] Joseph Stiglitz, *op. cit.*, pp. 60–61.
[73] Joan E Spero and Jeffrey A Hart, *op. cit.*, p. 258.
[74] Kishore Mahbubani, *The New Asian Hemisphere: The Irresistible Shift of Global Power to the East* (New York: Public Affairs, 2008), p. 38.

agricultural subsidies, access to industrialized markets for non-agricultural goods, special and differential treatment, the special case of cotton and the so-called "Singapore issues" (investments, competition, public markets transparency and trade easing). This eye-to-eye relation with the developed world represented the sign of a new time.

There was no way forward during the Doha Round; while the United States remained inflexible regarding the subsidy to its cotton producers, Japan did the same with its producers of rice and the European Union continued to be the most protracted provider of agricultural subsidies. In other words, there was no way forward for the Doha Round. In 2008, a breakdown in negotiations took place and any possibility of progress stalled. In the middle of this no-man land situation, WTO cannot lend much support to the advancement of international trade rules, but neither does it have the capacity to be partial towards the Western world and market economy, as it happened in GATT's time.

There is an area, nonetheless, where WTO still provides a unique contribution to globalization. Through its dispute settlement mechanisms, the organization remains the main arbiter among its 164 member countries. Since 1995, over 500 disputes have been brought to this organization and 350 rulings have been issued.

The Lazarus Effect

As for the IMF, discredit was unavoidable due to the many disruptions it brought about with its inflexibility and its "one size fits all" approach. As a result, there followed another, if shorter, lethargic period for the organization. An even bigger financial crisis, though, had a second Lazarus effect on the IMF.

A summit of the newly created G20, that gathered the largest developed and emerging economies, was held in Washington D.C. on November 15, 2008. Its aim was to articulate a response to the financial crisis that was overwhelming the world. Countries representing 90 percent of the global economy and around 75 percent of the world's population, agreed on a 3,600 words document of seven points. Points 5 and 7 of said aid document assigned to the IMF a very important role in confronting the crisis.

The IMF deployed its newly reinforced financial power and its cross-country experience, mobilizing resources to support its member countries. Its financial might on this occasion amounted to US$700 billion. This time, the IMF left aside the one-size-fits-all prescriptions, tailoring loan terms to countries in accordance to their varying strength and circumstances. And, even if structural reforms for borrowing countries continued to be part of its support programs, they became more focused on areas critical for recovery purposes. Moreover, having learned the lesson derived from the Washington Consensus period, the IMF has tried to protect social spending in borrowing countries.

Nonetheless, as the Southern European debt crisis showed, the IMF still supported, albeit reluctantly, the policy of putting all the burden on debtor countries and in demanding from them strict austerity policies. According to Stephen D. King: "Thereafter, the governments of the creditor nations (most obviously Germany, but also the Netherlands and Finland) alongside the so-called Troika (the European Commission, the European Central Bank and, reluctantly, the IMF) demanded that the 'borrower nations' should shoulder the burden of adjustment. Austerity imposed upon the debtors was seen as the best way of minimizing the creditors' loss — and reserving the stability of the financial system — even though the creditors themselves had been part of the problem, too happy to send their savings to other parts of the world without thinking carefully enough about how those savings would be invested".[75]

This means that even if the IMF has become more flexible and plural than its former self, many of its old habits still remain. However, its approach to globalization is not as rigid as it used to be. Market economy fundamentalism is certainly out of the picture and, according to the statements of its President Christine Lagarde, resistance against the siren call of protectionism have to be supported by a fight against social inequality, particularly in developed economies.

Even though WTO and IMF are the entrusted guardians of globalization, their strength has been diminished. The dispute settlement mechanism remains as the sole area where WTO remains really relevant. The IMF, even if assigned big responsibilities by the November 2008 G20

---

[75] Stephen D King, *op. cit.*, p. 74.

summit, only plays a real protagonist role in Europe, and even there it has been dependent on Germany's lead. Today, these institutions are but shadows of their former self. In terms of their meaning for the future of globalization, they are not in the same league as Chiindia and the Indo-Pacific region.

But the list of supporters of globalization is larger. If we were to include in it the financial and insurance interests involved in international trade, many additional pages would need to be written. The pro-globalization camp is, then, a lax and hugely diverse coalition, characterized by its plurality. Not all of its members, though, have the same strength or the capacity to actively promote it. In the next chapter, we shall see where the greater possibilities of advancement converge.

CHAPTER THREE

CHINA: GLOBALIZATION'S DRIVING FORCE

The Transatlantic Trade and Investment Partnership (TTIP), whose negotiation began in 2013, could have been an important driving force for globalization. If so, a more balanced situation might have existed between the Atlantic and the Pacific basins. However, negotiations between the United States and the European Union were halted indefinitely following the 2016 US presidential election. Moreover, both Europe and the US have become inauspicious places for globalization, as governments and populations have become weary of its social costs.

That being the case, Asia and particularly the Indo-Pacific region have turned into the new epicenters of globalization. Sheer numbers alone elevate the importance of the Indo-Pacific region and its global influence. It is home to more than 65 percent of the world's population and collectively produces more than 60 percent of global GDP. Over half of the world's trade passes through this region, which will have a disproportionately high contribution to global growth in the decades ahead.[1] It is here where the relaunching of globalization meets all the right opportunities: big funds, huge projects and shared conviction on its merits by both governments and populations. It is here, as well, where the emergence of a potent middle class opens the largest opportunities for its expansion.

---

[1] Samir Saran, "India's future as world power depends on 4 key relationships", World Economic Forum, 23 July 2018, https://www.weforum.org/agenda/2018/07/india-power-democratic-geoestrategic-relationships/. Accessed 27 July 2018.

Chindia

Within the Indo-Pacific region, Chindia plays the leading role. The first thought that comes to mind when reflecting about the future of globalization is indeed the contraction Chindia. This becomes a mighty term that evokes the two biggest emerging markets of the world. Countless opportunities for international trade will be found, indeed, when the middle classes of these countries reach their full potential.

Chindia makes reference to the combined force of two countries that until 1820 represented almost 50 percent of the world GDP, and which are on their way to reclaim their former preeminence. As Kishore Mahbubani states: "...the kind of incredible domination of the world that America and the West enjoyed for the last 200 years was a hugely artificial moment of history. For 1,800 of the last 2,000 years, the two largest economies in the world were consistently China and India. So by 2050, or earlier, the No. 1 economy will be China, No. 2 India, No. 3 the United States of America — that's the normal scheme of things".[2]

Edward Luce adds to the forecast: "By 2050 — a century after its communist revolution — China's economy is likely to be twice the size of America's and larger than all the Western economies combined...And, by then, India's economy will be roughly the size as America's".[3] But he also refers to the past economic might: "For roughly seven centuries, between 1100, shortly after the Norman Conquest, and 1800, when the Industrial Revolution took off, China accounted for roughly a quarter of global economy — and an even higher share of its estimated production. By one recent historical measure, China and India in 1750 produced three-quarters of the world's manufactures".[4]

According to Phillip S. Golub, in 1750, the combined manufacturing production of China and India represented 57.3 percent of the global output, while Europe just accounted for 23.2 percent.[5] At that point in time,

---

[2] Kishore Mahbubani, "The seesaw of power: A conversation with Joseph Nye, Dambisa Moyo and Kisshore Mahbubani", *International Herald Tribune Magazine*, 24 June 2011.
[3] Edward Luce, *op. cit.*, p. 316/4115.
[4] *Ibid*, p. 234/4115.
[5] Philip S Golub, "Quand la Chine et L'Inde dominaent le monde", *Maniere de Voir*, París, Janvier-March 2006.

these two countries represented the "central" regions of the world.[6] In 1700, India was responsible for 24 percent of the world's manufacturing output while Great Britain just represented 3 percent.[7] According to Adam Smith, in 1776, China was richer than all of Europe put together.[8] However, in 1900, China and India jointly represented just 7 percent of the world's manufacturing output.[9] Fifty years later, their combined GDP share of the world economy was only 8.8 percent.[10]After much humiliation and pillage by Western powers (including the deindustrialization imposed upon them through coercion and unfair trade treaties), and after huge mistakes of their own making as well, China and India are back. If we were to believe Kishore Mahbubani's assertion, Western predominance may well end up being a brief 200-year interlude, within Asia's multimillenary economic supremacy.

According to Morgan Stanley Smith Barney, in 2030, China's share of world GDP is expected to reach 23.1 percent and India's 10.4 percent, i.e., a combined 33.5 percent. Ten years later, in 2040, China should attain 40 percent and India 12 percent. In other words, with an expected combined percentage of 52 percent of the world's GDP in 2040, they will be surpassing its combined GDP global share of 1820, which was 48.9 percent.[11] The Organization of Economic Cooperation and Development (OECD), on its side, estimates that in 2030 China will gather 28 percent of the global GDP, while India will reach 11 percent. That is, 39 percent of the global GDP.[12]

---

[6]Gunder Frank Andre, "The world economic system in Asia before European hegemony", *The Historian*, 1994, Volume 56, Issue 2, pp. 259–276.

[7]Niall Ferguson, *Empire: How Britain Made the Modern World* (London: Penguin Books, 2004).

[8]Philip S Golub, *op. cit.*

[9]*Ibid.*

[10]T. N. Srinivasan, *Growth, Sustainability, and India's Economic Reforms* (Oxford: Oxford University Press, 2011).

[11]Edward M Kerschener and Naeema Huq, "Asian Affluence: The Emerging 21st Century Middle Class", New York, June 2011, http://www.morganstanleyfa.com/public/projectfies/35257b34-b160-45e4-980d-8bca327db92b.pdf. Accessed 13 July 2017.

[12]Åsa Johansson, *et al.*, "Looking to 2060: Long-term global growth prospects", OECD Economic Policy Papers, N. 03, 2012, http://www.oecd.org/eco/outlook/2060%20policy%20paper%20final.pdf. Accessed 25 February 2017.

As referred to by Anil K. Gupta and Haiyan Wang: "Starkly put China and India are changing the rules of the global game. They are two of the world's ten largest and the two fastest growing economies. Thus, they account for the two biggest growth opportunities for almost any product or service...They are two of the world's poorest economies in terms of per capita income. Thus, they offer some of the lowest wage rates for blue-and white-collar work-wage rates that can have a transformational effect on competitive advantage. They are the world's two largest producers of science and engineering graduates. Thus, they represent an opportunity to radically expand a company's intellectual capabilities without a proportionate increase in cost structure. And finally, they are the breeding ground for a new cohort of ambitious, aggressive, and fast-moving global champions".[13]

At the same time, the combination of rapid growth and big population that characterizes both offers them a spectacular advantage. Despite its fast growth in previous decades, Japan could have never expected to surpass US's GDP for the simple reason that is population is hardly 40 percent of that of the United States. On the contrary, China would only require that its per capita income becomes a quarter of that of the United States, in order to surpass that country's GDP. Hereafter, its population dimension would allow China to guarantee itself several additional decades of sustained economic growth at high rates. Something similar could be said about India.

In GDP per capita terms, China is today where Japan was in 1965, while India is where Japan was in 1950, which means that there is still a lot of tissue to cut upon. Not surprisingly, it has been estimated that during the decade of 2040, both countries will represent 40 percent of the total world market. Indeed, according to the OECD, China's middle class spending in 2020 will surpass that of the United States and in 2027 that of the 27 countries of the European Union, whereas India will move ahead of the United States in 2021 and the European Union in 2026, respectively.[14]

According to a Euromonitor International study, China's middle class will reach 700 million people in 2020, representing 48 percent of the total population of the country, whereas McKinsey estimates that by 2025

---

[13] Anil K Gupta and Haiyan Wang, *op. cit.*, pp. 1–2.

[14] *Ibid*; Jacques Attali, "Regional Outlook Forum", Institute of Southeast Asian Studies Lecture, Singapore, 12 January 2011; Edward M Kerschener and Naeema Huq, *op. cit.*

India's middle class will reach 583 million people, representing 41 percent of its total population. In other words, this embodies a combined middle-class consumer market of 1,283 million people.[15] However, using lower income estimates, the World Economic Forum reports that India's middle class reached 600 million in 2012, after having doubled from 300 million in 2004. According to them: "From 2027 India's population is set to overtake China's and the middle class will overtake that of the United States, Europe and China".[16] In either case, numbers are simply staggering. No other consuming market in the world will stand up to Chiindia.

China's Steps of the Route

But within Chindia, China's unstoppable drive to a position of leadership in the expansion of globalization has been fundamental. This route towards leadership, though, has not been easy, obvious or linear. It began as the natural by-product of its explosive international commercial interconnectedness, after its access to WTO in 2001. It continued as an expression of the country's willingness to create a parallel institutional framework to the Western controlled multilaterals. It went on as a mean of transforming the country in the center of an expanding supply chain and as the nucleus of the Asian economic integration process. It kept on by way of promoting its cities and companies into a position of world leadership. And, finally, it has become expression of a torch passing, as the United States is forfeiting its willingness to lead the international economy. Let us try to look closer into each step of that route.

In 2011, the United Nations Economic Commission for Latin America and the Caribbean, ECLAC, pointed out that the South–South exchange, headed by China, was the main driving force of global trade growth. The volume of exports from developing countries had, indeed, grown by

---

[15] *People's Daily Online*, 20 July 2010, http://english.people.com.cn/90001/90778/90862/7072426.html. Accessed 12 May 2013; "The 'Bird of Gold': The rise of India's consumer market", McKinsey Global Institute, May 2007, http://www.mckinsey.com/featured-insights/asia-pacific/the-bird-of-gold. Accessed 14 March 2018.

[16] Keith Breene, "6 surprising facts about India's exploding middle class", World Economic Forum, 7 November 2016, https://www.weforum.org/agenda/2016/11/6-surprising-facts-about-india-s-exploding-middle-class/. Accessed 14 March 2018.

17 percent in 2010 compared with 13 percent in developed countries.[17] The year before, Gordon Brown had written: "This weakening of the European, American and Japanese growth rate also reflects the fundamental shift taking place across the world in the location of production and the direction of trade...And with China leading the growth of South–South trade, globalization will no longer be dominated by trade between today's developed countries".[18] In 2012, indeed, China had become the first or the second trade partner for 78 countries, representing 55 percent of the global GDP.[19]

Some good examples of the above were the trade expansions experienced between China and Latin America and China and Africa. The former had gone from US$8.3 billion in 1999 to US$233.7 billion in 2011, while the latter grew from US$10 billion in 2000 to US$114.81 billion in the period between January and November 2010. At that point, China had already surpassed the United States as the largest trade partner with Africa, while its trade with Latin America was growing at nearly twice the level of that region with the United States. Trade between China and India had also gone from US$1.8 billion in 2001 to US$60 billion in 2010.[20]

The increase in trade between China and the Arab world was so impressive that experts were already talking about the reconstitution of the Silk Road: "The door between the Arab world and China, which was shut

---

[17] "Exports from Latin America and the Caribbean will increase in 27% in 2011", Economic Commission for Latin America and the Caribbean, Santiago de Chile, Press Release, 31 August 2011, https://www.cepal.org/en/pressreleases/exports-latin-america-and-the-caribbean-will-increase-27-2011. Accessed 27 March 2013.

[18] Gordon Brown, *Beyond the Crash: Overcoming the First Crisis of Globalisation* (London: Simon & Schuster, 2010), p. 136.

[19] Sistema Económico Latinoamericano, "Las relaciones entre China y América Latina y El Caribe en la actual coyuntura económica mundial" (Caracas: Ediciones SELA, septiembre 2012).

[20] John Naisbitt and Doris Naisbitt, *op. cit.*; Ruth Morris, "China: Latin America trade jumps", *LBC Latin Business Chronicle*, 9 May 2011; Comisión Económica para América Latina y El Caribe, *La República Popular China y América Latina y el Caribe: Diálogo y Cooperación ante los Nuevos Desafíos de la Economía Mundial* (Santiago de Chile: Junio de 2012); "China, Africa trade increase in 2010", Africa News.com, http://www.africanews.com/site/list_message32503. Accessed 12 January 2012; Chi Ravi Vellor, "India's passage to China", *The Straits Times*, 7 January 2011.

for centuries, is now open again".[21] China's exports to Arab countries worth US$6 billion in 2000 had reached US$60 billion in 2010. In the process, China had overtaken the United Kingdom in 2002, Germany in 2006 and the United States in 2008, as the larger exporter to this region.[22]

Edward Luce gives us the proper context of what was happening: "From barely a statistical rounding error in 1978, with less than 1 percent of global trade, China rose to become in 2013 the world's leading trading nation with almost a quarter of its annual flows...Nothing on this scale or speed has been witnessed before in history".[23]

At that time, unsurprisingly, China accounted for 13.6 percent of the global GDP. What is surprising, though, is the lack of connection between this figure and its percentage share and voting power within the IMF, which remained at just 3.8 percent. In fact, in 2014, China surpassed the US in GDP measured in Purchasing Power Parity (PPP).[24] Indeed, while the US accounted for US$17.4 trillion, China had reached US$17.6 trillion. Nonetheless, China's paltry voting power of 3.8 percent stood against 17.9 percent for the United States, which was short of absurd.

The Western Cabal

China's possibilities of increasing this utterly unfair ceiling, proved to be dim. Indeed, on two occasions the country tried to obtain a better positioning within the IMF, to no avail. One came a result of the talks for recapitalizing the International Monetary Fund, on occasion of the 2007–2008 financial crisis. The other came during the Eurozone Crisis in 2011.

In the first instance, the US Congress rejected any reorganization of the IMF quotas that could translate into a larger voting power for emerging economies, and particularly for China. In the second instance, China offered to provide US$100 billion to help ease the Eurozone crisis, and in return it asked Europe for support in obtaining more influence at the IMF. The European Union also spurned Beijing's demands.

---

[21] Ben Simpfendorfer, *The New Silk Road* (New York: Pelgrave Macmillan, 2011), p. 160.
[22] *Ibid.*
[23] Edward Luce, *op. cit.*, p. 219/4115.
[24] The PPP exchange rate translates into the equal amount of goods and services that can be bought by using two different currencies.

In relation to the second of these two cases, Benjamin Lim and Nick Edwards, Reuters' Correspondents in Beijing, wrote: "The IMF route would have been the simplest diplomatically, especially after European Union (EU) leaders last month laid out a plan to leverage up the resources of its crisis-fighting fund through an IMF-backed investment vehicle. But the sources in Beijing said this option was abruptly closed to China when it became clear to EU politicians that any investment from China would be contingent on gaining a greater say in IMF decision-making and a more rapid path to inclusion of China's Yuan in the IMF's special drawing rights (SDR) currency unit. Increasing China's say at the IMF would mean reducing EU representation and possibly diluting the influence of the United States, which enjoys veto-power status given its voting rights at the IMF".[25]

So embedded is the notion that such institutions "belong" to developed economies, that even common-sense proposals such as the previous one were flatly rejected. In the words of Joseph Stiglitz: "To maintain a cabal among developed countries, whereby the US appoints the World Bank president and Europe picks the International Monetary Fund's head, seems particularly anachronistic and perplexing today, when the bank and the fund are turning to emerging-market countries as a source of funds".[26]

Indeed, both the elections of Christine Lagarde from France at the head of IMF and Jim Yong Kim from the United States as chief of the World Bank, were seen as expressions of times gone by. The fact that the latter was confronted by two obviously better qualified candidates from Nigeria and Colombia, which stood no chance as a result of the prevailing situation, made the iniquity even greater.

As Kishore Mahbubani said, it is futile for the 12 percent of the world's population who live in the West to imagine that they can determine the destinies of the remaining 88 percent, many of whom feel newly energized and empowered. However, if the West tries to continue its domination, he concludes, a backlash will become inevitable.[27]

---

[25] Benjamin Lim and Nick Edwards, "Politics stymie China's EU aid offer", *Reuters*, 11 November 2011, http://www.reuters.com/article/2011/11/11/us-china-europe-f-idUSTRE7AA2DU20111111. Accessed 20 March 2014.

[26] Joseph Stiglitz, "Picking the next chief: Whose World Bank is it?", *The Straits Times*, 12 April 2012.

[27] Kishore Mahbubani, *op. cit.*

Daniel W. Drezner clearly describes the situation in the following terms: "But unless rising powers such as China and India are incorporated into this framework, the future of these international regimes will be uncomfortably uncertain (....) If China and India are not made to feel welcome inside existing international institutions, they might create new ones — leaving the United States on the outside looking in (....) Global institutions cease to be appropriate when the allocation of decision-making authority within them no longer corresponds to the distribution of power".[28]

China's Led Parallel Multilateralism

In a foreseeable attempt, in their summit at the end of March 2012, the leaders of the BRICS member countries agreed to move towards creating a new development bank that would improve access to capital for developing nations, while agreeing as well to do deals with one another in their local currencies. China, as we shall see, played a leading role in this matter.

As Radhika Deasi clearly explains, without fanfare, the main emerging economies began to bypass the economic institutional architecture of the West: "The BRICS and emerging economies have already set in train a wider set of changes in the institutional architecture of the world order. Since Western powers maintain their grip on its major institutions, these rising powers have simply side-stepped them, setting up new institutions and using old minor ones in new ways. The result is a decentralised institutional structure that doesn't look like a rival to Western-dominated centralised and worldwide institutions at first sight. But it is. For example, it bypasses the US dollar-cantered world monetary and financial regime... Over this period, the International Monetary Fund's influence fell and it had to compromise key policy prescriptions — pre-eminently on capital controls — as regional development banks and arrangements between two or more developing economies to conduct trade in their own currencies undermined its monopoly".[29]

---

[28] Daniel W Drezner, "The new new world order", *Foreign Affairs*, 2007, Volume 86, pp. 34, 36, 39.
[29] Radhika Deasi, "The West must wake up to the growing power of the brics", *The Guardian*, 2 April 2012.

In 2014, China was instrumental in the creation of the BRICS' New Development Bank, whose headquarters are in Shanghai. The bank is called to support public and private projects through loans, guarantees and other financial instruments. Moreover, the bank aims at cooperating with international organizations and other financial entities, in order to provide technical assistance to projects supported by the bank. The initial authorized capital of the bank was US$100 billion, distributed in equal parts among its five members.

In 2015, the BRICS member countries established a Contingency Reserve Arrangement to provide protection against global liquidity pressures. This arrangement is seen as a competitor to the IMF. Within its capital of US$100,000 billion, the majority, US$39.95 billion, corresponds to China.

But before being instrumental in these initiatives, China was already asserting an important international role through the China Development Bank. Created in 1994, as an engine called to power the government's economic development, the bank was involved in the international financial positioning of the country. Besides being the second bond issuer in China, after the Ministry of Finance, it became a key international lender. Solely in Latin America, Chinese loan commitments between 2005 and 2013, reached US$130 billion. That amount represented more than what the World Bank, the Inter-American Bank and the World Bank, combined, lent to the region during that period. The majority of those resources, dedicated to infrastructure and energy projects in commodity exporting nations, came from the China Development Bank.[30]

At the same time, the country became a member of many multilateral institutions within emerging nations. According to Erik Berglof: "In fact, Chinese international engagement is now occurring on a scale and at a rate never seen before. China is a member of many multilateral institutions — including several regional players like the African Development Bank (AfDB) and the Inter-American Development Bank (IDB) — with which it is deepening its relationships, especially through co-investment in projects around the world. For example, China significantly ratcheted up its

---

[30] Jorge Guajardo, "A Latin American perspective on China's growing presence in the region", in Roett, R. and Paz, G. (eds.), *Latin America and the Asian Giants: Evolving Ties with China and India.* Washington D.C.: Brookings Institution Press, p. 69.

commitment to the AfDB last year through the $2 billion African Growing Together Fund".[31]

In the global financial sphere, China has been very active as well. The country has moved in two directions — on the one hand, pushing forward the internationalization of its currency, the renminbi; on the other hand, trying to position Shanghai as a global financial center. In relation to the former, it has tried to tie the renminbi as much as possible to its wide international trade network, which is the largest in the world.

The following quote by Oliver Stuenkel says much in relation to the second of these initiatives: "...one of the Chinese government's most ambitious and fascinating strategies, which symbolizes the extent to which China is willing to alter global structures: To turn Shanghai, a regional center running behind other geographically close cities like Hong Kong, into a global financial center capable of challenging New York and London, the world's only truly global financial centers. According to China's State Council, this should be achieved by 2020".[32]

China also played an important role in the creation of the Shanghai Cooperation Organization (SCO), whose organizational charter was signed in June 2002, entering into force on September 2003. This is a multifaceted organization, which, beyond the mutually agreed economic support, also covers security and political support. SCO is integrated by eight Eurasian member states that, in addition to China, also include India, Russia, Pakistan and several Central Asian states. This organization superseded the Shanghai Five Group, which had been founded in 1996 under the stewardship of China.

Funding Asia's Infrastructural Development

Moreover, China was the driving force behind the Asian Infrastructure Investment Bank (AIIB) and the Silk Road Fund. The first is a multilateral

---

[31] Erik Berglof, "Will China change the world's financial institutions?", World Economic Forum, 25 November 2015, https://www.weforum.org/agenda/2015/11/will-china-change-the-worlds-financial-institutions/. Accessed 19 March 2018.

[32] Oliver Stuenkel, "Can Shanghai become a global financial center?", Post-Western World, 24 August 2015, http://www.postwesternworld.com/2015/08/24/shanghai-global-financial/. Accessed 19 March 2018.

development bank that aims at supporting the building of infrastructures in the Asia-Pacific region. The initiative gathered support from 37 regional and 20 non-regional members. Currently the bank has 61 member states, while another 23 are prospective members. That could take the bank to 84 members, which by all accounts is a very representative number. Moreover, the capital of the bank is US$100 billion, which is half of that of the Word Bank. China pledged US$50 billion to the AIIB special fund, which will help low-income countries in developing infrastructure projects.

AIIB was proposed by China in 2013, and its launching initiative took place in Beijing in October 2014. Since the inception of the project, the United States opposed the initiative and tried to avoid the participation of its main European and Asian allies. The simple fact that China could have attained such a degree of financial might, in the fastest growing region of the planet, was seen as a threat by Washington.

The boycott's fortune, however, fell together with the first domino piece that did not buckle under the US's pressure: the United Kingdom. As soon as London decided to be a founding member of AIIB, before the foreclosure of its initial subscription period on March 31, 2015, the rest of the domino row followed: Germany, France, Italy, Netherlands, Switzerland, Spain, Australia, New Zealand, South Korea, etc. Washington's opposition proved to be insufficient against the opportunities offered by China's initiative.

The Silk Road Fund, differently from AIIB, is not a multilateral financial institution. It is a Chinese state-owned investment fund, whose aim is to foster investments in the countries along the One Belt One Road project. The Chinese government pledged US$40 billion for the creation of this investment fund, which was established in December 2014. The recipients of these investments will not only be Asian countries, but also European ones. The Silk Road Fund will complement AIIB in relation to infrastructure developments along the One Belt, One Road route. These initiatives are bound to close the door to Washington-based financial institutions in this gigantic project.

The One Belt, One Road Initiative, itself, is a development strategy proposed by the Chinese government that focuses on connectivity and cooperation between Asian, African and European countries. It was unveiled by President Xi Jinping in September and October of 2013. This mega infrastructure development plan covers more than 65 countries in Asia, Africa and Asia, and bears a price tag estimated at a trillion dollars.

One Belt, One Road

This mega-project which comprises a land route ("Silk Road Economic Belt") and a maritime route ("Maritime Silk Road"), aims at building highways, railways, pipelines, ports and industrial ports. The land route will go from Lianyungang in China to Rotterdam in the Netherlands, while the maritime one will depart from Quanzhou in China and end in Venice, Italy. The One Belt, One Road Initiative combines several land and maritime corridors that would link Central Asia, South East Asia, West Asia, the Indian Ocean, the Arabic Sea, the Persian Gulf, the Middle East, the Red Sea, the Mediterranean Sea, Eastern, Central and Western Europe and the Horn of Africa.

In relation to China's reasons behind the One Belt, One Road Initiative, Hugh White expresses: "China wants to consolidate its position at the centre of the global supply and manufacturing networks which will be the key to the global economy over the coming decades. Beijing understands that as China's economy matures and its income levels rise, the lower-wage industries which have fueled China's growth so far, will migrate to less-developed countries where labour costs are lower. China's economic planners don't want to fight that trend, but turn it to China's advantage by building itself an inexpugnable place at the centre of the expanding supply-chain web which will result from it".[33]

The One Belt, One Road project encompasses 65 percent of the world's population, about one third of the world's gross domestic product and about a quarter of the world's trade.[34] Making this bold vision a reality will require an extraordinary alignment of financial resources, political commitment,

---

[33] Hugh White, "China's One Belt, One Road to challenge US-led order", *The Straits Times*, 27 April 2017.
[34] Goh Sui Noi, "China makes tracks on modern Silk Road", *The Straits Times*, 11 May, 2017.

technical skills and international cooperation. It is by no means an easy task. However, the benefits that it may bring to so many are so significant, that numerous countries have shown their interest in this project.

It comes as no surprise that 110 countries were represented, some of them at the highest level, at the mid-May 2017 Beijing meeting to discuss the initiative. With commodities showing their lowest prices in more than a decade, the incentive to build an intercontinental web of infrastructure and trade links has been greatly enhanced. The China Development Bank alone has earmarked US$890 billion for some 900 projects herein involved.[35]

Anabel Gonzalez, from the World Economic Forum, provides an overly ambitious picture of the Belt and Road initiative and of its expansive possibilities: "It is the most ambitious initiative to improve regional economic integration and connectivity on a transcontinental scale: involving 'hard' infrastructure along six overland corridors, and the 21st Century Maritime Silk Road; 'soft' infrastructure, such as the financial system, to enhance efficiency and facilitate economic flows; and policy reforms and institution-building to promote trade and foreign direct investment among the 70 or so BRI countries. There is talk now of expanding it to Latin America or to shipping routes across the Artic, dubbed the 'Polar Silk Road'".[36]

Trade Agreements, Global Cities and Innovative Companies

Beijing has also been playing a major role in the proposed free trade agreement known as the Regional Comprehensive Economic Partnership (RCEP). This would include the 10 member states of ASEAN (Brunei, Cambodia, Indonesia, Laos, Malaysia, the Philippines, Singapore, Thailand, Myanmar and Vietnam), plus the six states with which ASEAN has existing free trade agreements: Australia, China, India, Japan, South Korea and New Zealand.

Formal negotiations for RCEP began in November 2012, and it is expected that it will be formally launched in Singapore, in November 2018.

---

[35] Belt and Road Forum, "Projects span rail, ports, industrial parks", *The Straits Times*, 15 May, 2017.

[36] Anabel Gonzalez, "Brexit, the US, China and the future of global trade", *World Economic Forum*, 12 February 2018, https://www.weforum.org/agenda/2018/02/brexit-china-global-trade/. Accessed 4 March 2018.

RCEP has been seen, and consequently Beijing's particular interest in it, as an alternative to the Trans-Pacific Partnership (TPP) which excluded China. Once in force, RCEP will be open to new members. As a conventional free trade agreement, it will have a lax structure when compared to the TPP.

RCEP member states will account for a population of 3.4 billion people and a combined GDP of US$49.5 trillion, which is approximately tantamount to 39 percent of the world's GDP. It will become the largest trading bloc on the planet and its importance will keep increasing in direct relation to the GDP increase of its member states.

At the 2014 APEC Economic Leaders' Meeting, held in Beijing, President Xi Jinping urged the group economies to approve a roadmap for achieving a Free Trade Area of the Asia-Pacific (FTAAP). As a result, a so-called Beijing Roadmap was adopted in order to push forward the FTAAP process. A collective strategic study of this plan was subsequently approved at the 2016 APEC summit in Lima, Peru.

In Lima, President Xi delivered a keynote speech in which he urged the building of the FTAAP, as protectionism had dented global trade and economic integration. Moreover, he urged APEC members to stay committed to taking economic globalization forward and to transform the Asia-Pacific region in a growth engine within an "innovative, invigorated, interconnected and inclusive world economy".[37]

Looking at China's international positioning from another perspective, reference has to be made to its global cities. Earlier this decade, Joseph Stiglitz proclaimed that the two significant forces that would shape global prosperity in the twenty-first century would be US technological innovation, and urbanization in China. The Chinese regime has been doing its homework in order to turn the Stiglitz prediction into reality. This implies a clear effort to improve the international competitiveness of its cities. A raft of initiatives has focused on increasing the ease of doing business and attracting more global investments into them.

China's big cities have been overly successful in attracting multinationals. According to a 2018 report from the consultants AT Kearney, China's cities are more competitive than those in any other region of the

---

[37]President Xi, "Highlights of President Xi's attendance at the Lima APEC Meeting", *Xinhua*, 21 November 2016.

world. Moreover, the number of Chinese cities included in the 2018 Global Cities Index, soared from seven in 2008 to 27, 10 years later. The index measures aspects like business activity, human capital, information exchange and cultural experience.[38]

On the other hand, Brookings' Global Metro Monitor draws on GDP and employment data from Oxford Economics to track the economic performance of the world's 300 largest metropolitan economies. In 2014, China accounted for fewer than 50 metropolitan areas within the top 300. In the 2018 monitor, measured using 2016 data, this number had increased to 103. This was more than North America and Western Europe combined. Moreover, again according to Brookings, in 2018, five Chinese cities were among the world's 10 best performing metropolitan economies.[39] Even if Chinese economy growth slowed by recent standards, its cities significantly outpaced the rest of the world.[40]

But jointly to the impressive projection of China's global cities, we find the equally impressive innovative character of its companies. According to *MIT Sloan Management Review*: "Chinese performers are undergoing a rapid transformation of their own as they seek to evolve from backroom producers to the world's leading face of innovation. Over the past five years, domestic Chinese companies have been innovating unlike ever before. In 2016, the National Supercomputer Center in Wuxi, China, unveiled the Sunway TaihuLight, the world's fastest supercomputer, with 10.65 million CPU cores, Meanwhile, Chinese company Ehang Inc., based in Guangzhou, launched the world's first aerial passenger drone, the Ehang 184, capable of autonomously transporting a person in the air for 23 minutes. These feats of Chinese ingenuity join many other

---

[38] Briony Harris, "Chinas cities are rapidly becoming more competitive. Here's why", World Economic Forum, 15 June 2018, https://www.weforum.org/agenda/2018/06/china-cities-more-economically-competitive/. Accessed 20 June 2018.

[39] Max Bouchet and Joseph Padilla, "The world's ten best performing metropolitan economies: 2018 edition", Brookings, July 12, 2018, https://www.brookings.edu/blog/the-avenue/2018/07/11/the-worlds-ten-best-performing-metropolitan-economies-2018-edition/?. Accessed 17 July 2018.

[40] Sifan Liu and Joseph Padilla, "Meet the five urban China", Brookings, 20 June 2018, https://www.brookings.edu/blog/the-avenue/2018/06/19/meet-the-five-urban-chinas/?. Accessed 22 June 2018.

recent innovations in a range of industries. Western companies beware. This is not the China you are accustomed to, and the ramifications for your research and development strategies may be profound".[41]

This has been the result of China's well-defined technological strategy, based on the following seven steps. First, concentrating efforts, investments and synergies in 17 specific productive sectors and in a group of key state companies, the so-called "national champions". Second, massively investing in Research and Development. Third, by way of a stick and carrot policy that promoted technological transfer from foreign corporations investing in China. Fourth, buying corporations with useful technology abroad. Fifth, attracting back Chinese scientists residing in other countries by way of generous incentives. Sixth, investing copiously in education and in the formation of technological cadres, including substantial investments in their universities. Seventh, setting up high-technology incubators that provide finance, physical facilities and advisory services to technology start-up companies.

Moreover, on September 10, 2014, Prime Minister Li Keqiang defined a clear roadmap under the phrase "Mass Entrepreneurship and Mass Innovation". This became the slogan for a momentous government push to foster start-up ecosystems and prioritize technological innovation. China's central government laid out a goal, whose implementation was left up to thousands of mayors and local officials scattered around the country.

At the end of the day, Chinese innovation has become evident in the most diverse sectors: artificial intelligence, robotics, telecommunications, software, financial technology, Internet business models, nanotechnology, high-end equipment and green technologies. As referred to by *MIT Sloan Management Review*: "Foreign companies are starting to recognize these changes. In a 2014 survey, two thirds of foreign executives said that Chinese companies are 'just as innovative or more innovative' than their own companies".[42] The time in which China was simply a foreign enclave economy is long behind. Today, Chinese companies are forcefully

---

[41] Dan Prud'homme and Max Von Zedtwitz, The changing face of innovation in China, *MIT Sloan Management Review*, 2018, Volume 59, Issue 4, p. 24.
[42] *Ibid*, p. 26.

competing with the best examples of ingenuity that the West can offer. The caveat, though, is that while this enhances China's position in the global economic stage, it also makes it more autonomous in relation to its trade with developing economies.

The Trans-Pacific Partnership

But beyond China's leadership in so many areas, we find the TPP. This was, precisely, the United States' answer to Chinese assertiveness. Indeed, President Obama's Administration wanted to confront China's rise by giving shape to an Asia-Pacific security and prosperity area for the twenty-first century. This project had two aims at large.

The first of them sought sustainable security by enrolling the US and its traditional allies in the region, so as to counterbalance China's emergence. The second objective was to promote what Obama called "our shared prosperity", essentially through an enlarged trans-Pacific trade and economic liberalization agreement: the TPP. Hugh White, professor of strategic studies at the Australian University of Canberra talked of an "Obama containment doctrine to China", describing it as "America's most ambitious new strategic doctrine since Truman committed America to contain the Soviet Union".[43]

The TPP went in the opposite direction to the Asia-Pacific economic strategy purposefully followed by China for many years. East Asian countries, thus, were placed in a difficult balancing act. On the one side they had China, and on the other the United States. According to Kwan Weng Kin: "Security analyst Yukio Okamoto warned... 'The TPP raises the question of whether the region should aim for a US-style free trade area or to co-exist with China'".[44]

President Trump's first act in office, though, was to withdraw his country from the TPP. Hence, Obama's "shared prosperity" approach suddenly disappeared from the equation. Henceforward, there would be just be the security leg to counterbalance China's emergence. This one leg seems clearly insufficient to fulfill that role, as probably many countries

---

[43] Hugh White, "Contain China?", *The Straits Times*, 26 November 2011.
[44] Kwan Weng Kin, "Japan's balancing act", *The Straits Times*, 23 November 2011.

of the region would be ready to accept a certain degree of "Finlandization" if China is the only one offering them good economic opportunities.

Counterbalancing the United States

TPP moved on towards completion, with its 11 remaining members. But instead of becoming a counterbalance to China, TPP has become an economic counterbalance to President Trump's protectionism. According to Ernesto Londoño and Motoko Rich: "A trade act originally conceived by the United States to counter China's growing economic might in Asia now has a new target: President Trump's embrace of protectionism. A group of 11 nations — including major allies of the United States like Japan, Canada and Australia — signed a broad trade deal on Thursday in Chile's capital, Santiago, that challenges Mr. Trump's view of trade as a zero-sum game filled with winners and losers. Covering 500 million people on either side of the Pacific Ocean, the pact represents a new vision of global trade as the United States imposes steel and aluminum tariffs on even some of its closest friends".[45]

As a Working Paper by the Peterson Institute for International Economics stated, the absence of the United States in the TPP presented both costs and benefits. Among the costs was the obvious loss of access to the US domestic market, which had been an important incentive for many of the members (particularly Vietnam). Among the benefits, though, were not only less rigorous provisions (as it is the case of discarding the controversial eight-year data exclusivity protection for biologic drugs, advocated by the US), but also even stronger incentives for others to join. The fact is that Indonesia, South Korea, the Philippines, Taiwan, Thailand and, even China, have all expressed interest in being members.[46]

As a result of negotiations, the 11 remaining countries, coming from both shores of the Pacific Basin and representing a combined GDP of US$13.7 trillion and a joint population of 500 million people, were able to

---

[45] Ernesto Londoño and Motoko Rich, "U.S. Allies sign sweeping trade deal in challenge to Trump", *The New York Times*, 8 March 2018.

[46] Peter Pietri, Michael G Plummer, Shujiro Urata and Fan Zhai, "Going it lone in the Asia-Pacific: Regional trade agreements without the United States", October 2017, https://papers.ssrn.com/sol3/papers.cfm?abstract_id=3047895. Accessed 19 March 2018.

eliminate more than 98 percent of tariffs between them. The agreement was finally signed in March 2018. Rebranded as the Comprehensive and Progressive Agreement for TPP, it came to life the same day President Trump signed steel and aluminum tariffs.

The table is now served for China to take advantage of the TPP. Again, in the words of Londoño and Rich: "When Obama was advocating the deal, he said that 'America should call the shots' instead of China. Now, signatories are opening the door for China to join. Heraldo Muñoz, Chile's foreign minister, told reporters on Thursday afternoon that Chinese officials have been weighing the possibility of signing on. 'This will be open to anyone who accepts its components' Mr. Muñoz said. 'It's not an agreement against anyone. It's in favor of open trade'".[47]

It is possible that in the end China might not be interested in joining TPP. This is a deep and comprehensive "new generation" trade agreement, which covers issues that transcend the kind of traditional free trade agreements preferred by Beijing. However, TPP is no longer a threat for China, nor does it present an adversarial approach to its leadership in the region. Much to the contrary, TPP signatories have become China's natural allies in counterbalancing Trump's protectionism. Londoño and Rich, quote Professor Jeffrey Wilson, head of the US–Asia Center at the University of Western Australia: "If you're a trade policy maker in Asia, your number one fear is that Trump is going to take a swing at you...The U.S. is really delivering the region to China at the moment".[48]

The Withdrawal Doctrine

But more than simply delivering Asia or the Pacific Basin, Trump has been delivering the leadership on globalization to China. According to Richard Hass: "When great powers fade, as they inevitably must, it's normally for one or two reasons. Some powers exhaust themselves trough overreach abroad, underinvestment at home, or a mixture of the two. This was the case of the Soviet Union. Other powers lose their privileged position with the emergence of a new, stronger power. This describes what

---

[47] Ernesto Londono and Motoko Rich, *op. cit.*
[48] *Ibid.*

happened with France and Great Britain in the case of Germany's emergence after World War I and, more benignly, with the European powers and the rise of the United States during and after World War II. To some extent America is facing a version of this — amid what Farid Zakaria has dubbed 'the rise of the rest' — with China's ascendance as the most significant development. But the United States has now introduced a third mean by which a major power forfeits international advantage. It is abdication, the voluntary relinquishing of power and responsibility. It is brought about more by choice than by circumstances either at home or abroad (…) Abdication is as unwarranted as it is unwise. It is a basic fact of living in a global world that no country can insulate itself from much of what happens elsewhere. A foreign policy based on sovereignty alone will not provide security in a global, interconnected world".[49]

Richard Hass, President of the Council on Foreign Relations, later coined the term "withdrawal doctrine" to describe this abdication. Daniel Quinn Mills and Steven Rosefielde labeled this introspective process as "democratic nationalism". According to them, this conception assumes that America is a large family in which the needs of the members of the family should not be sacrificed to those of people abroad, or to a US establishment in tune with such cosmopolitan interests.[50] Robert Kagan elucidates the reasons why American withdrawal would be the worst possible response to disturbing events around the world, especially so as it is based on a fundamental and dangerous misreading of such events. He talks about a "jungle growing back", to refer to that situation.[51]

As a result of these different interpretations of the same phenomenon, Trump retired his country from TPP and imposed sanctions on steel and aluminum to its closest trade partners, in a move reminiscent of the infamous Smoot–Hawley Act of 1930, which launched an international trade war. The list, though, is much longer than that. Trump also withdrew his country from the Paris Climate accord and from the United Nations

---

[49] Richard Hass, "America and the great abdication", *The Atlantic Magazine*, 28 December 2017.

[50] Daniel Quinn Mills and Rosefielde Steven, *The Trump Phenomenon and the Future of US Foreign Policy* (New Jersey: World Scientific, 2016).

[51] Robert Kagan, *The Jungle Grows Back: America and Our Imperiled World* (New York: Knopf Publishing Group, 2018).

Human Rights Commission. He threatened to pull out from NAFTA, while initiating a tough renegotiation of the treaty. He imposed tariffs on Chinese goods representing US$50 billion and, when Beijing reciprocated, it targeted for tariffs Chinese goods representing US$200 billion. Meanwhile, while threatening to reduce US's participation in NATO, Trump referred to Germany as a "captive of Russia", and gave some of America's closest NATO partners the label of "delinquents". While visiting Britain, he purposefully detonated a pro-Brexit bomb that weakened his hosts, and made his anti-European Union sentiment sufficiently clear. Moreover, during the same visit, he called the EU an economic "foe" to the United Sates. He has threatened to impose a 25 percent tariff on the automotive imports coming from the European Union, which represent more than 28 percent of all European exports to the United States. At the same time, he has threatened to withdraw from WTO, while aiming at killing its dispute settlement mechanism. And so on and so forth. The great disruptor seems to know no boundaries.

As a result, Trump's relations with its main allies have become atrocious. As James Kirchick explains: "Donald Trump ascended to the presidency challenging the basic precepts of America's relationship with Europe: NATO he proclaimed, was not only 'obsolete', but Washington should make its security commitment contingent upon alliance members paying 'their fair share'. The European Union was not an ally but a competitor that had 'been formed, partially to beat the United States on trade'. Against the express wishes of every European government — including, at the time, Britain's — Trump cheered along Brexit and conveyed ambivalence as to whether the European Union should continue to exist".[52]

Not surprisingly, the US's three closest allies in Europe, the UK, Germany and France, issued an official statement on April 2018, saying that they would forcefully defend their interests against Washington's protectionism. Moreover, on May 10, 2018, Angela Merkel declared in Aquisgran that the time in which Europe could trust the United States had ended.

---

[52] James Kirchick, "Europeans want to break with America: They'd do so at their peril", Brookings, 25 May 2018, https://www.brookings.edu/blog/order-from-chaos/2018/05/25/europeans-want-to-break-up-with-america-theyd-do-so-at-their-peril/. Accessed 26 May 2018.

On the same token, Canada and Mexico, US partners at NAFTA, expressed their outrage on May 31, 2018 at being targeted by the steel and aluminum taxes (as the temporal exception that benefited them and the EU was not extended). According to the BBC News: "Mr. Trump has justified the tariffs by arguing that US steel and aluminum producers are vital to national security…The Canadian Prime Minister Justin Trudeau described that claim as an affront. 'That Canada could be considered a national security threat to the United States is inconceivable', he said…Mexican Foreign Minister Luis Videgaray said his country would also impose duties".[53]

Step by step, thus, Donald Trump has been alienating all US major trade partners. As was to be expected, the G7 fractured in two groups. On the one hand the United States. On the other, all the rest. In relation to the June 2018 summit of the group, *The New York Times* reported: "Earlier Thursday, President Emmanuel Macron of France and Prime Minister Justin Trudeau of Canada lashed out at Mr. Trump for imposing tariffs on their steel and aluminum industries… 'The American President may not mind being isolated, but neither do we mind signing a 6 country agreement if need be'".[54] And, indeed, that was the case, as the six other members signed the final G7 document, while the US abstained from doing so.

Donald Tusk, the President of the European Council, has expressed his bewilderment with this situation in the following terms: "What worries me the most is the fact that the rules-based international order is being challenged, quite surprisingly not by the usual suspects, but by its main architect and guarantor, the US…Undermining this order makes no sense at all, because it will only play into the hands of those who seek a new post-West order…".[55]

China's Taking of the Torch

And, indeed, President Xi Jinping has taken advantage of every possible opportunity to assert his country's willingness to take the torch from a

---

[53] "Trade tariffs: Chorus of condemnation intensifies", 31 May 2018.
[54] Michael D Shear, "Anger flares up as group of 7 heads to Quebec", 7 June 2018.
[55] Julian Borger and Anne Perkins, "Donald Trump calls for the G7 to readmit Russia", *The Guardian*, 8 June 2018.

withdrawing United States, within a new post-West order. At the Da Nang Asia-Pacific Cooperation Forum in November 2017, he told the assembly: "We should uphold multilateralism, pursue shared growth through consultation and collaboration, forge closer partnerships, and build a community with a shared future for mankind".[56]

A month before, at the 19th Communist Party Congress in October 2017, Mr. Xi proclaimed: "China will take the lead in international cooperation on climate change". Moreover, he added that "this is an era that will see China move closer to the centre of the world and make more contributions to humankind".[57] In January of the same year, at the World Economic Forum in Davos, Xi stated: "It is true that economic globalization has created new problems. But this is no justification to write off economic globalization altogether. Rather we should adapt and guide globalization, cushion its negative impact, and deliver its benefits to all countries and all nations (...) The global economy is the big ocean you cannot escape from...China has learned how to swim (...) We should commit ourselves to growing an open global economy (...) World history shows that the road of human civilization has never been a smooth one and that mankind has made progress by surmounting difficulty...When encountering difficulty we should not complain, blame others, or run away from responsibilities. Instead we should join hands and see to the challenge. History is made by the brave".[58]

Also, in June of 2017, China and the European Union prepared a joint statement to uphold the Paris Agreement on Climate Change, as the US pulled out from its commitment to it. On that occasion, *The Guardian* wrote: "The expected announcement in Brussels illustrates China's determination to take a leadership role in the world".[59]

---

[56] Nayan Chanda, "Trump Abdicates Global Leadership to China's Xi", *AsiaSentinel*, 17 November 2017, https://www.asiasentinel.com/opinion/donald-trump-passes-abdicates-global-leadership-xi-jinping/. Accessed 20 March 2018.

[57] Tay Hwee Peng, "19th party congress: 7 key themes from President Xi Jinping's work report", *The Straits Times*, 18 October 2017.

[58] Ceri Parker, "China's Xi Jnping defends globalization from the Davos stage", World Economic Forum, 17 January 2017, https://www.weforum.org/agenda/2017/01/chinas-xi-jinping-defends-globalization-from-the-davos-stage/. Accessed 20 March 2018.

[59] Daniel Boffey and Arthur Nelsen, "China and EU strengthen promise to Paris deal with US poised to step away", *The Guardian*, 1 June 2017.

In July 2018, at the BRICS summit held in Johannesburg, President Xi forcefully defended economic multilateralism and free trade, alerting against the dangers of unilateralism and protectionism. Addressing the existing dilemma between cooperation and conflict, he insisted in the need of working together on behalf of the common good.

As Anthony J. Blinken reluctantly recognizes: "All of this positions China to become, in Mr. Xi's words, 'a new choice for other countries' and the principal arbiter of something long associated with the United States: the international order. China has a profound stake in that order and a globalized world (…) I'd never bet against the United States, but if the Trump-led retreat into nationalism, protectionism, unilateralism and xenophobia continues, China's model could carry the day".[60] Even a country like Germany, as close to Washington as it is possible, is accepting this new reality. A poll released on May 2018, found that while 14 percent of Germans still believed that the United States was a "reliable partner", 43 percent (the highest mark) saw China as the new privileged ally.[61]

What a decade ago would have been unimaginable, the generalized acceptance of China as the leader of the globalized economy, is becoming a reality. In the process, the parallel globalization that China developed to overcome the constraints imposed upon its emergence by Western powers, has moved into center stage. The window of opportunity opened by the sudden withdrawal of the US found China ready. As a good surfer, Beijing had the surfboard in place when the big wave appeared. This, of course, would have not been possible had globalization not evolved from its initial market economy orientation into a more plural and multicultural content.

However, as we shall see next, while China has emerged as the leading driving force of globalization, many of its traditional Western supporters, and not just the United States, are weathering and eroding it.

---

[60] Anthony J Blinken, "Trump is ceding global leadership to China", *The New York Times*, 8 November 2017.
[61] James Kirchick, *op. cit.*

CHAPTER FOUR

THE ANTI-GLOBALIZERS

Against globalization plays the conviction that this phenomenon has had a very negative impact on the economies and the social tissues of countless countries, developed ones in particular, that, it has represented a zero-sum game in which emerging economies have unilaterally benefited, at the expense of the decline of traditionally rich societies. Above all, there exists the view that globalization identifies itself with greedy elites and corporations from developed economies, which have disproportionally enriched themselves, at the expense of the middle classes and the common citizen, who have carried the burden of disappearing jobs, economic insecurity and a declining life style. These beliefs and sentiments are associated with populist political parties and movements, left-wing politics and with Putinism.

The Embattled Fortress

It was not so at the beginning, when confidence that developed economies could become the natural beneficiaries of globalization prevailed. As Charles Kupchan clearly explains it: "A crisis of governability has beset the Western world. It is no accident that the United States, Europe and Japan are simultaneously experiencing political breakdown; globalization is producing a widening gap between what electorates are asking of their governments and what those governments can deliver...Globalization was supposed to have played to the advantage of liberal societies, which were presumably best suited to capitalize on the fast and fluid global marketplace. But instead, for the better part of two decades, middle-class wages in the world's leading democracies have been stagnant and economic inequality is rising sharply. The plight of the West middle class is the consequence primarily of the integration into global markets of billions of low-wage workers from developing economies".[1]

Indeed, by promoting the inclusion into the labor global equation of 1.3 billion Chinese, 1.2 billion Indians or 250 million Indonesians, within the context of a race to the bottom of production costs, Western nations created huge economic and social problems for themselves, while becoming embattled fortresses. Not surprisingly, a June 2008 Harvard Business School study reported that up to 42 percent of American jobs, which represented more than 50 million of them, were vulnerable to being sent offshore. The creative destruction associated with the market economy model, unforeseeable at the beginning, brought with it a lot of creation for emerging economies, and substantial destruction to developed ones.

The leverage of emerging economies significantly increased. In addition to their preponderance in commodities and new markets, they have gotten a substantial hold on manufacturing industries, brainwork, technology and cash, whereas Western economies have just cornered themselves. In Kishore Mahbubani's words, "The rest of the world, paradoxically, is more ready than Americans for a globalization that Americans themselves are creating".[2]

Slicing the Salami

Like slicing a salami, this process went through several stages. Western economies began by offshoring their blue-collar jobs to developing economies, which was tantamount to transferring part of their industrial might to those economies. Since 2001, nearly 60,000 manufacturing plants left the US and boarded up in emerging economies.[3] Around 450 of the largest

---

[1] Charles A Kupchan, "Refunding good governance", *The New York Times*, 19 December 2011.

[2] Kishore Mahbubani, "The seesaw of power: A conversation with Joseph Nye, Dambisa Moyo and Kisshore Mahbubani", *International Herald Tribune Magazine*, 24 June 2011.

[3] Bernie Sanders, *Our Revolution: A Future to Believe In* (London: Profile Books, 2017), p. 280.

500 multinationals invested in China.[4] Moreover, a fundamental part of China's trade with the world, since the beginning of the millennium, stemmed from foreign firms producing in China in order to sell their products somewhere else. More than 50 percent of China's exports were paid for by foreign firms, and were the result of foreign investments in China.[5]

Subsequently, Western economies offshored their white-collar jobs to developing economies. This implied relying on the strength of foreign brains, at the expense of making their own brains increasingly redundant. A 2006 study by the consulting firm Booz Allen Hamilton stated that white-collar offshoring included high-end work, which had traditionally been considered "core" to the business, such as chip design, financial and legal research, clinical trial management, book editing and so forth. The convergence of lower costs and the huge pool of available talent in emerging economies, such as India, led in that direction and implied the risk of tens of millions of jobs migrating from the West. Moreover, it was argued that high-wage jobs, performed by highly educated employees in the United States were, if anything, more offshorable than other service jobs.[6]

In the next phase, Western economies massively transferred their technology to China. This was done in two ways. First, it became a mean of gaining access to that country's gigantic market. Second, the technology was sold directly to Chinese firms. General Electric was a good example of the former, as it handed over its most sophisticated aeronautical electronic technology, in order to benefit from the Chinese aeronautical market, one expected to generate 400 billion dollars in sales during the next 20 years. The sale of technology to China, by American or European companies, frequently implied selling the companies that were producing it. This went from Volvo to MG and from IBM's Personal Computers

---

[4] Xulio Ríos, "Crédito y descrédito en América Latina", *Jiexi Zhonguuo: Análisis y Pensamiento Iberoamericano sobre China*, Número 2, Primer Trimestre 2012, pp. 23–24.

[5] Zachary Karabell, *op. cit.*, pp. 156–157.

[6] Alan S Blinder "Offshoring: The next industrial revolution", *Foreign Affairs,* 2006, Volume 85, pp. 113–128; Alan S Blinder and Alan B Krueger, "Alternative measures of offshorability", National Bureau of Economic Research, Working Paper 15287 (August 2009), http://www.nber.org/papers/w15287. Accessed 25 July 2015; Arianna Huffington, *Third World America* (New York: Crown Publishers, 2010).

Division and France's Thompson to numerous medium-sized Silicon Valley corporations.

From Job-Killing Offshoring to Job-Killing Automation

In the process, as it was to be expected, Western corporations obtained disproportionate profit margins. According to Ohio-based hedge fund manager John Hussman, in 2011, profit margins by US companies were 50 percent above historical levels.[7] However, when faced with the competition of good quality but lower-priced foreign products — resulting from the combination of offshoring and technology transfer — Western corporations responded by multiplying job-killing technologies home.

As Rana Foroohar remarked in 2011: "That so many of the jobs we now create are low end, underscores a growing debate over technology and its role. Many of the jobs that have disappeared from the U.S. economy have done so not only because they were outsourced but also because they are now done by computers or robots".[8] Not surprisingly, a well-known 2013 Oxford University report predicted that up to 47 percent of existing employment in the United States would disappear within the next one to two decades as a consequence of digital technology.[9]

On the same note, Edward Luce wrote, also in 2011: "The jobs that are currently being created in the United States are those relatively low-skilled and low-paid that cannot be replaced either by offshoring or job-killing technologies. In short, the middle-skilled jobs that once formed the ballast of the world's wealthiest middle class are disappearing...a growing share of whatever job the economy is still managing to create is in the least productive areas. Of the five occupations forecast by the Bureau of Labour Statistics to be the fastest growing between now and 2018, none requires a degree. These are registered nurses, 'home health aides',

---

[7] Andy Mukherjee, "Work and wages versus wealth and welfare", *The Straits Times*, 17 November 2011.

[8] Rana Foroohar, "What ever happened to upward mobility?", *Time*, 14 November 2011.

[9] Carl Benedikt Frey and Michael E Osborne, "The future of employment: How susceptible are jobs to computerization", Oxford University, 17 September 2013. http://www.oxfordmartin.ox.ac.uk/downloads/academic/The_Future_of_Employment.pdf. Accessed 25 July 2016.

customer services representatives, food preparation workers and 'personal home care aides'...If there is an explanation as to why middle-class incomes have stagnated in the past generation, this is it: Whatever jobs the US is able to create are in the least efficient sectors — the types that neither computers nor China have yet found a way of eliminating."[10]

Not surprisingly, corporate profits today are at their highest levels, as a percentage of GDP, in more than 85 years. At the same time, wages and salaries for American workers have reached one of their lowest points in more than 60 years.[11]

Turning the Rich, Richer

While corporations have been suppressing jobs at home, they have simultaneously been arguing against tax increases in the United States. Labeling those increases as "class warfare", they have managed to massively evade taxes at home while lobbying for tax benefits. The results have been impressive. In 2015, IBM made nearly US$6 billion in profits in the US and yet, instead of paying federal taxes, it got 321 million in tax refund. Also, in 2015, Xerox made US$537 million in profits but received 23 million in tax refund. The same year, American Airlines earned US$4.6 billion, receiving nearly 3 billion from the Internal Revenue Service. Citigroup had earnings of US$6.6 billion in 2013 and yet received a tax refund of 260 million. From 2010 to 2012, Pfizer made US$43 billion in profits worldwide, but received 2.2 billion from the IRS. And the list goes on.[12]

At the same time, American corporations have invested vastly in buybacks of their own stocks, instead of creating new jobs. The principle behind this awkward use of funds is simple. With fewer shares in the market, earnings per share tend to rise and, by investing in their own stocks, companies benefit from short-term jump in stock prices. This, of course, reflects well in their quarterly reports. Needless to say is that, as

---

[10] Edward Luce, "Is America working?" *Financial Times*, 11 December 2011.

[11] Senator Cory Booker, "The American dream deferred", Brookings, June 2018, https://www.brookings.edu/essay/senator-booker-american-dream-deferred/?. Accessed 30 June 2018.

[12] Bernie Sanders, *op. cit.*, pp. 275–276.

top executives are normally shareholders of the companies under their control, they benefit from these short-term jumps. This also helps senior management collect millions in cash and stock incentive payments, by meeting earnings-per-share goals.

In 2011, Nelson D. Schwartz wrote: "After diving in the wake of the financial crisis, buybacks have made a remarkable comeback in recent years, with $445 billion authorized this year, the most since 2007, when repurchases peaked at $914 billion".[13] As Cory Booker, Democrat Senator from New Jersey, pointed out: between 2003 and 2012, companies on the S&P 500 dedicated 91 percent of their total net earnings to stock buybacks and corporate dividends. That left just nine percent for the rest. The rest not only means new plants and developments, but also payment and investments in the workforce, including expanded training.[14]

Senator Booker also mentions how companies are relying on a range of practices to avoid workers from moving into better pay employment. In his words: "One of the core issues that has arisen in recent years in 'monopsony power', whereby one or a handful of employers have become so dominant in their market or their region that they can exercise enormous control not just over their worker's wages and their terms of employment, but even over where they can work. Corporations are increasingly exercising monopsony power through purposeful practices specifically aimed at weakening worker mobility and keeping a lid on wages. Workers all across the country, and in a wide range of occupations...are being held back under the threat of restrictive covenants that limit their ability to change jobs and get ahead".[15]

Monopsony power materializes through instruments like the so-called "non-compete" clauses and "no-poaching agreements". On the one hand, non-compete clauses are agreements between employers and employees that were originally intended to protect trade secrets and hold on to workers who had highly technical training. But now, this clause is being used

---

[13] Nelson D Schwartz, "In U.S., stock buybacks win out over jobs", *International Herald Tribune*, 23 November 2011.
[14] Senator Cory Booker, *op. cit.*
[15] *Ibid.*

not to protect trade secrets and retain highly qualified employees, but as a means to keep low-wage workers under their employer's total control. Not only are they contractually forbidden to move into higher paid jobs in similar industries or activities, but being at the mercy of their employers, they cannot even expect to obtain better wages within the same company. As mentioned by Senator Booker, sometimes workers sign non-compete clauses unknowingly, while others they do it for lack of options.

No-poaching agreements, on the other hand, prohibit the franchisees of a large company to recruit and hire away another's workers. This prevents employees from finding higher paying jobs within the same chain. As a result, the employees' leverage to negotiate for a raise is reduced to a minimum. In 2016, 58 percent of the US larger franchisors had in place no-poaching agreements.

The 2008 Financial Crisis

The result of this dramatic process has been a gigantic economic polarization in the United States. And on top of it all, this polarization was compounded by an additional event: the worst financial crisis since the Great Depression of 1929. The prevailing *laissez faire* environment was, again, the reason behind the 2008 financial crisis. Lax financial regulations allowed indeed for all kinds and shapes of excesses to be committed.

This course got on a fast track with the repeal of the Glass–Steagall Law in 1999. Its abolition threw down the fence that had so far prevented commercial banks into entering the investment banking business, and thus promoted their off-balance-sheet activities. Nonetheless, the major problems did not result from the excesses committed by deregulated commercial banks, but from those of other institutions which never been subjected to regulations: the so-called shadow banks.

The shadow banking system was constituted by a group of institutions (hedge funds firms, private equity firms, among others), which acted as banks without being so. They were involved in high-risk financial instruments such as hedge funds, auction rates, repo-tripartite, bonds with options, structured investment vehicles and the like. It is hardly surprising that without any kind of supervision, shadow banks simply went wild. Authoritative figures like Brooksley Brown, head of the Commodity

Futures Trading Commission, had issued loud warnings about the consequences of failing to regulate the financial derivatives in the late 1990s. However, the Commodity Futures Modernization Act, passed by Congress in December 2000, under the auspices of Treasury Secretary Larry Summers and Federal Reserve Bank Chairman Alan Greenspan, banned any attempt to regulate derivatives and new investment instruments.[16]

This environment was perfectly symbolized by a 2003 photo session in which representatives of different federal regulatory bodies cut piles of regulations with power saws and pincers. According to the prevailing dogma of the day, markets were perfectly able to self-regulate. In the words of Dambisa Moyo: "In the US, Chairman Greenspan, as a convert and proselytizer for self-regulation, oversaw the rise of what came to be termed the shadow banking system. This was the network of hedge funds, private equity firms and off-balance-sheet entities that where outside the purview of the Fed....Such was the byzantine nature of the derivative complex that no one actually appreciated the size and indeed the whereabouts of this labyrinth of debt".[17]

Such extremes were much helped by the underestimation of risk that came from easy money. In C. Fred Bergsten words: "These huge inflows of foreign capital, however, turned out to be an important cause of the current economic crisis, because they contributed to the low interest rates, excessive liquidity, and loose monetary policies that brought the overleveraging and underpricing of risk...".[18]

Indeed, after having promoted China's trade surplus, through the offshoring of blue-collar jobs, the United States let China finance its own spending binge. As Fareed Zakaria pointed out: "Through their accumulation of massive quantities of American debt, the Chinese ended up subsidizing the behavior that caused it — American consumption. They financed our spending binge and built up a vast hoard of dollars IOUs".[19] China's lending was not only responsible for the United States living beyond their means, but also created the cheap money that encouraged financial excesses in that country.

---

[16] Edward Luce, *op. cit.*
[17] Dambisa Moyo, *How the West was Lost* (London: Allen Lane, 2011), pp. 66–67.
[18] Fred C Bergsten, "The dollar and the deficits", *Foreign Affairs*, 2009, Volume 88, p. 24.
[19] Fareed Zakaria, *The Post-American World and the Rise of the Rest* (London: Penguin Books, 2009), p. xx.

The Mortgage Crisis Carnage

This was the underlying reason why the mortgage market in the United States was so full of cash that it became possible to obtain a 100 percent mortgage without an income, a job or even assets. As such, this became the spark that unleashed the American financial fire.

The immediate cause of it, though, were the so-called "securizations", in which different kinds of mortgages were bundled together, repackaged and converted into securities that went into the financial market. Bad mortgages were prevalent due to two main considerations. Firstly, because the larger the mortgage was, the larger the fee that the banks, as mortgage originators, got paid. Secondly, because lending banks did not bear the risk if the borrower did not repay. Thanks to securization, irresponsible lending became the norm.

The toxic securities therein derived were subsequently sold as highly trustable financial products. When this distorted system imploded, as it was bound to do sooner or later, countless American middle-class citizens not only saw their pensions evaporate, but millions of middle-class families who were led to believe that they could become homeowners, suffered foreclosures and evictions.

As Joseph Stiglitz explained, the banks' influence dominated almost every decision the government made within the subsequent rescue efforts. Not only did the banks and the U.S. Treasury have a common interest in not writing down the principal of the mortgages, as that would have forced the banks to recognize the loss, but the banks actually objected to homeowners under stress borrowing at low interest rates as they themselves were doing from the Federal Reserve. In sum, both the Bush and Obama administrations followed the same course of action: concentrating their efforts on the rescue of the banks, and not the indebted homeowners.[20] The result, as Elizabeth Warren reported, was that more than 120,000 families were filing for bankruptcy every month.[21]

Atif Mian and Amir Sufi, economists at Princeton and the University of Chicago, have argued that the government's efforts should have gone to families and the collapsed housing market, rather than the financial sector.

---

[20] Joseph Stiglitz, *Freefall: Free Markets and the Sinking of the Global Economy* (London: Penguin Books, 2015).

[21] Alfredo Toro Hardy, *op. cit.*, p. 81.

In their view, the core of the problem should have been the relationship existing between indebtedness, falling consumption and high unemployment, and not financial loses. Foreclosures, according to their argument, drove down housing prices and generated a vicious cycle. More people underwater, wallowing in debt and unwilling to spend money meant higher unemployment, which, in turn, led to further foreclosures. This not only affected people and communities, but the real economy as well. As they concluded, there was nothing healing in this perverse cycle induced by the government's distorted priorities.[22]

The Numbers Behind Social Polarization

How to be surprised, then, by the numbers revealed behind this social polarization? Since the end of the 1970s, the earnings of the upper 1 percent have increased by 156 percent, and that of the 0.1 percent at the top by 362 percent, while the 40 percent at the bottom owes more than it owns.[23] Moreover, the top 1 percent owns almost as much wealth as the bottom 90 percent. The salary of the majority of the working population, meanwhile, has remained stagnant since the end of the 1970s.[24]

But the numbers keep uncovering an alarming divide. Billionaires in the US grew tenfold between 2000 and 2015. In 2000, the US had 51 billionaires with a combined net worth of US$480 billion. In 2015, the country had a record-breaking 540 billionaires with a combined net worth of US$2.4 trillion. Moreover, the 20 wealthiest Americans own more wealth than the bottom 150 million people.[25]

Between 2002 and 2007, the 1 percent at the top obtained two-thirds of the gains resulting from the economic growth experienced during that period. However, the richest 0.1 percent got the two-thirds of that 1 percent received. In 2010, the six heirs of Sam Walton, Walmart's founder,

---

[22] Atif Mian and Amir Sufi, *House of Debt* (Chicago: The University of Chicago Press, 2014).
[23] Alvin Powell, "The cost of inequality: When a fair shake isn't", *Harvard Gazzete*, 1 February 2016, https://news.harvard.edu/gazette/story/2016/02/the-costs-of-inequality-when-a-fair-shake-isnt/. Accessed 27 January 2017.
[24] Nicholas Kristof, "Occupy Wall Street' and inequality", *New York Times*, 15 October 2011; Bernie Sanders, *op. cit.,* p. 207.
[25] Bernie Sanders, *op. cit.,* pp. 207–208.

had a combined wealth superior to the 40 percent at the bottom of America's society. Meanwhile, in 2009, 80 percent of the country's population had shown a net decrease of its patrimony in relation to 1983.[26]

As a result of this economic polarization, only two types of jobs have increased in numbers in the last few years. On the one hand, Wall Street financiers, Silicon Valley entrepreneurs, corporate managers, doctoral engineers and physicists and the like, are doing extremely well. On the other hand, there are the low-end services undertaken by nurses, domestic aides, food preparers, janitors, auto repair workers, nutritionists and such. Between both types of jobs there is a gap labeled as the missing middle. A middle of more than 100 million people who, according to Roger Cohen, in 2011, were falling in a downward spiral close to or below the poverty line.[27]

Bernie Sanders says that the median income in the US, i.e., the amount of money of the household right in the middle, is almost US$1,400 less than it was in 1999, after adjusting for inflation. At the same time, the real median income of full-time male workers is US$2,144 less than it was 43 years ago. Over the past decade, 81 percent of US households saw "flat" or "failing" incomes.[28] As Martin Ford mentions, income inequality in the US has soared to levels not seen since 1929.[29]

Martin Ford also remarks on how economic polarization translates into deeply unequal consumption patterns. In his words: "The top 5 percent of the households are currently responsible for nearly 40 percent of spending, and that trend towards increased concentration at the top seems almost certain to continue".[30]

The Regional Divide

It is worth noting that this economic polarization is directly linked to a regional divide as fundamental differences exist between large coastal

---

[26] Erik Brynjolfsson and Andrew McAffe, *The Second Machine Age* (New York: W.W. Norton & Company, 2014).

[27] Roger Cohen, "Decline and fall", *International Herald Tribune*, 22 November 2011.

[28] Bernie Sanders, *op. cit.*, pp. 210–211.

[29] Martin Ford, *Rise of the Robots: Technology and the Threat of a Jobless Future* (Electronic book, New York: Basic Books, 2015), p. 91/6743.

[30] *Ibid*, p. 176/6743.

cities, essentially global cities, and inland United States. In Paul Krugman's words: "On the economic side, some parts of America, mainly big coastal cities, have been getting much richer, but other parts have been left behind (...) In the most part I'm in agreement with Berkeley's Enrico Moretti, whose 2012 book T*he New Geography of Jobs*, is must reading for anyone trying to understand the state of America. Moretti argues that structural changes in the economy have favored industries that employ highly educated workers — and that these industries do best in locations where there are a lot of these workers. As a result, these regions are experiencing a virtuous circle of growth: Their knowledge-intensive industries prosper, drawing even more educated workers, which reinforces their advantage. And at the same time, regions that started with a poorly educated work force are in a downward spiral, both because they're stuck in the wrong industries and because they're experiencing what amounts to brain drain".[31]

On the one hand, then, there are busy, favored coastal cities; on the other hand, the left-behind areas of the US, which are beginning to show alarming signs of social decay. A Harvard University analysis of 1.4 billion Internal Revenue Service records on income and life expectancy, showed amazing differences in life expectancy between the richest and the poorest. People living in wealthy cities such as New York City, Boston, Los Angeles or San Francisco have life expectancies significantly longer that those in poorer inland regions. Life expectancy in the latter is now equal to places like Sudan or Pakistan. When data was laid over maps of the United States, low life expectancy concentrated not in the Deep South, but across the Midwest Rust Belt. People in New York or San Francisco live longer than in the industrial Midwest. Among men, the gap is around 15 years.[32]

Paul Krugman gets into further detail as to the reason of this life expectancy gap between big coastal cities and the Midwest Rust Belt. In his words: "To be sure, social collapse in the white working class is a deadly

---

[31] Paul Krugman, "What's the matter with Trumpland?", *The New York Times*, 2 April 2018.

[32] Peter Reuell, "For life expectancy, money matters", *The Harvard Gazette*, 11 April 2016, https://news.harvard.edu/gazette/story/2016/04/for-life-expectancy-money-matters/. Accessed 27 January 2017.

serious issue. Literally. Last fall, the economists Anne Case and Agnus Deaton attracted widespread attention with a paper showing that mortality among middle-aged white Americans, which had been declining for generations, started rising circa 2000. This rising death rate mainly reflected suicide, alcohol and overdoses of drugs, notably prescriptions opioids... And other signs of social unraveling, from deteriorating health to growing isolation, are also on the rise among American whites. Something is going seriously wrong in the heartland".[33]

The mind-blowing extent of this economic inequality is described by Martin Ford in the following terms: "While inequality has been increasing in nearly all industrialized countries the United States remains a clear outlier. According to the Central Intelligence Agency's analysis, income inequality in America is roughly on par with that of the Philippines and significantly exceeds that of Egypt, Yemen and Tunisia".[34]

The causes of this social inequality are many. Beyond those mentioned in previous pages, others like significant tax reduction for the wealthiest, the decreasing power of unions, social divestment, austerity policies derived from the financial crisis, plus a huge public debt, are also in line. The majority of these causes are closely related to the market economy policies that date back to the Reagan Administration. However, there is an important additional element that has to be put in the mix: the flexibilization of campaign financing rules by the Supreme Court.

The Koch Brothers

The conjunction between the disappearance of donation limits and the possibility to shield the identity of donors has exponentially increased campaign contributions and, with it, their political leverage. As a result, politics and big business have become intermingled as never before. As if Iron Triangles, lobbies and Political Action Committees were not enough to influence the decision-making process on behalf of big money, Supreme Court's "Citizens United" decision of 2010 consolidated this symbiotic

---

[33] Paul Krugman, "Republican elite's reign of disdain", *The New York Times*, 18 March 2016.
[34] Martin Ford, *op. cit.*, p. 868/6743.

relation. Thanks to the so-called "independent expenditures", the wealthiest people and the largest corporations of the United States can now spend unlimited sums of money on their preferred candidates.

As a result of this, the Republican Party came to be controlled by the Koch brothers (the second wealthiest family in the US), and a group of no fewer than 18 billionaires acting under the stewardship of the Kochs. The Grand Old Party was forced to bow low before a conjunction of oil, banking, defense, chemical, pharmaceutical and brewing interests, and to their extreme right agenda.

Their agenda includes, among other things, the abolition of Medicare and Medicaid programs; the abolition of any compulsory insurance or tax-supported plan to provide health services; the repeal of the Social Security system; the abolition of the governmental Postal Service; the repeal of minimum wage laws; the elimination of governmental ownership, operation, regulation and subsidy of schools and colleges; the end of compulsory education laws; the privatization of the public roads and the national highway system and all government welfare and aid to the poor programs. In other words, a political agenda that clearly reflects their patrimonial interests.[35]

In Jane Meyer terms: "The Kochs were not alone. As they sought ways to steer American politics hard to the right…they got valuable reinforcement from a small cadre of like-minded wealthy conservative families who were harnessing their own corporate fortunes toward the same end…But their goal was patently political: to undo not just Lyndon Johnson's Great Society and Franklin Roosevelt's New Deal but Teddy Roosevelt's Progressive Era, too".[36] John J. Miller, quoted by Jane Meyer, adds: "What they started is the most potent machinery ever assembled in a democracy to promote a set of beliefs and to control the reins of government."[37]

Noreena Hertz clearly explains the implications herein involved, when she says: "Wherever we look, corporations are capturing the responsibilities of governments…Governments, by not even recognizing this capture, are putting at risk the implicit contract that exists between them

---

[35] Jane Meyer, *Dark Money: How a Secretive Group of Billionaires is Trying to Buy Political Control in he US* (Electronic book, New York: Doubleday, 2016).
[36] *Ibid*, p. 1104/9091.
[37] *Ibid*, p. 1774/9091.

and the citizens, and which represents the essence of every democratic society".[38] The breakdown of this social contract has profound political implications, as citizens feel increasingly estranged from the political system.

How to be surprised by the fact that already in 2008, 80 percent of Americans surveyed told the Program on International Policy Attitudes that they believed that "a few big interests, looking for themselves" controlled the government.[39] Confidence in the political system has plummeted as a result of this situation. Trust in Congress, indeed, dropped from 42 percent in 1973 to just 8 percent in 2015, an approval rating lower than any other institution, including banks or big business.[40] The significance of this is enormous, as the connivance of the political class with banks and big business, seems to be considered even more reprehensible than the greediness and selfishness of the latter.

The European Union Conundrum

Many of the aforementioned elements are also reproduced within the European Union, especially those related to their corporations' offshoring of countless jobs to China and other emerging economies, and to job killing technologies in response to the foreign competition that they helped to nurture. As the McKinsey Global Institute reports, in the United States and in the 15 core European Union countries, otherwise known as EU-15, there are 285 million adults who are not in the labor force.[41] However, it must be said, the extreme social inequality that characterizes the US, is mainly absent from Europe.

Lucas Chancel provides the right context of the European social divide when saying: "Inequality is on the rise across the world, but it's not increasing everywhere at the same pace. In many ways Europe stands out as a positive exception. Despite the criticism thrown out at the EU, it is a global

---

[38] Noreena Hertz, *The Silent Takeover* (London: William Heinemann, 2011), p. 11.

[39] Arianna Huffington, *op. cit.*, p. 129.

[40] Stephen D King, *op. cit.*, p. 21.

[41] James Manyika, "Technology, jobs, and the future of work", McKinsey Global Institute, Executive Briefing, May 2017, https://www.mckinsey.com/featured-insights/employment-and-growth/technology-jobs-and-the-future-of-work. Accessed 23 April 2018.

leader in preserving a degree of fairness in the social fabric…Today, the top 1% in Europe take 12% of the income…while the bottom 50% have 22%… Put bluntly, the EU has resisted the notion of turning its market economy into a market society. It has partly rejected the thinking of Ronald Reagan and Margaret Thatcher, in which market forces, in the absence of any regulation, provide the best of all worlds in areas such as education, health and wages. There are large differences within Europe, though: the UK and Ireland have followed the American path more closely than continental Europe…That said, social healthcare systems in most European countries still guarantee universal protection for all — hardly the case in the US. Many of those countries offer free access to university…Labour markets are also more favourable in Europe than in the US, where the minimum wage has fallen by a third in real terms since the 1970s (in France it has risen fourfold). In Sweden and Germany, trade unions are represented in corporate governance bodies, taking part in strategic decision-making".[42]

In spite of all this, the European Union still presents two serious problems: undemocratic decision-making at the top and the application of austerity measures all around Europe, particularly harsh in peripheral nations, where there has been a burdensome debt crisis. Both these problems have alienated a large part of its population.

European institutions, governments and elites have clearly underestimated the popular will. Under this premise, several of its governments, and particularly the British one, ignored the overwhelming rejection of its population, expressed both in the polls and in the streets, in relation to the Iraq invasion in 2003. A couple of years later, in 2005, and as a result of the widespread dissatisfaction with the EU's structure by its member states, the federation's leadership presented the draft of a new Constitution for approval purposes. Such approval was to come by direct consultation of its populations, by way of referendum. However, that same year, 54.9 percent of French voters and 61.5 percent of Dutch voters rejected the proposed Constitution. At that point, the European Council decided to relabel the constitutional proposal as a Treaty, so that it would not have to be subjected to popular ratification.

---

[42]Lucas Chancel, "The fairest of them all: Why Europe beats the US on equality", *The Guardian*, 24 January 2018.

This bureaucratic manipulation translated into the Lisbon Treaty, approved in October 2007. The reason for this relabeling was clear. In order to pass a treaty, only the affirmative will of the governments and the ratification of the parliaments were needed. However, for its own constitutional reasons, the Irish government decided to submit the Treaty of Lisbon to a popular referendum. This meant going back to round one.

Again, popular consultation provided the same results that it had given in France and in the Netherlands in 2005. In 2008, indeed, the treaty was rejected by 53.4 percent of the Irish voters. Other EU governments met this rejection by putting an overwhelming pressure upon the Irish one to hold another referendum. As a consequence, a new direct consultation of the Irish citizens was held in 2009, this time with positive results. The logic that worked in the end was this: keep the citizens voting until they vote right. This underestimation of the people's will is tantamount to a clear democratic deficit. As a result, both EU institutions and national governments have become the target of popular anger.

The second problem, originating in the application of austerity policies within the block is dual in nature: it relates to the management of the debt crisis in highly indebted Eurozone counties, and is the result of the EU's decision to cut national deficits in all of its 27 member states.

The Austerity Nightmare

The management of the debt crisis was, of the two, the bigger problem and was directly linked to the complexity of the so-called Eurozone, that is, the 19 nations with varying degrees of economic developments where the € is the official currency. To put things in context in relation to this crisis, we have to go back to the early 2000s, when several of its economies, the so-called PIIGS (Portugal, Italy, Ireland, Greece and Spain), ran large trade deficits.

Germany and other EU countries, which enjoyed trade surpluses, helped these indebted economies through loans and bond purchases. However, when the financial crisis of 2008 hit hard and credit dried up internationally, creditors began collecting their loans. Behind this situation, there were several reasons worth taking note of.

The first was projecting a wrong impression regarding the nature of the sovereign debt amid the members of the Eurozone. According to Gordon Brown: "Financial markets assumed from the outset that the European Central Bank was ready to accept at its discount window the sovereign debt of all member countries on equal terms, thus fostering the impression that all euro sovereign debt was of equal quality".[43]

It should have been obvious, though, that if both the German and the Greek debts were seen on an equal footing, the result would be low interest rates as well as happy borrowing by the weaker economies of the zone. For the latter, to borrow in the same conditions as its core members became a temptation difficult to resist.

The second reason was the macroeconomic straitjacket that the € imposed upon its member countries, who were forbidden to devaluate. Again, in Gordon Brown's terms: "It was a risk...because Europe's countries did not appear to have the flexibility necessary to adjust their economies to crises".[44] Indeed, countries like Japan or the United States, which run large deficits, have been able to finance them by simply printing more of their currencies. Not being able to devaluate takes away all room for maneuver from indebted countries, leaving austerity measures as the only alternative.

The third reason was lurking in the European Central Bank (ECB) statues, which limited its role. Instead of enjoying an ample mandate to deal with the different problems that the € might have experienced, its mandate focused primarily on keeping inflation under control. The € became, thus, the only international currency that did not have a lender of last resort.

As a result, the only institution that could have acted unilaterally and decisively to avert the crisis, by buying the sovereign bonds of the affected economies, was not able to do so. As John Quiggin explained: "Unlike any previous central banks in history, the bank has disclaimed any responsibility for the European financial system it effectively controls, or even for the viability of the euro as a currency. Instead, it has focused entirely on the

---

[43] Gordon Brown, *op. cit.*, pp. 183–184.
[44] *Ibid*, p. 186.

formal objective of keeping inflation rates to a 2 percent target".[45] It must be added, nonetheless, that under the increasing pressure of the crisis, the institutional boundaries of the bank were subsequently expanded.

Indebted countries could not dig themselves out of a fiscal hole through devaluation, unless they abandoned the Eurozone altogether. However, that looked like jumping off a cliff. The only available option left to them was to convince the creditor countries to forgive part of the debt, which proved easier said than done as Angela Merkel's Germany loudly opposed any bailout. In this, Berlin was followed by other Northern European economies.

Merkel's Harshness

Merkel's harshness stands awkwardly out against the treatment that her own country got in 1953. In a historical meeting in London, the 20 countries that were owed by the Federal Republic of Germany decided to erase from their credit books more than half its debt. Had this half not been forgiven, would the Federal Republic have evolved differently, at a different pace maybe? We are entering here into the realm of counterfactual history, and this is not the purpose of the book. What is certainly verifiable is that Hitler's emergence into power was directly linked to the social costs associated with the World War I reparation debt, and this was obviously taken into account in 1953.

The fact remains, however, that passing over the objections of the majority of EU's member countries and the IMF itself, Merkel's Germany was instrumental in imposing upon Athens one of the most painful structural packages in recent history. The "Troika" of the European Commission, ECB and IMF, was very much the visible face of the negotiations with Greece and later with Spain, imposing draconian austerity measures upon them both. However, the leading force behind the "Troika" was Germany.

Two of the most important economists of our day, Nobel Laureates Joseph Stiglitz and Pal Krugman, reacted against such senseless austerity measures, their multiplier economic effect and their social and political

---

[45] John Quiggin, "Enabling the euro crisis", *International Herald Tribune*, 11 October 2011.

implications. According to Stiglitz: "...austerity has been an unmitigated disaster, which has become increasingly apparent as European Union economies once again face stagnation, if not a triple-dip recession, with unemployment persisting at record highs and per capita real (inflation-adjusted) GDP in many countries remaining below recession levels. In even the best-performing economies such as Germany, growth since the 2008 crisis has been so slow that, in any other circumstance, it would be rated as dismal. The most afflicted countries are in depression. There is no other word to describe an economy like that of Spain or Greece, where nearly one in four people — and more than 50% of young people — cannot find work...Meanwhile, Germany is forcing other countries to follow policies that are weakening their economies — and their democracies".[46]

Paul Krugman, on his side, expressed: "...Germany is demanding that Greece keep trying to pay its debts in full by imposing incredibly harsh austerity...Chaos in Greece could fuel the sinister political forces that have been gaining influence as Europe's Second Great Depression goes on and on...Looking forward, however, how much can Greece take? Clearly it can't pay the debt in full; that's obvious to anyone who has done the math. Unfortunately, German politicians have never explained the math to their constituents. Instead, they've taken the lazy path: moralizing about the irresponsibility of the borrowers, declaring that debts must and will be paid in full, playing into stereotypes about shiftless southern Europeans".[47]

But of course, austerity policies were also harsh in the other highly indebted countries, namely, Portugal, Ireland, Italy and Spain. Nonetheless, as mentioned above, there was another dimension to austerity that came from the strict limits imposed upon the EU members' deficits. These were to be reduced, in all of its 27 member states, to a maximum of 3 percent by the financial year 2014–2015.

EU Austerity Policies

This, of course, imposed variable degrees of sacrifice upon the different countries of the union. The Conservative–Liberal Democrat coalition in

---

[46] Joseph Stiglitz, "Austerity has been an utter disaster for the Eurozone", *The Guardian*, 1 October 2014.

[47] Paul Krugman, "A game of chicken", *The New York Times*, 6 February 2015.

the UK announced the largest cuts in State spending since World War II. In Germany, and notwithstanding the fact that unemployment was at 7 percent at the time, plans were made to cut the deficit in €80 billion by 2014. No one in the region got it lightly.[48]

These austerity measures were being imposed on populations that were already suffering the effects of the economic contraction due to the United States financial crisis, globalization and automation. Edward Luce refers to the most affected sectors as follows: "In Britain we call them the 'left-behinds'. In France, they are the *'couches moyennes'*. In America they are the 'squeezed middle'. A better term is the 'precariat' — those whose life is dominated by economic insecurity".[49]

Not surprisingly, the accumulated grievances of this "precariat", and of the unheard citizens, have created a sort of counter-society, which looks at fresh and more inclusive political options. Thanks to it, the political fringes are becoming mainstream and newly created parties are moving into center stage. Meanwhile, traditional parties are quickly eroding (as it is the case in Europe), or moving towards the extremes of the political spectrum.

While conservative parties are evolving into the extreme right, many center-left parties seem to be imploding. The Socialists in France went from holding government to receiving just 7 percent of the vote in the 2017 presidential election. In the Netherlands, the Labor Party share of the vote fell from 24.8 percent in the 2012 general election to just 5.7 percent in 2017, dropping from 150 members of Parliament to just nine. Germany's historic Social Democratic Party fell behind the newly formed Alternative for Germany. The Czech Social Democrats, who had received around one-third of the popular vote in 2006, collapsed in the 2017 elections, winning only 7.3 percent of the vote. And so the list goes on.[50]

Both in Europe and the United States, economic disruption sparked social unrest, which in turn produced major political disruption. Even the

---

[48] "EU austerity drive country by country", BBC News, 21 May 2012.
[49] Edward Luce, *op. cit.*, p. 136/4115.
[50] William A Galston, "The Rise of European populism and the collapse of the center-left", Brookings, 8 March 2018, https://www.brookings.edu/blog/order-from-chaos/2018/03/08/the-rise-of-european-populism-and-the-collapse-of-the-center-left/. Accessed 10 April 2018.

World Economic Forum recognizes this: "The growing gap between the rich and the poor, the old and the young, has been largely ignored by policymakers and investors until the recent rise of anti-establishment votes, including those for Brexit in the UK and for President Trump in the US... Inequality is much more than a side-effect of free market capitalism. It is a symptom of policy negligence...Capitalism has been incredibly successful at boosting wealth, but it has failed at redistributing it".[51]

Populism, indeed, is becoming the new political home for an emerging majority in both Europe and in the United States. For many populists, though, a world socially and economically turned upside down only accounts for half of their resentment story. Immigration tells the other half. As David Brooks says: "In times of anxiety and distrust, it's a lot easier to sell us/them distinctions than tolerance for cultural diversity".[52] If so, the anxiety of economic exclusion becomes the ideal breeding ground for intolerance against the foreigner. Particularly so, when ethnic and cultural diversities are involved.

Immigration: The Other Half of the Resentment Story

Current immigrants to the United States mostly come from China, India, the Philippines, Vietnam and Latin America. Almost a fifth of total legal immigrants, and the majority of the illegal ones, come from one single country: Mexico. The impact of the "Latino Americanization" of the United States is transforming the US into a bilingual society. By 2015, there were almost as many Spanish speakers in that country as in Spain itself: 41 million. According to the US Census, there will be 138 million Spanish-speaking US citizens in 2050.[53]

Much to the point, Samuel P. Huntington wrote about the strong possibility of the United States becoming a bifurcated society "...in terms of language (English and Spanish) and culture (the Anglo-Saxon and the

---

[51] Alberto Gallo, "How the American dream turned into greed and inequality", World Economic Forum, https://www.weforum.org/agenda/2017/11/the-pursuit-of-happiness-how-the-american-dream-turned-into-greed-and-inequality/. Accessed 12 December 2017.
[52] "Vladimir Putin, the most influential man in the world", *The New York Times*, 2 April 2018.
[53] Stephen D King, *op. cit.,* p. 156.

Hispanic) ...Substantial portions of the United States, particularly Florida and the Southwest, would end up being essentially Hispanics both in terms of culture and language, with both cultures and languages coexisting. The United States, hence, would loose its cultural and linguistic unity, transforming itself into a bilingual and bicultural society such as Canada, Switzerland or Belgium".[54]

What Huntington failed to mention, and many of the current rejecters of Latin American presence in the US seem to forget, is that what drives Hispanic population growth is the children or grandchildren of the immigrants. Conversely, the number of Latino immigrants into the country continues to decline. Two out of every three Hispanics in the United States today were born there. Indeed, every year one out of four babies born in the United States is born to a Latino mother. Three-quarters of Hispanics or Latinos are thus US citizens.

Moreover, many members of the Latino community trace their ancestry to places that were incorporated into the United States by conquest or war. In other words, their forefathers lived there before those territories became part of the United States. The descendants of families, who inhabited what is now Southwestern United States, could very well say "We didn't cross the border. The border crossed us". This means that they belong to families that for generations have enjoyed US citizenship.

The extreme measures against Southern immigrants taken by the Trump Administration bear no relation to the actual magnitude of the said immigration. On the contrary, they seem to be more in tune with the anxieties related to the changing racial landscape of the United States. According to Brookings Institute: "What is new is that Trump is clearly capitalizing on what *The New York Times* columnists Charles Blow has termed 'white extinction anxiety'. 'For the first time since the Census Bureau has released these annual statistics' wrote Brooking demographer William Frey, 'they show an absolute decline in the nation's white non-Hispanic population — accelerating a phenomenon that was not projected to occur until the next decade'...The racial makeup of the United States

---

[54] Samuel P Hungtinton, *Quiénes Somos? Los Desafíos de la Identidad Nacional Estadounidense* (Barcelona: Paidós, 2004), p. 45.

may change, but when white power lies in the balance, the unspeakable becomes acceptable".[55]

So, it seems that Trump achieves his ongoing popularity, within his Republican base, by way of reassuring them against the anxieties of the white population losing its majority status in the United States. Hispanic immigrants may turn out to be, under this argument, simple scapegoats within a larger picture. As Brookings stated: "A second noteworthy finding from the new census estimates is that, for the first time, minorities outnumber whites nationally for each age under 10".[56]

Within the European Union, the dramatic eastward expansion and the lack of border controls established by the Schengen Agreement (of which only the UK and Ireland are not part), were sources of malaise for many. In the UK, where the former but not the latter was a huge problem, the prevailing uneasiness was explained by Rowena Mason as follows: "Public unease has been fuelled by a failure to prevent immigration from piling pressure on jobs markets and public services, and a refusal by politicians to acknowledge the sheer numbers of Europeans making new homes in the UK after the EU's expansion to the east in 2004 and 2007".[57]

Being overflowed by Romanian or Polish citizens was indeed resented by many Western Europeans. However, this pales in comparison to the indiscriminate arrival of people from the Middle East or Africa. In 2015, more than twice as many people as in the previous year sought asylum in the European Union. Syria, Iraq and Afghanistan, the three least peaceful countries in the world, were the three biggest sources of asylum seekers in Europe that year.[58]

In Stephen D. King words: "Whatever the humanitarian need of the refugees themselves, the numbers arriving in the EU created a serious challenge to Schengen and, by implication, to the EU's very existence".[59]

---

[55] Andrew M Perry, "Trump reveals 'zero tolerance' for democracy", 25 June 2018, https://www.brookings.edu/blog/the-avenue/2018/06/25/trump-reveals-zero-tolerance-for-democracy/?. Accessed 27 June 2018.

[56] *Ibid.*

[57] Rowena Mason, "How did UK end up voting to leave the European Union?", *The Guardian*, 24 June 2016.

[58] Rowena Mason, *Ibid.*

[59] Stephen D King, *op. cit*, pp. 165–166.

Indeed, Schengen represented a very different proposition when Eastern Europeans could freely move to Western Europe, than when admitted Middle Eastern immigrants can freely circulate within the whole European Union.

With her generous policy towards Syrians refugees, Angela Merkel compounded the situation. After taking in more than 1 million refugees and asylum seekers in the previous two years, in August 2015, she declared that her country was prepared to receive hundreds of thousands more. This not only transformed Europe into a magnet for displaced Syrians and Middle Easters, but also was accompanied by Germany's pressure to have an EU mandatory quota system for refugees.

There is no need to point out that her immigration initiatives, combined with her policy towards Greece (and the PIIGS in general), and her staunch support for austerity measures capable of maintaining national deficits under control, helped to ignite the populist insurgence in Europe. And so, by a rather curious historical twist, Ms. Merkel, the most important globalizer of the day, became the main promoter of European populism.

The Populist Flood

Therefore, immigration adds to the list of grievances for many dissatisfied citizens. Populism, as said, has become the great beneficiary of this huge dissatisfaction against the status quo, unleashing a political wave that currently floods both the United States and Europe. The common denominator of all these populist parties and movements is their anti-system character. They present themselves as expressions of the people and of its interests against the traditional elites. Within their credo, a dichotomy exists between the forgotten social majority and the privileged few, meaning, the establishment, the oligarchy, the plutocracy or the "cast". Their grievance is directed against deaf, selfish, arrogant and corrupt political elites, which are complicit with the excesses and greediness of big corporations and a wealthy class.

Although common to them all, their notion of "people" is rather lax. All sorts of groups may represent "the people": depressed social sectors, displaced workers, indebted students, threatened small retailers, and such like, hence the predilection of so many of these parties for direct democ-racy, in which the people are able to express their will through plebiscitary mechanisms, and without the constraints of an elite's controlled repre-sentative democracy.

And then, there is the common element of the perceived foreign threat. For all of them, globalization plays that role, having become the main disruptor of their societies and the main enemy of their middle classes. This enmity encompasses, by extension, a wide array of interna-tional or multinational institutions or initiatives that goes from the World Trade Organization to Davos; from the international financial markets to free trade agreements and the International Monetary Fund.

For European populists, this includes the European Union as well, an institution that systematically underestimates the will of the people, and is being seen as a neoliberal-oriented organization in tune with the business elites. Moreover, the austerity policies established under its guard were profoundly resented. The ECB also falls under this category.

The foreign threat also has for many, if not for all, another face: immi-gration. For this group of populists, immigrants are seen as a true plague that is transforming and deforming the traditions and the national charac-ter of their societies, while presenting an unfair competition for their own workers. The animosity against it encompasses, by extension, traditional parties, governments or supranational organizations, seen as supportive of this foreign avalanche.

In John B. Judis words: "Populist parties and candidates are on the move in the United States and Europe. Donald Trump has won the Republican nomination; Bernie Sanders came in a very strong second to Hillary Clinton for the Democratic nomination. And these candidacies came on the heels of the Tea Party and Occupy Wall Street movements. In Europe populist parties in France, Sweden, Norway, Finland, Denmark, Austria, Greece, Italy, Spain and Switzerland are contending for power or are already part of the government".[60] Soon after John B. Judis' appraisal of the situation, Trump obtained the presidency of the most powerful nation on Earth and populism became the main opposition force in Germany.

---

[60] John B Judis, *op. cit.*, p. 12.

On the Move

During the run up to the American election, populism from both parties played a forceful role. Sander's populist bid almost got him the nomination of the Democratic Party, while Trump's got him the White House. This show of strength was also replicated on the other side of the Atlantic, where populism is shaking the status quo both from the hard right and from the extreme left. While in the US, the two traditional parties have been assaulted from the inside by populism, in Europe fringe or newly created populist parties have become mainstream, attaining power in many cases.

In Italy's March 2018 parliamentary election, the Five Star Movement won 32.7 percent of the vote, while the League (formerly the Northern League), obtained 17 percent. Populism, in its different versions, clearly dominated the country. Extreme right- and left-wing Italian populists reached an agreement to form a consensus government among them. This was preceded by the election of a new Speaker of the Chamber of Deputies agreeable to both.

The President of the Italian Republic, though, refused to appoint the Prime Minister that they had selected and went on for a caretaker government who would be responsible of summoning fresh elections. It was the establishment's reaction against the populist triumph, wanting to put in motion the well-known practice of keeping the citizens voting until they did it "right". As events unfolded, however, the caretaker government could not be formed and the President was forced to appoint a populist government under the Prime Minister that he had initially rejected.

The party Alternative for Germany, which started in 2013 as a protest movement, won up to 25 percent of the vote in the German state elections of March 2016. Moreover, in Germany's parliamentary elections of September 2017, the party, widely known by its German initials AfD, obtained 92 MPs and around 13 percent of the vote. Conversely, the ruling Christian Democrats got the worst result since 1949, while the Social Democrats, its main opponents, scored their lowest electoral results in a century.

The political cataclysm caused by this sudden emergence of populism in Germany brought with it several consequences. After six months of negotiations, Angela Merkel barely managed to form a government with a frail coalition. Populist AfG on its side, became the main opposition party. According to *The New York Times*: "Ms. Merkel will limp on as chancellor. For how long is unclear. The nationalism and anti-migrants sentiment that has challenged multilateralism elsewhere in Europe is taking root — fast — in mainstream German politics".[61] The country, long regarded as Europe's model of stability and political maturity, has definitely changed.

In France, the National Front (FN) came first in the regional elections of December 2015, obtaining 27.73 percent of the vote, although all other parties joined forces to prevent its victory. The previous year, it also had arrived first in the European parliamentary election with 24.8 percent of the ballots. Its candidate was one of the two frontrunners in the first round of the 2017 presidential election, arriving second in the final round with 34 percent of the vote. Although its opponent was elected President, the norm being that whoever opposes FN's candidate in the second round concentrates the rest of the electorate, the FN won both in the North and the South of the country.

In Denmark, the People's Party (DF) came in second in the June 2015 parliamentary elections obtaining 21.1 percent of the vote. In Austria's presidential election, the Freedom Party (FPO) candidate came first in the first round of the April 2016 presidential election, being defeated by few points in the second round. However, FPO won the parliamentary election of October 2017. In Switzerland, the Swiss People's Party (SVP) came in first in the October 2015 parliamentary election, with almost 30 percent of the vote.

In Norway, the Progress Party (FrP) has been part of the governmental ruling coalition since 2013. In Sweden, the Sweden Democrats party (SD), won about 13 percent of the vote in the parliamentary elections of September 2014. Because none of the traditional parties would form a coalition with them, the country has been governed by a shaky minority coalition. In the Netherlands, the Freedom Party (PVV) arrived at the second position in the March 2017 parliamentary elections.

Britain's United Kingdom Independence Party (UKIP) was at the forefront of the successful Brexit campaign of June 2016. In Rowena Mason

---

[61] Katrin Benhold and Melissa Eddy, "Merkel to survive, agrees to border camps for migrants", 2 July 2018.

words: "Cameron might never have called the referendum had it not been for the rise of Nigel Farage and UKIP. By January 2013, when the prime minister called the EU vote, UKIP had started to gain traction in local elections and was polling double digits for the first time...Even after promising the referendum, Farage managed to gain millions of votes in the 2015 election, many of them in Labour areas as well as Conservatives".[62]

In Spain, in the December 2015 and June 2016 parliamentary elections, the Podemos Party created in 2014, arrived third and at a short distance from the Socialist Party (PSOE) and of the winning Popular Party (PP). It won 22 percent and 21 percent of the vote, respectively. In Greece also, the recently founded Syriza Party came first in the two parliamentary elections held in 2015 with around 35 percent of the vote, thus taking charge of the government.

According to Steven Erlanger: "The four countries of the European Union's East that made older member anxious — Poland, Hungary, the Czech Republic and Slovakia — are all led by populists of one stripe or the other...And the fact that populists now run governments in Eastern and Central Europe threatens to further legitimize movements that once sat on the political fringe".[63] It must be added that in the elections held in June 2018, the populist also won the majority of the vote and formed a government in another Eastern member country of the EU: Slovenia.

Law and Justice in Poland, Fidesz in Hungary, Action of Dissatisfied Citizens (ANO) and Freedom and Direct Democracy in the Czech Republic, the Slovak National Party, the People's Party of Slovakia and We Are Family in Slovakia and the Slovenian Democratic Party in Slovenia, are all expressions of this tide.

What Does Populism Stands for?

In order to understand better what populism stands for, a double distinction is in line. On the one side, there is left-wing populism and right-wing populism; on the other side, there is European populism and US populism.

---

[62] Rowena Mason, *op. cit.*
[63] Steven Erlanger, "In Eastern Europe, populism lives, widening a split in the EU", *The New York Times*, 28 November 2017.

John B. Judis believes that the main difference between left-wing and right-wing populism is the following one: "Leftwing populists champion the people against an elite or an establishment. Theirs is a vertical politics of the bottom and middle arrayed against the top. Rightwing populists champion the people against the elite that they accuse of coddling a third group, which can consist, for instance, of immigrants, Islamists or African American militants. Leftwing populism is dyadic. Rightwing populism is triadic. It looks upward, but also down upon an out group".[64]

This looking down upon a certain group of people, essentially immigrants, makes the fundamental difference between both kinds of populism. While right-wing populism makes a strong distinction between the "we versus them", Sanders' populism overtly advocates for a "humane immigration reform", by "creating a path for the 11 million undocumented people in our country to become lawful permanent residents, and eventually citizens".[65]

However, there is more to that distinction than immigration. Leftwing populists are clearly favorable to public spending and economic redistribution, which tends not to be the case with their right-wing counterparts. In Europe, theirs would essentially be a soft Euroscepticism in contrast to a hard Euroscepticism or Europhobia, more common to right-wing populism. Nationalistic and xenophobic expressions and messages would be common in right-wing populism, whereas its leftist version avoids nationalistic or xenophobic undertones.

Also, in the case of Europe, left-wing populism is identified with late or least developed countries or regions, which essentially identifies with Southern Europe. This would be the case of Greece and Spain. Italy is more of a hybrid, as it reproduces this dichotomy within its own territory. The northern part, which is more developed and richer, shows strong right-wing populism, whereas the southern part follows essentially a left-wing one.

The per capita income in prosperous northern Italy, at around €32,000, is on par with Germany, France and the UK. Per capita incomes in southern Italy — the so-called Mezzogiorno — are only around €7,000, on par

---

[64] John B Judis, *op. cit.*, p. 14.
[65] John B Judis, *Ibid*, p. 400.

with Slovenia, Greece and Portugal. The gap that exists within Italy, thus, is as big as the gaps across much of Europe.[66]

It is important to add, nonetheless, that the Five Star Movement which dominates the Italian "Mezzogiorno", considers itself to be a transversal party rather than a left-wing one, meaning by this to be a political aggrupation where disillusioned citizens, from left or the right, can find a space. The same applies to Spain's Podemos. Nonetheless, both of those parties are considered to be left-wing because their constituencies are mostly aligned in that direction, and their policies clearly differ from those of the right-wing counterparts.

As numbers go, compared to left-wing populism, the right-wing one is a much bigger group. From Trumpism, which is today the new face of the Republican Party, to the rest of the European right-wing populists, theirs is indeed a larger gathering. Right-wing, though, may not be the correct category to include these parties in, as they are clearly hard right.

Several of the parties of this European hard right populism are grouped in the so-called Movement for a Europe of Nations and Freedom (MENL). They work together as a parliamentary group within the European Parliament, where they were recognized as a political block in 2015. However, not all of them are equally interested in actively participating at this level, given their prevailing contempt towards the European Union.

European Populism vs. American Populism

There also exists an important distinction between European populism and its US counterpart. The plurality of political parties within the European political scene, in tune with the parliamentary political system of the majority of its countries, allows for fringe parties to survive. It also allows for the creation of new parties.

As a result, many populist parties existed for quite some time on the outskirts of their political systems before thriving, in the same manner in which others moved into the mainstream after having been recently created. In Stephen D. King's words: "...parties have either emerged from

---

[66] Stephen D King, *op. cit.*, p. 219.

nowhere or chased electability from the political fringes".[67] This undoubtedly eased their steadfast moving into center stage when the right conditions emerged.

In the United States, the rigid two-party system and the existence of the Electoral College, takes away any chance of success by a populist party. Even Ross Perot, who ran two of the strongest presidential showings by a third party or an independent candidate in US history, had no chance of success. In the 1992 election, he received 18.9 percent of the popular vote, about 19,741,065 votes, but did not get any Electoral College vote. In 1996, after having founded the Reform Party, he received 8 percent of the popular vote, but again not a single Electoral College vote. He showed that populism had an important support in the country, although he also made evident the impossibility of winning the presidency from outside the two-party system.

Hence, the only chance that populism has in the US is by conquering one of the two traditional political parties from the inside. The first recent populist movement that tried to do that was the Tea Party. Although its grasp on the Republican Party proved to be very important, with 62 vociferous members in the House of Representatives, it remained clearly insufficient to obtain the control of the party. The 2016 Presidential Election was to become a landmark, as both Bernie Sanders and Donald Trump emerged as formidable populist candidates within the two-party system.

In June 2016, David Brooks wrote a very important piece in his *The New York Times* column. According to him, Donald Trump completely changed the nature of the political debate in the United States. Until then, and for the last 80 years, the debate had been centered in the dichotomy more State vs. less State. While Democrats represented the former, Republicans called for the latter. Trump was able to move the debate into a completely different direction: a dichotomy between openness vs. closeness. That meant being open to the world and to a globalized international society or, alternatively, putting strict limits to free trade, establishing rigid barriers to immigration, diminishing international commitments and giving free rein to the mistrust against all

---

[67] Stephen D King, *op. cit.*, p. 101.

things foreign. This new debate, in Brooks' view, was to remain in place for decades to come.

Bernie Sanders also represented a variation of the traditional debate, but in a much more restrained form. He rejected globalization to be certain, and proposed a much more nationalistic approach to economics. However, he did not have a quarrel with immigration, nor did he mistrust the foreign world *per se*. Moreover, he was very much into the traditional argument of more State, although with a populist tone: "We have to forcefully take on the arrogance and greed of the ruling class".[68]

With a difference of degrees, thus, 2016 was a different campaign, as strong candidates in both parties had a message that until then had essentially remained on the fringe of American politics. The new message, though, was directly related to poll numbers. In 2002, Pew Research found that 78 percent of Americans supported global trade. In 2008, that percentage had fallen to 53 percent. In 2014, when Pew asked if international trade improved the livelihood of Americans, only 17 percent thought that it led to higher wages, while only 20 percent believed that it created new jobs.[69]

Bernie Sanders did not only display an impressive show of force, but even while losing the candidacy, he was able to bend the globalizer per excellence, Hillary Clinton, to his anti-globalizing proposals. Moreover, such a stance has arrived to stay. The so-called Progressive wing of the Democratic Party is currently providing it with a boost of activism and energy and, if Donald Trump is to be defeated in 2020, it would be likely by way of a populist attack to his left flank.

Indeed, it seems unlikely that traditional politics and traditional messages will get Trump out of the White House. In Edward Luce terms: "Many comfort themselves that Trump's victory was an accident delivered by the dying gasp of America's white majority — and abetted by Putin. History will resume normal business after a brief interruption. How I wish they were right. I fear they are not".[70]

---

[68] Bernie Sanders, *op. cit.*, p. 87.

[69] T. X. Hames, "Will technological convergence reverse globalization", Strategic Forum, National Defense University, July 2016, http://ndupress.ndu.edu/Portals/68/Documents/stratforum/SF-297.pdf. Accessed 12 May 2018.

[70] Edward Luce, *op. cit.*, p. 138/4115.

The Trump Factor

The reasons for this are clear. According to a Pew Research Center poll, 81 percent of Trump supporters thought life for people like them had gotten worse over the previous 50 years, while only 11 percent thought it had got better. Moreover, Trump supporters were deeply pessimistic about the future, with 68 percent believing that the lives of the next generation would be even worse.[71] Not surprisingly, *The Economist* said: "Populism wave has yet to crest".[72]

Populism, indeed, will take time to crest, as the reasons that gave it rise are not bound to disappear any time soon. With robots and computers taking down jobs at amazing speed (replacing in the process the competition of low-cost workers such as those from Vietnam or Indonesia), and with immigration following its course, as wars and hunger abroad are a fact of life, populism seems to have become the new normal.

Trump was not only capable of winning the White House but, subsequently, of conquering the Republican Party most thoroughly. Asking himself about the reasons that made Trump so successful, Martin Woolf explains: "Yet, as Robert Kagan, a neoconservative intellectual argues in a powerful column in the Washington Post, Mr. Trump 'is also the GOP's Frankenstein monster'. He is, says Mr. Kagan, the monstrous result of the party's 'wild obstructionism', its demonization of political institutions, its filtration with bigotry and its 'racially tinged derangement syndrome' over President Barak Obama…Why has this happened? The answer is that this is how a wealthy donor class, dedicated to the aims of slashing taxes and shrinking the state, obtained the foot soldiers and voters it required, This, then, is 'pluto-populism': the marriage of plutocracy with right-wing populism. Mr. Trump embodies this union. But he has done so by partially dumping the free-market, low tax, shrunken government aims of the party establishment, to which his financially dependent rivals remain wedded".[73]

In other words, Trump not only gave voice to the anger of America's squeezed middle, but he profited from the table that the Koch brothers had

---

[71] Stephen D King, *op. cit.*, p. 241.
[72] "Left behind", *The Economist*, 21–27 October 2017.
[73] "Donald Trump embodies how great republics meet their end", *Financial Times*, 1 March 2016.

already served. They had been playing with political fire in order to get the "foot soldiers and voters" to support their patrimonial agenda. Trump just needed to turn that fire against the plutocrats and the establishment. And he did so quite adroitly. Being a billionaire himself, he did not need the Koch's money, and hence was free to define his own rules of the game. Being an expert in reality shows, he was able to take advantage of the anger that they had been flirting with, projecting it to maximum intensity decibels. His was, no doubt about it, a hostile takeover of Koch Inc., meaning the Republican Party.

And, indeed, it has been a successful takeover. As expressed by *The Economist*: "All presidents, Republican and Democrats, seek to remake their party in their own image. Donald Trump has been more successful than most. From the start, the voters he mesmerized in the campaign embraced him more fervently than congressional Republicans were ready to admit. After 15 months in power, as our briefing explains, he has taken ownership of the party".[74] *The New York Times* agrees: "The President transformation of the G.O.P. — its policies, its tone, even the fate of its candidates — has never been so evident. A party that once championed free trade has become protectionist under Mr. Trump. Sermons about inclusivity have been replaced with demagogic attacks on immigrants…".[75]

Thomas L. Friedman goes further: "The U.S. Republican Party has blown up in all but name, going overnight from an internationalist, free trade, deficit-hawk party to a protectionist, anti-immigrant, deficit-dove party — all to accommodate the instincts of Donald Trump and his base. As the former House Speaker John Boehner noted: 'There is no Republican Party. There's a Trump party'".[76] President Trump, as *The New York Times* reported on June 24, 2018, enjoys the support of 90 percent of his party.

Again, *The Economist* says: "Because the party was becoming Trumpian long before Mr. Trump took over, it will no more go back to the

---

[74] "What has become of the Republican Party", *The Economist*, 21st–27th April 2018.
[75] Jonathan Martin and Michael Tackett, "Republicans absorb new lesson: Cross president Trump at their peril", 13 June 2018.
[76] Thomas L Friedman, "Why are so many political parties blowing up? (Part 1)", *The New York Times*, 26 June 2018.

1980s in his absence than to 1880s...But the attitudes he has ridden to office will still outlive him".[77] Not surprisingly, the same article quotes Andrea Volkens, of the Berlin Social Science Center, saying that the Republican Party sits much closer today to France's FN than to the Conservatives in Britain. Hence, the Republican Party, and not just the current occupant of the White House, are within the populist camp. As such, and for the foreseeable future in the United States, populism will be a force to reckon with.

But the anti-globalization camp does not stop here. From both extremes of the political spectrum, rejection to all that this movement represents is very much alive. As much of the hard right within the developed economies has fusioned itself with populism, there does not seem to be much else to look for in that direction. On the contrary, several expressions of left-wing anti-globalization still subsist outside the frame of populism. This is clearly the case of Jeremy Corbyn in the United Kingdom and, to a lesser extent, that of Jean-Luc Mélenchon in France.

The Comeback of the Extreme Left

Jeremy Corbyn's positions are very much in tune with UK policies of the 1970s: nationalization, council house building and government-planned industrial strategy. Moreover, they seem to come from a very specific source within the Labour Party itself: Tony Benn. He was the architect of the 1983 Labour manifesto, which in those years shaped much of the party's ideas. Far left-wing politics of the 1970s and the 1980s are thus back in fashion, courtesy of the social disruptions brought up by globalization. As Thomas L. Friedman correctly points out: "Britain's Labour Party has gone from the center-left to quasi-Marxist".[78]

As a result, a marginal figure within the Labour Party of the past three decades like Jeremy Corbyn, has moved into the center stage of British politics. Under his leadership, the party won 40 percent of the vote in the 2007 general election, its highest since 2001, and came close to dislodging the Conservatives from power. Meanwhile, his presence at the top of the

---

[77] *"How the elephant got its Trump"*, *The Economist, op. cit.*
[78] Thomas L Friedman, *op. cit.*

party has been instrumental in doubling its ranks to 552,000 members. But it was not the nostalgic oldies who brought him there, but the millennials, who as in the case of Bernie Sanders, are his more enthusiastic supporters. A grassroots activist group, known as Momentum, played a key role in electing Corbyn as leader by energizing a young and online base. His success was the product of an internal insurgency, which has allowed him to be in the anteroom of 10 Downing Street, in spite of having been rejected by much of the establishment of his party. That says much about the strength of the anti-globalization movement in the UK.[79]

Corbyn's stance in this matter is emblematic. Even Gordon Brown, curiously enough, recognizes the significance of his anti-globalization position. Referring to Brown's opinion, Rob Merrik says: "Mr Corbyn was successfully tapping into rising public anger over the unfair effects of globalization, after centrists appeared to show they had 'no answers', Mr. Brown said. 'People feel rightly or wrongly that the problems that they have — stagnant wages, inequality, polarization between rich and poor, public service not being properly financed — they ascribed that to the failures of governments, centrist governments that have not been able to manage globalization', he said. On Mr Corbyn shock rise, Mr Brown said: 'He has come through because he expresses people's anger at what's happened — the discontent. When he attacks universal credit, he is speaking for many people, when he says the health service is underfunded, he is speaking for many people'…In the interview, Mr Brown denied he was moving to the left, but argued Mr Corbyn's success was because New Labour 'did not finish the job of curbing inequality and bad banking practices. He has 'articulated a view of a fairer society' by pinching the 'for the many not the few', he noted'".[80]

Another important European anti-globalization far-left figure is France's Jean-Luc Mélenchon. After splitting from the Socialist Party, following its defeat in the 2007 election against Sarkozy, he formed the Left Party, which lingered on the sidelines of French politics for a few

---

[79] Naomi O'Leary, "Europe left looks to Jeremy Corbyn", Politico, 29 July 2018, https://www.politico.eu/article/jeremy-corbyn-labour-left-left-look-to-corbyn/. Accessed 4 August 2018.

[80] Rob Merrik, "Gordon Brown backs Jeremy Corbyn as Labour leader: 'People want to see change'", *The Independent*, 10 November 2017.

years. However, during the 2012 presidential election, Mélenchon received 11.1 percent of the vote, being placed in the fourth position on the first round. Having founded a new party called La France Insoumise in 2016, he was again a candidate for the presidential election of 2017.

He received 19.58 percent of the votes in the first round of that election, being again placed number four but at a short distance from the other competitors. Indeed, he was just 4.5 points away from Emmanuel Macron and less than two points from Marine Le Pen, who went on to the second round. Moreover, he tripled the score of the mainstream Socialist Party, whose collapse elevated Mélenchon as the *de facto* leader of the French left.

For many analysts, though, Mélenchon's strong standing in the last presidential election was due to the fact that he moved from traditional left-wing positions into populist ones, immigration excluded. He can, indeed, be considered borderline in relation to populism.

What admits no doubts, though, is Mélenchon's anti-globalization stance, or better put, his alter-globalization one. The difference being that the latter supports global cooperation and interaction, but opposes what it describes as the negative aspects of economic globalization. In other words, it does not oppose economic globalization *per se*, but the fact that major corporations enrich themselves at the expense of common people and the environment. Alter-globalization is also highly critical of the role played by international organizations such as the World Trade Organization or the International Monetary Fund.

In his last presidential campaign, Mélenchon threatened with taking France out of WTO, referred to bankers as "parasites" who "produce nothing", while saying that free trade "destroys everything" and leads to the "total perversity" of social dumping.[81] Moreover, he expressed that "the leveling of the world economy will lead ineluctably to a global race-to-the-bottom…as workers in developed countries are forced to compete with foreign workers who can produce the same goods at a fraction of the price". He also called for "the radical renegotiation or abandonment of European treaties".[82]

---

[81] Michel Stothard, "Jean-Luc Mélenchon barges way into tight French presidential race", *Financial Time*, 17 April 2017.
[82] Harrison Stetler, "The Rise of Jean-Luc Mélenchon and France's 'Post-Democracy'", *The New Republic*, 18 April 2018.

If the favorite child of Western globalization, Emmanuel Macron, fails to deliver the many expectations that he created in the 2017 campaign, there will not be a safe net for establishmentarian parties. Backlash will be inevitable. As both the Republicans and the Socialist parties suffered historical defeats and fragmented in the 2017 elections, they appear to be far too weak for leadership in the 2021 presidential elections. Hence, Marine Le Pen and Jean-Luc Mélenchon could end up being the frontrunners that year, which entails undoubtedly a dim prospect for globalization.

Putin: The Godfather of Populism

And then, in a totally different category, we find Vladimir Putin. His ideas have much in common with those of hard-right populists. Of course, not that Russia matters all that much in the global trade equation, energy excluded, but it becomes relevant due to its closeness to Western populists. This closeness expresses itself in three ways: first, through the Kremlin cyber-campaigns on their behalf; second, by their looking at Putin's ideas as role models; third, by seeing Russia as a natural ally.

As Sholmo Ben-Ami puts it: "According to Gerard Araud, France's ambassador to the United States, Russian electoral interference and manipulation, if left unchecked, could pose an 'existential threat' to Western democracies. In other words, an autocrat ruling over an impoverished country with an oil-addicted economy smaller than that of Brazil is supposed to be capable of bringing down the world's major democracies… Russia's cyber-campaign against the centrist Emmanuel Macron — meant to aid the far-right candidate Marine Le Pen — included everything from the publication of baseless claims that Macron is gay to the diffusion of fake documents claiming that he has an offshore bank account".[83] The list of Russian political interference on behalf of Western populist candidates is long. That, of course, includes Donald Trump.

On the other hand, Putin has articulated a group of conservative ideas — attacking the "fetishization" of tolerance and diversity, the

---

[83] Sholmo Ben-Ami, "The threat to Western democracy starts at home", *The Strategist*, Canberra: Australian Strategic Policy Institute, 31 March 2018, https://www.aspistrategist. org.au/threat-western-democracy-starts-home. Accessed 14 May 2018.

excesses of moral relativism, the denying of traditional identities, same-sex partnerships and marriages, etc. This has transformed him into the hero of far-right populism. In Franklin Foer words: "But right-wing leaders around the world — from Rodrigo Duterte in the Philippines to Nigel Farage in Britain to Donald Trump in the U.S. — now speak of Putin in heroic terms".[84]

But were those ideas sincere or opportunistic? Again, according to Foer: "After the global crisis of 2008, populist uprisings had sprouted across Europe. Putin and his strategists sensed the beginnings of a larger uprising that could upend the Continent and make life uncomfortable for his geostrategic competitors...With the traditionalist masses ripe for revolt, the Russian president had an opportunity. He could become... 'The New World Leader of Conservatism'".[85] Opportunism, it seems, was the nature of the game.

For hard right populists, though, the perceived commonalities with Putin make of him a natural ally. As Ronal Brownstein expresses: "But conservative-populist nationalists in both the United States and Europe view Putin as a potential ally because they are focused on a sharply contrasting set of international priorities: resisting Islamic radicalization, unwinding global economic integration, and fighting the secularization of Western societies...European populist parties share a common set of priorities focused on restricting immigration, unwinding global economic and political integration (by renouncing the European Union, and, for some of these parties, NATO as well), taking tougher steps to fight Islamic radicalism, and, in most cases, opposing cultural liberalism and secularization at home. On all those fronts, they view Putin not as a threat, but as an ally".[86]

While referring to the Trump–Putin summit, held in Helsinki in July of 2018, Robert Kagan confirms the above: "What observers could not see, was that this was not a meeting between adversaries. It was a meeting between allies, with convergent interests and common goals. These, incidentally, have nothing to do with the 2016 election. They have to do with

---

[84] Franklin Foer, "Its Putin World", *The Atlantic*, March 2017.
[85] *Ibid.*
[86] Ronal Brownstein, "Putin and the Populists", *The Atlantic*, 6 January 2017.

a common view of the liberal world order that the United States helped create seven decades ago. Both leaders seek its destruction".[87]

It would be naïve not to assume that what really matters to Putin's Russia is the objective of undermining, from the inside, Western power and stability. This, by way of deconstructing the Western's democratic post-war establishment, through the weakening of the American-led network of alliances and rules (particularly NATO) and by the collapse of the European Union. Populism becomes, under this perspective, a formidable tool on behalf of Russia's geopolitical aims.

Putin's anti-globalization stance, though, is of secondary relevance, given Russia's modest role within it. What really matters, from a globalizing perspective, is his manipulation of the anti-establishment sentiment prevailing in Western societies so as to disrupt the *status quo* most thoroughly. The following assertion by David Brooks seems, thus, to make sense: "Who is the most influential human being on the planet? My vote goes to Vladimir Putin".[88]

In conclusion, Western post-cold war consensus on globalization is falling apart as a result of the divisive nationalism that a rising populism is bringing with it. As the French Minister of Finance Bruno Le Maire warned at the G20 summit at the end of July 2018: "World trade cannot base itself on the law of the jungle…The law of the jungle, the law of the fittest. This cannot be the future of the global trade relations. The law of the jungle will only turn out losers, it will weaken growth, threaten the most fragile countries and have disastrous political consequences".[89] Unfortunately, we have indeed entered into the law of the jungle with major economies imposing massive tariffs among themselves, while punishing emerging economies. However, as we shall see next, technological leaps also add up to the weakening of international trade in a substantial way.

---

[87] Robert Kagan, "The United States and Russia aren't Allies. But Trump and Putin are", NPR, 17 July 2018, https://www.npr.org/2018/07/17/629598855/opinion-the-united-states-and-russia-arent-allies-but-trump-and-putin-are?. Accessed 18 July 2018.

[88] David Brooks, *op. cit.*

[89] Bruno Le Maire, "'Trade war a reality' French Finance minister warns", BBC News, 22 July 2018.

CHAPTER FIVE

TECHNOLOGY: MAKING GLOBALIZATION REDUNDANT

On a periodical basis, humanity goes through groundbreaking phases where beliefs and certainties are shaken to their core and substituted by new set of convictions. The Western world has been through three of those periods during the last six centuries. These were the Renaissance in the fifteenth and sixteenth centuries, the Enlightenment during the eighteenth century and Modernism, which began at the end of the nineteenth century but reached its peak during the twentieth. In each of these phases, the way men thought about themselves and their physical environment changed considerably. If by comparison to these very creative periods the twenty first century looks unremarkable, we may have to think again.

Renaissance, Enlightenment and Modernism

Renaissance was a wide-ranging movement which generated fundamental changes in the fields of philosophy, art, culture and science (even if this last term didn't exist at the time). Its ideas on humanism placed the human being at a whole different level. For Renaissance thinkers, the center of the universe was no longer God and religion, but the human being as the measure of all things.

This radical shift from Theocentrism to Humanism was counterlevered by another major one in astronomy, where the Earth stopped being the center of the universe and the Sun became, more modestly, the center of a newly conceived solar system, with nine planets in orbit around it,

Earth among them. This was a sobering thought. Man on Earth was the measure of all things...but up to a point.

With those two major shifts in place, human beings set about looking at the world afresh, developing more appropriate ways of observing, registering observations and using inductive thinking. Thanks to these, other major leaps took place in disciplines such as mathematics, physics, biology, medicine, geography, mineralogy and cartography.

Enlightenment, also known as the Age of Reason, was another all-encompassing movement. Reason passed to be seen as the source of legitimacy of political power, determining ideals such as liberty, progress, tolerance or fraternity. It was a period of notable political advances in areas such as constitutional government or the separation between the Church and State. The arts entered in tune with the prevailing notion of harmony, while the sciences witnessed great transformations. Scientific method, under the realm of reason, was based on evidence and testing. Mathematics and the experimental method allowed to solve what until then had been mysteries. As well as the Renaissance, and with rival towering protagonists, it was a period of immense fecundity.

Modernism, understood as a movement of movements, had, to the contrary, the rejection of reason as its core value. This implied the repudiation of harmony, causality and realism, so dear to Enlightenment. A thorough questioning of preexisting certainties took place in the most diverse areas. Abstract art, atonal and dodecaphonic music, introspective narrative based on the free flow of consciousness, existentialism, surrealism, psychoanalysis or the theater of the absurd knocked down frames of reference everywhere.

The Sciences were not absent from this process. Following their own dynamic, but providing inspiration to artists, literary figures and thinkers, they threw down the pillars of the universe built up by Newton during the Enlightenment. Absolute notions of time and space lost all ground under the theory of Relativity, while quantic physics going even further made of the universe a place dominated by randomness.

Renaissance, Enlightenment and Modernism, all symbolized new ways to perceive the human being and his/her surroundings. Each confronted humanity with new levels of consciousness (or subconcsiousness in the case of Modernism), determining fresh values, attitudes and behaviors.

Human beings felt more or less valued in each of these periods and, subsequently, felt more self-assured or insecure in relation to their nature and place in the concert of things. However, there was a common denominator in all of these periods: humans were always at the center of the stage. Whereas studying or questioning themselves, or their surroundings, they could not be taken out of the equation.

Compared with the fundamental changes brought up by the three aforementioned periods, the twenty-first century looks really dull. There is nothing about it that recalls the iconoclastic combativeness of the past century. Nowhere can we find today major figures such as Einstein, Bohr, Picasso, Matisse, Freud, Jung, Stravinsky, Schoenberg, Joyce, Proust, Camus, Husserl or Wittgenstein. Besides the technological obsession, there does not seem to be anything truly significant going on.

Singularity

However, according to many, this technological obsession will bring with it, what by comparison would dwarf Renaissance, Enlightenment and Modernism put together. Indeed, this century is called to witness the most significant phenomenon since the appearance of *Homo sapiens*: Singularity. That is, that inconceivable moment in which Artificial Intelligence (AI) will surpass human intelligence. In other words, an explosion of non-human intelligence able to increase at such speed, that human beings will eventually become irrelevant. Humans will simply have to leave their much-cherished place at center stage.

Singularity will not probably be a big noticeable event, certainly not a Columbus discovery of the Americas type of thing. As Kevin Kelly correctly points out: "Until recently, conventional wisdom held that supercomputers would be the first to host this artificial mind...However, the first genuine AI will not be birthed in a stand-alone supercomputer, but in the superorganism of a billion computer chips known as the net...It will be hard to tell where its thoughts begin and ours end. Any device that touches this networked AI shares — and contributes to — its intelligence. A lonely off-the-grid AI cannot learn as fast, or as smartly, as one that its plugged into 7 billion human minds, plus quintillions of online transistors, plus hundreds of exabytes of real-life data, plus the self-correcting feedback loops of the entire civilization…When this emerging AI arrives, its very ubiquity will hide it. We will be able to reach this distributed intelligence in a million ways, through any digital screen anywhere on earth, so it will be hard to say where it is. And because this synthetic intelligence is a combination of human intelligence (all past human learning, all current humans online), it will be difficult to pinpoint exactly what it is as well".[1]

Indeed, as Yuval Noah Harari further elaborates: "The relentless flow of data sparks inventions and disruptions that nobody plans, controls or comprehend".[2] However, we will know that singularity is there, because human jobs will lose ground at incredible speed. This will happen because as humans remain locked in their biological jail, with limited possibilities to increase their mental prowess, AI will be expanding exponentially. This in turn, means that the gap between AI and our own intelligence will be increasing continuously, making human beings less and less relevant… until they are relegated to obsolescence.

Of course, initially the distance between AI and human intelligence will not be so obvious. As Kevin Kelly observed, it will be hard to locate or define AI. Moreover, exponential duplications can go unnoticed in their initial stages, as passing from 2 to 4 or from 8 to 16 is not very impressive. However, after 50 duplications, the jump goes up from 563 billion to 1.1 trillion. In other words, while human beings remain static at the point where they were overtaken, AI will keep advancing indefinitely and relentlessly according to Moore's Law parameters (doubling its capacity every 18 months). Not surprisingly, Stephen Hawking considered AI more dangerous for the future of humankind than nuclear bombs.

Common sense would advocate that the limits of AI should be defined by human needs, which by extension implies that they should not overcome human capacity to control it. Nonetheless, as Yuval Noah Harari refers, this is a subject where the governments of the world have relinquished leadership, on behalf of the market forces and of what he calls

---

[1] Kevin Kelly, *The Inevitable: Understanding the 12 Technological Forces that will Shape Our* Future (London: Penguin Books, 2016), pp. 29–30.
[2] Yuval Noah Harari, *Homo Deus: A Brief History of Tomorrow* (New York: Harper Collins, 2017), p. 385.

"dataism" (the belief that technology is an end in itself). Overwhelmed by the complexity or the volume of information herein involved, governments are simply looking elsewhere.[3]

In Harari's words: "The hand of the market is blind as well as invisible, and left to its own devices it may fail to do anything at all about the threat of global warming or the dangerous potential of artificial intelligence (…) Just as free-market capitalists believe in the invisible hand of the market, so Dataists believe in the invisible hand of the data flow".[4] In other words, market forces and technological gurus will also relinquish their control over this process.

But what about populists, who according to their manifestos want to protect the jobs of their citizens and reign over market forces? Populists, it would seem, are obsessed with wrong issues and bygone eras. One the one hand, the real threat to domestic employment does not come either from cheaper workforce in distant countries, or from immigrants willing to work for lower salaries. Automation is not only where the real danger is, but also the main cause why jobs are currently being lost.

On the other hand, whatever damage globalization might have done to developed societies, the damage has already been done. There is no way to go back in time. Attention should thus be given to attaining the proper balance between technology and employment. That is, to define how much technological disruption are the populists willing to accept in their societies.

As W. Brian Arthur correctly points out: "Offshoring in the last few decades has eaten up physical jobs and whole industries, jobs that were not replaced. The current transfer of jobs from the physical to the virtual economy is a different sort of offshoring, not to a foreign country but to a virtual one. If we follow recent history we can't assume these jobs will be replaced either".[5] The populists would do better focusing on these "virtual" countries.

Many of the populists, however, maintain a sanguine attitude in relation to disruptive technologies. Referring to Michael Katsios, Deputy

---

[3] Yuval Noah Harari, *op. cit.*
[4] *Ibid*, pp. 376 and 385.
[5] W. Brian Arthur, "Where is technology taking the economy", *McKinsey Quarterly*, October 2017, https://www.mckinsey.com/business-functions/mckinsey-analytics/our-insights/where-is-technology-taking-the-economy. Accessed 15 May 2018.

Assistant to President Trump and Deputy Chief Technology Officer at the White House, journalist Will Knight reported: "'To a certain degree job displacement is inevitable'... 'We must do what Americans have always done: adapt'... 'Today, there is a rebirth. People are transforming once empty factories into the cradle of America's industrial future', he said".[6] What Katsios failed to mention is that the cradle of America's industrial future threatens to be a jobless one. Just as traditional governments and political parties are leaving this subject on the hands of market forces or technological gurus, so are the populists, for the same reasons.

In summary, this is the context of the gigantic challenge that humankind will face in the twenty-first century. However, while singularity materializes, we will be feeling the impact of what Klaus Schwab has coined as the Fourth Industrial Revolution (the first industrial revolution was powered by steam, the second by electricity and the third, in the late twentieth century, by electronics).

The Fourth Industrial Revolution

In Schwab's words: "Contrary to previous industrial revolutions, this one is evolving at an exponential rather than linear pace...It builds on the digital revolution and combines multiple technologies that are leading to unprecedented paradigm shifts in the economy, business, society, and individually. It is not only changing the 'what' and 'how' of doing things but also 'who' we are. It involves the transformation of entire systems, across (and within) countries, companies, industries and society as a whole".[7] And he adds: "The danger is that the fourth industrial revolution would mean that a winner-takes-all dynamic plays out between countries as well as within them".[8]

To understand the meaning of exponential pace, we have to read what Ray Kurzweil, Director of Engineering at Google and founder of the

---

[6] Will Knight, "The White House says a new AI task force will protect workers and keep America first", *MIT Technology Review*, 10 May 2018, https://www.technologyreview.com/s/611118/the-white-house-ai-taskforce-will-keep-america-first-and-protect-its-workers/. Accessed 14 May 2018.
[7] Klaus Schwab, *The Fourth Industrial Revolution* (London: Portfolio Penguin, 2017), p. 3.
[8] *Ibid*, p. 63.

Singularity University, has to say: "Exponentials are quite seductive because they start out sub-linear. We sequenced one ten-thousandth of the human genome in 1990 and two ten-thousandth in 1991. Halfway through the genome project, 7 and a half years into it, we had sequenced 1 percent. People said, 'This is a failure. Seven years, 1 percent. It's going to take 700 years'. Seven years later it was done, because 1 percent is only seven doublings from 100 percent — and it has been doubling every year. We don't think in these exponential terms".[9]

And, as MIT scholars Erik Brynnjolfsson and Andrew McAffe have amply explained, when technological leaps surpass the adjustment capabilities of societies, social havoc might ensue.[10] Especially so, when radical changes not only affect a single productivity sector, but all of them at the same time. Let us just consider that within the sole sector of digital technology, as a well-known 2013 Oxford University report predicts, 47 percent of existing employments in the United States will be erased within the next one to two decades.[11] Moreover, according to the McKinsey Global Institute, currently demonstrated automation technologies could affect 50 percent of the world economy or 1.2 billion employees and US$14.6 trillion in wages.[12]

But of course, there is much more into it. It is the convergence and feedback of multiple technological leaps that makes the situation so utterly complex. Among such leaps, we could mention digital technology and robotics, additive manufacturing (3D printing), nanotechnology, bioengineering and genomics, the Internet of things and new energy technologies. Those technologies will project their impact in every imaginable direction.

---

[9] Leia Parker, "Google, Singularity University visionary Ray Kurzweil on the amazing future he sees", *Silicon Valley Business Journal*, 6 September 2016, http://www.bizjournals. com/sanjose/news/2016/09/06/exclusive-google-singularity-visionary-ray.html. Accessed 25 October 2017.

[10] Erik Brynnjolfsson and Andrew McAffe, *op. cit.*; Erik Brynnjolfsson and Andrew McAffe, *Race against the Machines: How Digital Revolution is Accelerating Innovation, Driving Productivity, and Irreversibly Transforming Employment and the Economy* (Lexington Mass.: Digital Frontier Press, 2011).

[11] Carl Benedikt Frey and Michael E Osborne, *op. cit.*

[12] James Manyika, *op. cit.*

The Sunset of the Assembly Line

Human assembly lines will be flattened down as a result of automation and robotics. Current comparison is of an all-in cost per hour of around €5 for automation, against €9 for manual Chinese labor.[13] Not surprisingly, robots are becoming an economic alternative even in labor-intensive China. In 2017, China became number one worldwide in robotic manufacturing capacity. Moreover, Foxconn, the company that among many other things manufactures the bits that go into iPhones, announced that it was replacing 1 million Chinese workers by robots.[14] As robots become more inexpensive, versatile, adaptive and flexible, no measure of cheap labor will be able to keep pace with them.

This implies, on the one hand, operating with the so-called "dark factories". In them, the line runs for 24 hours a day, without direct human intervention, with low-level monitoring and maintenance and no need for light, heating or air conditioning. And, on the other hand, operating with the so-called collaborative robots or "cobots", which emphasize their flexibility and capacity to work next to humans without putting them in danger.

While "dark factories" are ideal for big companies, cobots, at an average cost of US$24,000, are particularly useful to small companies that account for 70 percent of global manufacturing.[15] Human presence is practically eliminated in the first case, and substantially reduced in the second.

As McKinsey puts it: "Think of the differences between the factory of 2017 and 1937. Or 1997. Or even 2007. Think of the advances in automation, robotics, sensors, the Internet of Things, analytics, big data, artificial intelligence, and design methodologies. How much more will manufacturing change by 2027? By 2037?".[16]

Manufacturing will be also disrupted totally by additive manufacturing or 3D printing. Since things have been made with tools or machinery,

---

[13] Finbarr Livesey, *Ibid*, pp. 73–74.

[14] Martin Ford, "China's troubling robot revolution", *The New York Times*, 10 June 2015; Finbarr Livesey, *op. cit.*, p. 79.

[15] T. X. Hammes, *op. cit.*

[16] Erin Blackwell, Tony Gambell, *et al.*, "The great remake: Manufacturing for modern times", https://www.mckinsey.com/business-functions/operations/our-insights/the-great-remake-manufacturing-for-modern-times. Accessed 19 June 2018.

manufacture has been a subtractive game. A piece of material would have layers removed until the object in question reached the right shape. A new game player has now entered the field, allowing an object to be printed layer upon layer from a digital 3D model. This player is a game changer.

Instead of manufacturing multiple smaller parts to be joined together, a single final one can be printed directly. As Finbarr Livesey explains: "One of the lead adopters is General Electric (GE)…They now make a fuel nozzle using a 3D metal printer, meaning that a part once made by welding eighteen pieces together can now be printed of in one go…".[17] The first change it brings is eliminating numerous intermediary manufacturing steps.

It would seem that fewer pieces would mean smaller storage space. But what is involved is much more than that, as with 3D printing industrial pieces and parts can now be printed on demand. Hence, the second change is that inventories will soon become obsolete.

On the other hand, 3D printing leads to the mass customization and design for purpose of industrial parts and pieces. However, mass customization need not be of just pieces and parts, but also of final products. Again, Finbarr Livesey presents us with a good example: "You've just entered the world of mass customization. On the Adidas website you can choose a base design for a trainer and then customize every color, texture and style for each element, even adding in some text or photo print if that's what you fancy…But the key here is that those shoes were never going to be made unless you clicked the purchase button on the website, linking production directly to actual demand".[18]

Scale and standardization, the basis of the assembly line, will be in trouble when competing with mass customization. Not surprisingly, according to Rick Smith and Mitch Free: "Industrial 3D printing is the Second Wave of production technology. It is just beginning to disrupt a $14 trillion global manufacturing industry that is based on mass production".[19] This is the third change, which will be the equivalent of driving one's own car instead of using the public transportation system.

---

[17] *op. cit.*, p. 50.
[18] *op. cit.*, p. 52.
[19] Rick Smith and Mitch Free, *The Great Disruption: Competing and Surviving in the Second Wave of the Industrial Revolution* (New York: Thomas Dunne Books/St. Martin's Press, 2016), p. 16.

But in addition to eliminating intermediary manufacturing steps, and being able to mass customize, 3D printing can manage complex designs not available to the assembly line. Again in Rick Smith and Mitch Free words: "3D printers don't care about complexity. The additive process, building layer by tiny layer, produces extremely complicated objects just as easily as simple ones."[20] This is the fourth change: complex designs not available in the assembly line are now possible.

Finally, additive technology provides companies with two additional and fundamental benefits. One is speeding the production process (as long supply chains become unnecessary). The other is allowing for smaller volumes of production near to the consumption market. The cycle time between production and distribution is thus shortened considerably, while a decentralization in the production process allows for smaller-scale 3D factories close to the final costumer. This is the fifth change: the possibility of localizing production in the vicinity of the final consumer.

Because it used to take days to print a part, 3D printing was used primarily for prototyping and very high value parts. However, in April 2016, Carbon 3D released a commercial version of the machine that was 100 times faster. Moreover, some time after Carbon 3D announced its new technology to the world, a Canadian engineer named Diego Seoane unveiled his new 3D printing technology, which works twice as fast as the Carbon 3D printer.

Not surprisingly, 52 percent of the CEOs surveyed by PricewaterhouseCopers in 2016, expect to use 3D printing for high volume production within the next three to five years.[21] Moreover, the German government's plan for the future, known as "Industry 4.0", aims at customization and flexibilization in the production process, with the possibility of last-minute changes being introduced within the context of rational use of resources and minimal waste. This, of course, is a perfect definition of 3D printing.

The Sunset of Raw Materials

And then, there is nanotechnology. Iron and steel industries, mining, in general, and countless commodities will lose much ground, as the

---

[20] *Ibid*, p. 82.
[21] *Ibid*, p. 132; T. X. Hammes, *op. cit.*

introduction of new materials by nanotechnology fully materializes in the next few decades. According to K. Eric Drexler: "A nanoscale technology revolution has already arrived, bringing with it the radical abundance we call the Information Revolution...The same profound digital principles will enable a parallel revolution that will enable radical abundance, not just in the world of information, but in the world of tangible, physical products as well".[22]

Examples speak for themselves: carbon nanotubes with higher strength than any other known material and more conductive than copper; a lightweight material as firm as aircraft aluminum but one hundred times more resistant; a material stronger than steel with only one-fifth of its density; "microlattice", 99.99 percent air and yet incredibly hard to break; "graphene", an efficient conductor of heat and electricity 200 times stronger that steel and a million times thinner than a human hair.[23]

Drexler continues: "The extraordinary lightness and strength of materials like these has far-reaching consequences (...) In aerospace technology and a range of other spheres of engineering, the prospect of removing more than 80 percent of the structural mass promises a revolution in performance and efficiency. Performance aside, making products less massive reduces materials consumption, with a proportional impact on production costs".[24]

Traditional assembly lines will be deeply affected as well, as 3D printing and new materials seem to be made for each other. The possibility of commercial application of many of these materials brought up by nanotechnology would be out of reach, if it were not for 3D printing. The result can be none other than a combination of nearly unlimited amount of geometries with a nearly unlimited amount of material properties.[25]

Food production is also in the process of being revolutionized. Farming and livestock sectors can be turned upside down as genome technology advances in the direction of producing vegetables, fruits and meat *in vitro*. Synthetic biology will be able to write DNA, thus designing food

---

[22] K. Eric Drexler, *Radical Abundance: How Revolution in Nanotechnology Will Change Civilization* (New York: Public Affairs, 2013), p. 6.

[23] Klaus Schwab, *op. cit.*; Rick Smith and Mitch Free, *op. cit.*

[24] K. Eric Drexler, *op. cit.*, p. 163.

[25] Rick Smith and Mitch Free, *op. cit.*

that would be engineered from the ground up and then industrially produced.

Cultured meat could be produced from a single muscle stem cell, growing the steak without needing the cow. This technology, which is already scientifically viable, will keep improving and eventually become commercially viable. It will require 95 percent less water, 98 percent less land and 45 percent less energy, while generating 95 percent less greenhouse gases. The growing global market will provide a massive financial incentive to master the production of cultured meat.[26]

But cultured meat will not only affect the livestock sector but also the agricultural one. As T. X. Hammes refers: "When it succeeds, it will reduce the import/export not just of meat but also of the agricultural feed products necessary to raise animals. The top five soybean exporters shipped a total of over 60 million metric tons in 2015, most of it as animal feed".[27]

Together with the above advancements, there would be many other leaps in sensors, production automation, robot farming or engineering, which will radically transform the multimillenarian relation between human beings and soil.

Indoor farms, which are beginning to take shape in developed countries, are a good example of this. Indoor farms do not require herbicides or pesticides, use 97 percent less water, use 40 percent less power, waste 50 percent less food and are not subject to weather irregularities. Depending on their production, such farms can produce 11 to 15 crop cycles per year.[28]

One type of indoor farming is vertical farming. This method will be able to grow vegetables inside climate-controlled, light-controlled cylinders, located in towers. Without using pesticides, herbicides or synthetic

---

[26] Peter H Diamandis, "These 4 Tech Trends Are Driving US Toward Food Abundance", *Singularity Hub*, 18 May 2018, https://singularityhb.com/2018/05/18/these-4-trends-are-driving-us-toward-food-abundandance/#sm.0001kyij62wlkdw0yculio1plvs92. Accessed 12 May 2018; T. X. Hammes, *op. cit.*

[27] *Ibid.*

[28] Michael Zappa, "15 emerging agriculture technologies that will change the world", *Policy Horizons Canada*, 6 May 2015, http://www.businessinsider.sg/15-emerging-agriculture-technologies-2014-4/#18EzrTcMUDhrlBtw.97. Accessed 5 September 2016; Josie Garthwaite, "Beyond GMOs: The rise of synthetic biology", *The Atlantic*, 25 September 2014; T. X. Hammes, *op. cit.*

fertilizers, this method uses instead thousands of infrared cameras and collecting data sensors in order to optimize the growing of vegetables. One of its current developers, a Californian company call Plenty, claims that this technology can achieve yields of up 350 times greater than traditional agriculture while using 1 percent of the water and almost no land when compared to conventional methods.[29]

The energy sector also advances at amazing speed. In addition to technological advances in fracking and horizontal drilling, there have been impressive advances in clean energies. Solar and wind technologies, whose prices have fallen 85 percent since the beginning of this century or the last years of the preceding one, are duplicating their capacity every two years within the parameters of the Moore Law. According to well-known futurologist Jeremy Rifkin, such technologies are moving towards the zero marginal costs' stage where they will be able to run for free, once their development costs have been amortized.[30]

At the same time, biomass — now entering into its second generation — evolves rapidly, as rapidly as geothermic and wave technologies. Lithium batteries, whose price has fallen by 40 percent since 2009, and whose storage capacity has augmented dramatically, are beginning to provide profitability to electric cars. Chemical systems that can replicate photosynthesis artificially on a grand scale — and hence create solar collectors that produce fuel — are on their way. Biotechnology is also on its way to substituting oil in the production of plastics. Self-fertilizing plants, derived from synthetic biology, could decouple agriculture from the oil industry fertilizers. Synthetic-biological redesign of organisms could generate biofuel almost identical to gasoline. Moreover, such technological changes move in tandem with the decarburization requirements of the 2015 Paris Agreement on Climate Change.[31]

---

[29] Ronald Holden, "It's called vertical farming, and it could be the future of agriculture", *Forbes Magazine*, 4 November 2016.

[30] Jeremy Riffkin, *The Zero Marginal Cost Society: The Internet of Things, the Collaborative Commons, and the Eclipse of Capitalism* (New York: Pelgrave, 2014).

[31] McKinsey Global Institute "Disruptive technologies: Advances that will transform life, business, and the global economy", May 2013, https://www.mckinsey.com/business-functions/digital-mckinsey/our-insights/disruptive-technologies. Accessed 19 May 2018; Josie Garthwaite, *op. cit.*; Bruce Watson, *op. cit.*; T. X. Hammes, *op. cit.*

And what if Ray Kurzweil proves to be right in his prediction about the future of solar energy? According to him: "Solar energy is growing exponentially because we're applying nanotechnology to the construction of solar panels and energy storage. It's now 2 percent of the world's energy, so people dismiss it: 'It's 2 percent. It's a nice thing to do. It's a fringe player. That's not going to solve the problem'. They are ignoring the exponential growth. Two percent is only six doublings from 100 percent. We're doubling every two years. That's 12 years. We can meet all of our energy needs through solar".[32] A recent Stanford University report is somewhat less optimist than Kurzweil, as it predicts that, in 2050, the world could be able to fulfill its energy needs through a combination of solar, wind and water energy technologies, without hampering economic growth.[33]

The Sunset of the Human Service Sector

Meanwhile the service sector is threatened by digital technologies in every imaginable way. Not only repetitive and routine jobs will be displaced by such technologies, but also jobs that require analytical thinking and high educational levels are being targeted by "big data", deep learning the Internet of things and the automation of knowledge work.

The volume of digitalized information is so massive that it would fill five stacks of CD disks reaching as far as the moon. Big data allows that all that universe of stored digital information can be instantaneously collated. As a result, we are passing from the realm of cause–effect into that of correlation. For the last century, the handling of information was done by compiling and analyzing small plots of it. As the recollection of information was a complex, expensive and time-consuming process, the way of managing it was by focusing on reduced and random samples. This allowed inferring what happened in the whole by way of analyzing the particular. Samples, of course, had to be obtained and processed in a

---

[32] Leia Parker, *op. cit.*
[33] Mark Z Jacobson, Mark A Delucchi, Zack A. F. Bauer, *et al.*, "100% Clean and Renewable Wind, Water, and Sunlight All-Sector Energy Roadmaps for 139 Countries of the World", Joule, 6 September 2017, https://web.stanford.edu/group/efmh/jacobson/Articles/I/CountriesWWS.pdf. Accessed 19 May 2018.

careful and orderly manner. Thanks to big data, though, the whole can now be easily reviewed and correlated. Within this holistic approach, what matters is the probabilistic relation among things and not its causality.[34]

In David Runciman's words: "Machines that are capable of learning do not have to be capable of thinking the way we do. What they require are vast amount of data, which they can filter at incredible speed searching for patterns of which they make inferences, and then for further patterns in their own failures to draw the optimal inferences".[35]

Martin Ford explains this in the following terms: "By one estimate, the total amount of data stored globally is now measured in thousands of exabytes (an exabyte is equal to a billion gigabytes), and that figure is subject to its own Moore's Law — like acceleration, doubling roughly every three years. Nearly all that data is now stored in digital format and is therefore accessible to direct manipulation by computers (…) The vast majority of this data is what a computer scientist would call 'unstructured' (…) the ability to process a stream of unstructured information…is, after all, one of the things for which humans are uniquely adapted. The difference, of course, is that in the realm of big data, computers are able to do this on a scale that for a person, would be impossible. Big data is having a revolutionary impact in a wide range of areas including business, politics, medicine, and nearly every field of natural and social science".[36]

As for the implications of big data in the area of business, Martin Ford adds: "Whereas today there is a team of knowledge workers who collect information and present analysis to multiple levels of management, eventually there may be a single manager and a powerful algorithm. Organizations are likely to flatten. Layers of middle management will evaporate, and many jobs now performed by both clerical workers and skilled analysts will simply disappear".[37] And this type of situation would generalize in most intensive knowledge occupations. From medical

---

[34] Victor Mayer Schoenmberg and Kenneth Cukier, *Big Data: A Revolution That Will Transform How We Live, Work and Think* (London: John Murray, 2013).

[35] Alan Bennett, "Diary", *London Review of Books*, Volume 4, Issue 2, 2018.

[36] Martin Ford, *The Rise of Robots: Technology and the Threat of a Jobless Future* (New York: Basic Books), pp. 85–87.

[37] *Ibid*, p. 96.

internists to radiologists, from pharmacists to lawyers, from accountants to financial analysts, the list can be immense.

The case of IBM's Watson computer in the field of medical diagnosis is emblematic, being able to instantly process and correlate all digitalized information in medical textbooks, scientific journals, clinical studies and even physicians' notes for individual patients. Delving into a gigantic collection of data, and crossing the boundaries of medical specialties, it can make a diagnosis in matter of minutes. Watson, though, has been expanding its might into several other areas.

Big data is not only relevant in itself, but also as a precious source that feeds deep learning. That is, the process through which AI teaches itself. In deep learning, there is no date like more data. Data, lots of it, is indeed the new petroleum that will fuel the age of AT.

This Fourth Industrial Revolution is bringing with it two closely inter-related consequences that can drastically affect globalization. It will trigger, on the one hand, a decoupling between developed and emerging economies and, on the other hand, it will induce the onshoring of previously offshored manufacturing and service activities, while allowing for the local substitution of imported commodities.

A Decoupling World Economy

In 1991, Alvin Tofller wrote about a world divided into quick-moving and slow-moving nations; into nations with advanced economic and technological systems and outpaced economic and technological nations, subjected to huge economic limitations and social problems.[38]

Toffler's decoupling prediction would not last a decade, as 1.3 billion Chinese or 1.2 billion Indians joined the labor market within a context of a race to the bottom of production costs. As a result, Western nations began transforming themselves into embattled fortresses. Moreover, in 2008, lax and hawkish banking practices in the US unleashed an international recession. As Western nations emerged from this crisis, a concatenation of high indebtedness, sluggish growth and lack of confidence made its appearance. As a consequence, another decoupling,

---

[38] Alvin Toffler, *El Cambio de Poder* (Barcelona: Plaza y Janés Editores, 1991).

very different from that predicted by Toffler, began to take shape. Indeed, developing nations, lifted by China's phenomenal emergence, continued to grow despite the lackluster performance shown by the developed world.

However, the Fourth Industrial Revolution in sight will bring back the kind of decoupling envisaged by Toffler. Within it, the distinction between high- and low-cost production countries will become increasingly irrelevant. What will matter is the aptitude for innovation that each country has. Thus, a group of developed economies led by the US, this time with the active presence of China as well, will run the show.

This decoupling could be particularly tough for slow-moving nations. Technologically advanced economies will become much more autonomous in relation to the manufactures, commodities and services coming from the developing world. While globalization loses standing, as a result of the increasing autarchy of developed countries, emerging nations will become dramatically stressed.[39]

This incoming tsunami will impact them in all sorts of ways. Their labor-intensive assembly lines could be flattened down by the double disruption of robotics and additive manufacturing. Their mining sector, iron and steel industries and many other commodities will lose ground as nanotechnology substitutes old materials for new ones in the next few decades.

Their farming and livestock sectors can be turned upside down, as genome technology advances in the fields of vegetables, fruits and meat, while indoor farming, robot farming or production automation take over. As a result, the developed world will become increasingly self-sufficient in these areas. Live meat and milk, vegetables and fruits that have grown in the soil will be a quaint thing of the past. Much of the hydrocarbons reserves in emerging economies run the risk of remaining underground, as new technologies supply the developed world with the energy it needs.

Last but not least in the list of woes, their service sector, which has played such an important part in the welfare of the emerging nations, will be threatened by digital technology from all fronts. This shall derail or

---

[39] T. X. Hames, "The end of globalization? The international security implications", War on the Rocks, 2 August 2016, https://warontherocks.com/2016/08/the-end-of-globalization-the-international-security-implications/. Accessed 13 February 2017.

abort its integration into global value chains. The lower costs of their white-collar jobs, their "cheaper brains", will count for little, when confronted by the power of algorithms.

This is one side of the coin.

Returning Home

The other side of this same coin is the onshoring, reshoring or nearshoring of previously offshored manufacturing and service activities, as well as the local substitution of imported commodities. The new technologies are the ones doing this, motivating developed societies to produce near the area where consumption takes place, be it of objects, food and energy, while the same applies to services. Not surprisingly, Finbarr Livesey wrote: "We are running the global economy on a model that went out of date without anyone noticing at some point in the past decade".[40]

Labor-intensive assembly lines can only become obsolete if robotics and atomization can now work at the scale required, from the small to the large, at a lower cost. If robots can produce endlessly, and at a lower cost than the human worker, there can be no match for them. Why then have factories at the other end of the world, when it is possible to produce cheaper at home?

The math is clear to Foxconn, a quintessential labor-intensive producer in China. As mentioned before, this Taiwanese company decided to replace 1 million Chinese workers by robots. What was not mentioned is the fact that this company is planning to move a large part of its production to the United States. Indeed, it recently opened a facility in Pennsylvania and is planning to open more facilities in other US states.

If a Taiwanese company is willing to relocate close to its main consumer market, what argument is there for American companies not to do the same? The truth is that between 2010 and 2015, according to the Reshoring Initiative, over 1,300 American companies either brought production back to the United States or chose to source from home suppliers instead of remaining overseas.[41] Within an extensive survey of companies

---

[40] Finbarr Livesey, *op. cit.*, p. 1.
[41] *Ibid*, p. 125.

reported by Finbarr Lievesy, 71 percent believe that advance manufacturing processes will improve the economy of localized production.[42]

Additive technology will also erode, in a substantial way, labor-intensive assembly lines and faraway supply chains. Jeffrey Immelt, then General Electric's CEO stated: "We can basically make every product GE makes and do it economically in the US today".[43] And, as GE, countless companies in the developed world will produce locally finished products or the parts thereof, avoiding the delay of long supply chains, import fees and trapped inventory.

The implications of a contraction in the international trade of parts, as a result of local 3D printing, will be huge. According to PricewaterouseCoopers, that would put up to 40 percent of traditional air and shipping cargo under threat.[44] Intermediate trade of unfinished goods, it has to be outlined, accounts for approximately 60 percent of current world trade.[45]

Additive technology can be profoundly disruptive in this intermediate trade for two reasons. First, because numerous parts will be produced locally. Second, because 3D printing allows for the elimination of many previously needed parts and pieces in any given product.

But in addition to unfinished goods, 3D printing is evolving into the production of finished goods as well. This implies, of course, smaller volumes of production, but, at the same time, customized production. As a result, there would be a decentralization of the production process, with numerous 3D printing factories producing for localized markets. Companies would hence move toward having smaller production facilities in each of the markets in which they are selling.

A fundamental by-product of 3D printing factories near home will be speedy deliveries. This trend, introduced by Amazon Prime in 2005, allowed customers to pay US$79 for a two-day unlimited delivery. A recent Deloitte report asked over 4,000 US costumers what they considered to be fast shipping, to which 90 percent replied two days

---

[42] *Ibid*, p. 124.
[43] Rick Smith and Mitch Free, *op. cit.*, p. 145.
[44] *Ibid*, p. 108.
[45] Finbarr Livesey, *op. cit.*, p. 52.

or less.[46] Americans are no longer willing to wait for their products. Local 3D printing will be the answer to this quest for immediacy, making supply chains and long delays even more outmoded, especially when each item is uniquely customized, and not the product of mass standardization.

Local Substitution of Commodities

The traditional natural resources that developing economies have been extracting out of their grounds, tilling out of their fields or raising up in their farms for the consumption of the developed economies might turn out to be substituted by local alternatives. Technology simply could trump those gifts of nature. Molecular bonding between light atoms that result in new materials, cellular factories that replace the need of living animals, controlled environment agriculture in reduced spaces, renewable energy, are but a few examples of the way in which mass substitution of commodities can take place in developed economies.

Strong and lightweight materials resulting from nanotechnology are ideal for the construction of bridges and aircrafts, but are equally useful for many other applications, such as the construction of machine parts, tables, walls, circuit boards or textile fibers. Moreover, they are resistant to corrosion, fatigue, creep and fracture. In K. Eric Drexler words: "Because structures made of stronger, lighter materials can be made with less mass, the cost of raw materials and processing can be reduced in direct proportion".[47]

Being much lighter and stronger, they allow for the elimination of a substantial percentage of structural mass. Products less massive not only have a favorable impact on production costs but also, as in the case of aircrafts, considerably reduce the amount of fuel needed.

But it is not only in the area of aerospace where new materials allow for energy saving. Carbon nanotubes can outperform and replace copper as an electrical conductor. Photovoltaic cells can improve significantly with nanotechnology materials, thus allowing for greater improvement in

---

[46] *Ibid*, p. 137.
[47] K. Eric Drexler, *op. cit.*, p. 162.

solar conversion efficiency. As such, these new materials have the potential to change the energy economy, by lowering the cost of electric power. Nanotechnology will also be able to replace steel, aluminum and plastic structures with stronger and more efficient materials, hence making these commodities increasingly redundant. Again in K. Eric Drexler words: "In a wide range of products, performance depends of the strength and density of structural materials, and building with stronger, lighter materials can reduce product mass because structural materials make up almost all the mass of almost every industrial product".[48]

New structural materials resulting from nanomanufacturing, will have a profound impact. They are potentially able to replace numerous commodities, while at the same time save energy by reducing mass or improving conductivity. In other words, steel, aluminum, copper, oil, gas, among many other commodities, are being targeted for profound disruption by nanotechnology. This implies not only substitution of commodities in a mass scale, but also the capacity to produce their replacements locally.

This process of substitution does not stop at inanimate matter but targets live creatures as well. We are heading for what Elsa Sortiaris calls "the post animal economy".[49] Cellular agriculture, for instance, is a scientific field that uses genomics to replicate proteins and biomolecules produced by animals. These "cellular factories" can grow food and brew beverages locally and sustainable. Cow-free milk is an example of what can be produced. Within this post-animal feeding industry, we will find chicken-free chicken or beef-free beef. Cheap, scalable and locally produced meat only requires small biopsies from an animal to extract a group of cells to nurture them up.

Mass substitution of agricultural products is also in line. Controlled environment agriculture, represented by high-tech indoor farms, will be able to produce locally year-round higher yields. As Peter Diamandis says: "Imagine…growing all your food in a 50-story tall vertical farm in downtown LA or off-shore on the Great Lakes where the travel distance

---

[48] K. Eric Drexler, *op. cit.*, p. 162.
[49] Elsa Sortiaris, "5 wild biotech products of the future", Singularity Hub, 24 November 2017, https://singularityhub.com/2017/11/24/5-wild-biotech-products-of-the-future/#sm. 0001kyij62wlkw0ycu1io1plvs92. Accessed 29 May 2018.

is no longer 1,500 miles but 50 miles. Delocalized farming will minimize travel costs at the same time that it maximizes freshness".[50] And the examples go on.

As for the substitution of fossil energy, not only is the shale revolution leading towards US self-sufficiency, but renewable energy rapidly advances towards making the developed world much more autonomous in this area. Although electricity generated by wind, solar, geothermal and other renewable sources can be transmitted over long distances, it is mostly generated and consumed locally. Contrary to oil, gas and coal, it is not transported through extensive distances in tankers, ships or pipelines.

According to a 2014 report by the International Renewable Energy Agency (IRENA), solar photovoltaic costs fell by two-thirds between the end of 2009 and 2013, a speed of change comparable to that seen in the IT revolution. Indeed, in 2013, prices had fallen by 80 percent since 2008.[51] In addition, as expressed by a 2016 IRENA report "Biomass for power, hydropower, geothermal and onshore wind can all now provide electricity competitively, compared to fossil fuel-power generation".[52]

The best example of this locally generated renewable energy is provided by Jeremy Riffkin, who has served as advisor to Germany, the european union and China within the so-called Third Industrial Revolution framework. His master plan to implement post-carbon infrastructures, have been endorsed by national governments and multilateral institutions, including the European Parliament in 2007.

Today, as he expresses, Internet technology and renewable energies are beginning to merge, in order to create a new infrastructure for a Third Industrial Revolution. This should change the way power is distributed in the twenty-first century. In the coming era that he envisages, hundreds of millions of people will produce their own renewable energy in their

---

[50] Peter Diamandis, *op. cit.*

[51] Edgar Meza, "IRENA: PV prices have declined 80% since 2008", PV Magazine, 11 September 2014, https://www.pv-magazine.com/2014/09/11/irena-pv-prices-have-declined-80-since-2008_100016283/. Accessed 29 February 2018.

[52] International Renewable Energy Agency, "The power to change: Solar and wind cost reduction potential to 2025", 2016, http://www.irena.org/DocumentDownloads/Publications/IRENA_Power_to_Change_2016.pdf. Accessed 29 February 2018.

homes, offices and factories and share it with each other through an "Energy Internet".

This implies several steps: (a) shifting to renewable energy, (b) transforming the building stock into power plants to collect renewable energies on-site, (c) deploying hydrogen and other storage technologies in every building so as to store intermittent energy, (d) using Internet technology to transform the power grid into an energy Internet that acts just like the Internet (with millions of buildings generating small amount of renewable energy, whose surplus is sent to the grid so as to be shared with others) and (e) transitioning the transport fleet to electric plug-in and fuel cell vehicles, which can be charged at home.[53] Locally produced and distributed renewable energy, will make obsolete the era in which hydrocarbons traveled through long distances.

Algorithms Supplanting Low-cost Foreign Brains

Looking for cheaper white-collar jobs in distant places no longer shall make sense. Algorithms would provide the same kind of services locally, for even lower costs. Hence, searching for the better qualified designer, engineer, financial analyst or accountant, at the best available costs in faraway lands, will become useless. Not only long-distance low-end services such as call centers shall be turned upside down, but also high-end knowledge-intensive services such as chip design, market analytics, security analysis, software development and the like.

India's lead in IT services, based on factors such as extensive experience at remote delivery of IT services to global clients, highly developed process rigor, in-depth knowledge of specific industries and fluency in the English language, will tend to become irrelevant when confronted with big data and deep learning (the process by which machines try to mimic the brain functioning in order to understand patterns).

As Nida Najar explains: "India's information technology industry grew at a breakneck speed over the past two decades thanks to a trend commonly called offshoring...But the global tech industry is increasingly relying on

---

[53] Jeremy Rifkin, *The Third Industrial Revolution: How Lateral Power is Transforming Energy, the Economy, and the World* (New York: St. Martin's Press, 2011).

automation, robotics, big data analytics, machine learning and consulting —
technologies that threaten to bypass and even replace Indian workers...
'What we're seeing is an acceleration in shedding for jobs in India and an
adding of jobs inshore', said Sandra Notardonato, and analyst and research
vice president for Garter, a research and advisory company".[54]

It would seem, though, that those inshore jobs to which
Mrs. Notardonato refers to, will not be human ones. The inshoring or
reshoring trend shall clearly be felt in the white-collar jobs of emerging
economies. As a result, the best part of Stan Shih's "smile curve" (where
services were the most valuable component of the offshoring process) will
be returning to developed economies.

Onshoring Supporters

This onshoring or reshoring process will be reinforced by the support of
three groups of political actors: the populists, the environmentalists, and
the governors and mayors of economically decayed regions and cities in
the United States.

As mentioned at the beginning of the chapter, populists do not seem
to be at odds with disruptive technology. Moreover, their protectionist
policies are certainly adding to the economic reasons behind the onshoring process. The rise of economic nationalism as represented by Trump
and other economic leaders is indeed creating the political incentives for
the repatriation of economic activities.

Finnbarr Livesey puts this in the right terms when saying: "Companies
have always had to work with the political context of the day. It is possible
that companies became too used to the relative stability of the past decades, with a settled position on globalization for many politicians, pundits
and economists. The rapid change in the political context will make the
job of structuring companies harder, as managers will have to deal with
greater border restrictions and the uncertainty of how these will evolve".[55]

With the political context moving in the same direction as the potential benefits offered by new technologies, the possibilities of moving back
home will certainly increase. Hence, populism and technological change

---

[54] Nida Najar, *op. cit.*
[55] Finnbarr Livesey, *op. cit.*, p. 178.

seem to work in tandem to promote the reshoring of economic activities. The combination of new boundaries and new technologies indeed becomes a powerful instrument of change, strong enough to shake to its bones the relative stability of past decades.

There seem to be logical reasons as to why environmentalists would be happy with the onshoring of economic activities that the Fourth Industrial Revolution is bringing with it. Home production, especially if done by less polluting automatized factories, may diminish substantially the countless moving of innumerable parts and pieces around the world. This represents billions of tons of yearly CO_2 emissions that can be subtracted from the global warming equation.

The same goes with 3D printing, which drastically reduces the number of pieces and parts to be produced or moved around. Moreover, in traditional manufacturing, the main byproduct is waste, while additive 3D printing technology results in very little waste of raw materials.

True, additive technology is energy intensive. However, this results primarily from the heating of materials for printing purposes. Some of the biggest advances in this area, though, are being done by new nanotechnology materials, which do not need to be heated for printing. Moreover, the negative side of energy-intensive manufacturing will decrease as renewable sources of energy become more accessible.

In addition, the extra energy usage of 3D printing is offset by its many technical improvements, a good example of which would be the enormous savings in jet fuel consumption mentioned above. But also, 3D printing innovations can result in energy breakthroughs, especially in energy storage, as exemplified by its making batteries more efficient and by increasing energy conductivity and solar conversion efficiency. At the same time, these new materials can reduce the ecological impact derived from the digging up and extraction of the tens of billions of metals and minerals used by the industry yearly. This includes, as well, the long-distance transport of such materials.

Environmentalists can only welcome cultured meat factories or controlled environment agriculture. Cultured meat, as mentioned, is expected to require 95 percent less water, 98 percent less land and 45 percent less energy, while generating 95 percent less greenhouse gases. Indoor farms, on the other hand, do not require herbicides or pesticides, use 97 percent less water, 40 percent less power and waste 50 percent less food. And all of this shall be done without long-distance transport of commodities.

As for renewable energy to be generated and distributed locally, environmentalists must be exceedingly happy. Jeremy Riffkin's Third Industrial Revolution would be a dream come true for them. Leaving hydrocarbons reserves underground, the sun, wind, biomass and geothermal energies can be used to supply localized energy needs, and this would be the ideal answer to their quest for a cleaner planet.

Presumably, then, environmentalists would gladly add their weight to the onshoring trend that technological leaps are pushing for. Within this dissimilar group of supporters of the reshoring process tied to the Fourth Industrial Revolution, we should find as well the governors and mayors of those states and cities of the United States dragged down by economic decay.

As argued in a Brookings Institution report written by Cecile Murray and Alan Berube: "Amid this rising inequality, the question of how to revive broad-base economic growth in the middle of the country has received substantial attention...These places — including large urban areas like Detroit, Pittsburg, and Cleveland, as well as smaller communities like Albany, Ga., Janesville, Wisc., ad Dubuque, Iowa — once formed the backbone of America's manufacturing economy, but have since struggled to transition to a more digital economy (...) The technologically advanced economy is a major driver of economic growth. And older industrial cities (OICs) are research powerhouses. These communities receive more grant dollars per capita from the National Institute of Health and National Science Foundation than their peers, and are home to many of the world-famous private research universities of the Northeast as well as the renowned land-grant colleges and universities of the Midwest. Notably, many of these research universities are located in downtown areas. Recent research from our Brooking colleagues suggests that this proximity to employers, entrepreneurs, capital, and other amenities that facilitate research commercialization positions these institutions well to serve as regional hubs of innovation and growth".[56]

---

[56] Cecile Murray and Alan Berube, "The road to economic revival in the Heartland runs through older industrial cities", 15 May, 2018, https://www.brookings.edu/blog/the-avenue/2018/05/15/the-road-to-economic-revival-in-the-heartland-runs-through-older-industrial-cities/. Accessed 15 May 2018.

As this report shows, there is a strategy in place for the economic revival of America's heartland. The reconversion into digital manufacturing of these older industrial cities is a fundamental part of that strategy. The comparative advantages that many of these cities enjoy, as research powerhouses, could indeed position them well for such endeavor. Hence, they may become excellent places for the onshoring process that the Fourth Industrial Revolution is bringing with it. And although new technologies are not conducive to job creation, they might energize decaying communities in many other ways. As a result, as Cecile Murray and Alan Berube remark: "Local, regional and state leaders are stepping up to retool these economies for growth and inclusion by supporting firm creation and expansion".[57] These leaders can thus be added to this particular convergence of interests.

However, as we shall see next, there are no clear-cut situations. Complexity and ambivalence prevail in every direction.

---

[57] *Ibid.*

CHAPTER SIX

THE CONSISTENCY OF BOTH SIDES

The alignment of both sides is thus clear. However, this is not a linear confrontation as both the pro-globalization and anti-globalization trends are subjected to external and internal challenges, as well as to important contradictions. Hence, reviewing the solidity of the main forces in play can help us advance a step further in the understanding of the process in motion.

Essentially, the four fundamental forces pushing in both directions are the leadership of China and the economic strength of Asia, on the one side, and populism and the Fourth Industrial Revolution, on the other. Consequently, trying to ascertain the consistency of such forces can provide a more accurate picture of this fluid situation.

China, as explained in Chapter Three, is clearly becoming the leader of the globalized economy. It not only enjoys the necessary economic strength to play that role within the vacuum left by the US withdrawal, but also has the willingness and the vision to do so. Moreover, an increasing number of members of the international community are beginning to accept it as the natural option to succeed the United States in that role. That is why, if China does not prove to be up to this task, the pro-globalization side will clearly be affected.

Is China up to the Task?

China's positioning as a globalizing leader happens at a time in which the dichotomy openness vs. closeness is defining the internal debate of many

Western societies. The current confrontation between the small village and the global village shows an intensity not seen since fundamentalism emerged in Islamic societies. Populism wants to hang on to nationalist impulses, traditional roots and mistrust against all foreigners, while globalizers aim at a flat world characterized by uniformity and universality.

Curiously enough, the main globalizer of the day, China, reproduces within its society this debate with great intensity. What's more to the point, it also does this with immense originality. Indeed, China is clearly subjected to the contradictory forces of globalization and nationalism. Each of these forces, as a matter of interest, provides the Chinese Communist Party (CCP) with a different kind of legitimacy in relation to its society. Hence, the regime plays both cards at the same time.

Globalization, which has brought great prosperity to the country, identifies itself with the blessing of the heavens. That is, the ancestral formula according to which wealth and peace show that the gods have extended their protection to the rulers. Nationalism, on the other hand, identifies itself with the belief that China's ancient history and its never surpassed tradition of centrality, entitles the country to a position of privilege. Moreover, two centuries of humiliation by foreign powers imposes upon them the need to stand high. As a result, projecting the prominence of which they are considered to be worthy, and not allowing to be humiliated ever again, become fundamental legitimacy requirements.

The CCP, therefore, has to move adroitly within the constraints that these two contradictory forces impose. It has to move forward with globalization, which has allowed China to take 600 million people out of poverty, while transforming the country into the most commercially interconnected center of the world. Consequently, like a prestidigitator, it has to maintain this virtuous circle in continuous movement.

As Tim Marshall wrote: "The deal between the Party leaders and the people has been, for a generation now, 'We'll make you better off — you will follow our orders'. So long as the economy keeps growing, that bargain may last. If it stops, or goes in reverse, the deal is off. The current level of demonstrations and anger against corruption and inefficiency are testament to what would happen if the deal breaks".[1] The globalizing

---

[1] Tim Marshall, *Prisoners of Geography: The Maps that Tell You Everything You Need to Know About Global Politics* (London: Elliot and Thompson Limited, 2016), p. 51.

route, amply explained in Chapter Three, thus becomes a fundamental part of this societal deal.

But, at the same time, Beijing has to show its nationalist resolve. According to Robert D. Kaplan: "There was a latent fear that 'China was about to be dismembered, that it would cease to exist as a nation, and that the four thousand years of its recorded history would come to a jolting end'…China, having survived that nightmare, and having reached a zenith of land power and territorial stability not seen since the Ming dynasty of the sixteenth century and the Qing dynasty of the late eighteenth century, is now about to press outward at sea…China's very urge for an expanded strategy space is a declaration that it never again intends to let foreigners take advantage of it, as they did in the previous two centuries".[2]

Its assertive stance in the South China Sea, which it calls its "blue national soil" and claims 80 percent of its extension, confronts Beijing with Vietnam, The Philippines, Malaysia and Brunei. The so-called "Nine Dash Line", turned into 10 dashes in 2013 to include Taiwan, marks what China considers to be its territory. This generates a dispute over ownership of more than 200 islands and reefs, and poisons Beijing's relations with many of its neighbors. Moreover, this includes the huge energy supplies believed to be beneath the sea, which China already began to explore.

This dispute places China at counterflow of international legality, as expressed by the United Nations Convention on the Law of the Sea (UNCLOS) and The Hague Court Ruling of July 2016, regarding the rights of The Philippines in its contention with China. However, China insists that its ancestral rights over many parts of the area date back to the Han dynasty in the second century BC, while the various official maps made by the Nationalist Kuomintang governments, before and after World War II, incorporated South China Sea dryland formations into Chinese territories. Accordingly, they state that their rights precede the interpretations of the contemporary international law of the sea stipulated by UNCLOS.

In mid-2010, China labeled the South China Sea as a "core interest", which relates to the fact that 80 percent of the country's oil imports, passes through it. To protect its claims in the area, China has reclaimed land to the sea and built extensive military structures, airfields and helipads on

---

[2]Robert D Kaplan, *op. cit.*, p. 21.

several reefs and shoals. Even if China was not the first in occupying and militarizing insular spaces in the South China Sea, it has gone further and at a much faster pace than its neighbors in such undertaking. It has, for instance, reclaimed 17 times more land to the sea, than the rest of the contenders together.

Several authors, including Robert D. Kaplan and Hugh White, have suggested that Beijing wants to transform the South China Sea into China's Caribbean Sea.[3] In other words, to replicate the kind of hegemony that the United States has exerted over the Caribbean Basin's countries. Interestingly enough, the so-called Greater Caribbean is roughly the size of the South China Sea.

At the same time, Beijing is in the process of building a blue water navy, able to operate in "distant seas"; this for reasons of prestige and to protect its sea trade routes in the Indian Ocean. This implies becoming a two-ocean power (Pacific and Indian). With that aim in mind, China is undertaking the construction of deep-water ports in Burma, Bangladesh, Pakistan and Sri Lanka.

According to Robert D. Kaplan: "Moreover, the very launching of an aircraft carrier indicates that China has the ambition to transform its navy from the 'sea denial' type — in order to protect its coastline — to a more formidable 'sea control' type, which portends a blue-water oceanic force".[4] All of this, needless to say, has placed China on a collision course with India.

Such expansive geopolitics greatly affects China's globalizing efforts and, particularly, its regional economic integration process, including its One Belt, One Road Initiative. Moreover, its nationalistic assertiveness is generating a clear reaction. Not only have most of the South East Asian countries gotten closer to the United States for balancing purposes, but the United States, Japan, India and Australia are forging a coalition to counterbalance China. As a result, not only can its economic objectives be greatly complicated, but the country itself is being surrounded by a containment force. The blessing of the Heavens, thus, runs the risk of being overwhelmed by its nationalistic impulses.

---

[3] Robert D Kaplan and Hugh White, *op. cit.*; Hugh White, *The China Choice: Why America should Share Power* (Oxford: Oxford University Press, 2013).
[4] Robert D Kaplan, *op. cit.*, pp. 36–37.

Grabbing with the Two Hands

However, what makes China so especial is the fact that, as mentioned before, globalization and nationalism are not seen as antithetic forces but as interdependent expressions of State policy. They both converge with the aim of legitimizing the regime in the eyes of its citizens. As a matter of fact, this dual policy was conceptualized in times of Deng Xiaoping under his coined aphorism of "grabbing with the two hands".

According to Christopher R. Hughes: "The policy of 'grabbing with the two hands' may succeed in providing security for the CCP Party-state through a combination of economic growth and rising nationalist expectations. Yet this nationalism remains a 'two edged' instrument…and also enhances tensions with neighbouring states. Whether or not the CCP can maintain the right balance between nationalism and globalisation thus presents an interesting case study…".[5]

For the Chinese culture, where the complementarity of the opposites is seen as natural, this balance between openness and closeness must be seen very natural as well. Not so natural maybe is the daunting task of keeping the proper equilibrium between these hugely conflicting aims. One false step, one overreach, one overreaction, and everything might be blown to pieces.

And the risk of a false step increases with popular pressure. As stated by the Council on Foreign Relations: "Beyond the party's control, the emergence of the Internet in the last two decades has given nationalists more power to vent their anger at particular incidents… 'It makes much easier for the nationalistic rhetoric', says Minxin Pei (a senior associate in the China program at the Carnegie Endowment for International Peace). He says the young, urban and educated Chinese are more nationalistic and they are the ones using Internet (…) Pei says nationalism is certainly an obstacle in China's image as a responsible stakeholder. 'A very nationalistic public makes foreigners very wary of China and harms China's image', he says'…The Chinese leaders also fear nationalism could turn

---

[5]The London School of Economics and Political Sciences, "Globalisation and nationalism: Squaring the circle in Chinese international relations theory", LSE Research Online, March 2009, p. 23, http://eprints.lse.ac.uk/23038/1/Globalisation_and_nationalism%28 LSERO%29.pdf. Accessed 18 September 2016.

against them in the form of criticism if they failed to deliver on the nationalistic promises. *New York Times* columnist Nicholas D. Kristoff writes: 'All this makes nationalism a particularly interesting force in China, given its potential not just for offering legitimacy to the government but also for taking it away'".[6]

Should the regime let nationalism get out of control, big problems might ensue. The worst-case scenario would be war. This, by way of a confrontation with the United States, which sustains the right of free maritime circulation and insists on the need to respect international maritime law (although the American Congress has not yet ratified the UNCLOS). It could also translate into a confrontation against the colligated forces of US, Japan, India and Australia, or even into a new armed conflict with Vietnam. The most benign scenario, on the other hand, would be to be compared to Germany's Wilhelm II empire. This would imply losing its international credibility and its privileged standing as globalization leader.

One of the fundamental reasons for the derailment of globalization would be nationalism prevailing in China. A second main reason would be conflict prevailing over collaboration in Asia, thus neutralizing its economic strength and growth potential. In that case, as well, globalization would be deprived of one of its fundamental relaunching pads.

Is Asia up to the Task?

As amply explained in Chapter Three, Asia has become the new epicenter of globalization. It is there that this movement meets all the right opportunities: big funds, huge projects and shared conviction on its merits by both governments and populations. It is there, too, where the emergence of a potent middle class opens the largest opportunities for its expansion.

It is Asia, indeed, where an impressive middle class became the main beneficiary of globalization, obtaining the lion's share of the economic growth that this process generated. Branko Milanovic explains it well: "People at point A had the highest real income growth: some 80 percent during the twenty-year period...Who are the people in this group, the

---

[6] Jayshree Bajoria, Backgrounder, "Nationalism in China", 22 April 2008, https://www.cfr.org/backgrounder/nationalism-china. Accessed 6 June 2018.

obvious beneficiaries of globalization? In nine of ten cases, they are people from the emerging Asian economies, predominantly China, but also India, Thailand, Vietnam and Indonesia...They are the people around the middle of the distribution in their own countries (...) These groups were the main 'winners' of globalization between 1988 and 2008. For convenience, we call them the 'emerging middle class'".[7]

Moreover, according to the Organization for Economic Cooperation and Development (OECD), the world's middle class will increase from 3,300 million people in 2020 to 4,900 million in 2030. Of that amount, 80 percent of the increase will take place in Asia. As a result, a big share of global consumption and investment will move to Asia.[8] China and India will experience the largest increase, but other countries of the region will the see their middle classes grow at an amazing pace as well.

As expressed by Edward Luce: "By 2050 — a century after its communist revolution — China's economy is likely to be twice the size of America's and larger than all the Western economies combined...And, by then, India's economy will be roughly the size of America's".[9] According to PricewaterhouseCoopers, in 2050, the four largest economies of the world will be ranked in the following order: China, India, United States and Indonesia. In other words, three of the top four economies will be in Asia.[10]

However, opportunities and future expectations may all be frustrated, if conflict ends up prevailing in a region where economic expansion and the threat of war have moved side by side for a long time. According to Desmond Ball, professor at the Strategic Defence Studies Centre of the Australian National University, from the late 1980s to the late 1990s, Asia's share of global military expenditure almost doubled, passing from

---

[7] Branko Milanovic, *Global Inequality: A New Approach for the Age of Globalization*, Chapter 1 (Cambridge, MA.: The Belknap Press of Harvard University Press, 2016), p. 329.
[8] Homi Kharas, "The emerging middle class in developing countries", Working Paper No. 285 (2010), http://www.oecd.org/dev/44457738.pdf. Accessed 12 June 2018.
[9] Edward Luce, *op. cit.*, p. 316/4115.
[10] David Law, "Three scenarios for the future of geopolitics", World Economic Forum, 21 June 2018, https://www.weforum.org/agenda/2018/06/david-law-global-futures-3-scenarios/. Accessed 29 June 2018.

11 percent to 20 percent, while Asia's share of arms imports increased from 15 percent to 41 percent of the world total.[11] No other continent shares this dual capacity for impressive economic growth and potential for military destruction.

Even some ASEAN countries, considered as beacons of stability within the region, have seen their military budget increase in an impressive manner. Since 2000, arms import by Indonesia, Singapore and Malaysia have increased by 84 percent, 146 percent and 722 percent, respectively. At the same time, a more exposed country like South Korea, more than doubled its defense expenditures between 2006 and 2015, expending US$1.24 trillion. Given the military modernization programs under way in many of these countries, Asian nations are expected to purchase by 2030 as many as 111 submarines, by definition, instruments of sheer aggression. Just China is expected to have 75 submarines in the next few years as, since 2005, it has been outbuilding the US in new submarines by a relation of eight to one. By 2021, China will have three aircraft carriers as well, while it has increased the number of its four-generation aircrafts from 50 to 500 since 2000. China's total military related expenditures in 2009 were estimated to be of US$150 billion by the Pentagon, and have since moved higher.[12] Four Asian countries have nuclear arsenals: China, India, Pakistan and North Korea.

Asia's Fault Lines

But within the tensions that surround Asia, there are five milestones of instability that can lead to a major war at any time. Four of those cases are the result of previous conflicts. Those fault lines are North Korea–South Korea, China–Japan, China–India, India–Pakistan and Iran–Saudi Arabia.

A potential war between the Koreas could be particularly bloody. Nuclear arms aside, such war might entail the destruction of Seoul, which lies just 35 miles south of the 38th parallel and the demilitarized zone. Almost half of South Korea's 50 million inhabitants live in the greater Seoul region, where most of its industrial and financial centers are located.

---

[11] Robert D Kaplan, *op. cit.*, p. 33.
[12] *Ibid*, pp. 19, 33–35 and 38; Tim Marshall, *op. cit.*, p. 53.

Such a region is within range of the estimated 10,000 artillery pieces, dug in at the hills above the 148-mile-long demilitarized zone. According to some experts, North Korea could fire up to 500,000 rounds towards the city, just in the first hour of a conflict.[13] The destruction herein involved could ruin one of the largest economies of the world.

The 2017 test launches of intercontinental ballistic missiles by Pyongyang, its potential to miniaturize nuclear weapons and its development of missile launching submarines brought tensions to the roof. However, a respite was given to those tensions, as a result of the June 2018 summit in Singapore between presidents Trump and Kim Jong-un, and previously between the latter and South Korean President Moon-Jae-in.

The mercurial nature of Trump and Kim, compounded by the difference in perceptions between the parties, the vagueness and lack of verifiability on what has been agreed, plus negative past experiences and tough negotiations ahead, should caution against optimism. Especially so, as CNN reported on June 27, 2018, satellite images showed that North Korea kept upgrading its nuclear facility at Yongbyon Nuclear Center. In other words, weeks after the Singapore Summit, business in North Korea continued as usual. The risk of war in this area is not going to disappear any time soon. Especially so if an oversold but insufficiently grounded diplomacy fails, as the post-Singapore follow-on negotiations are proving to be.

The China–Japan conflict's trigger point is the islands called Senkaku (Japan) or Diaoyu (China). Obtained by Japan as a result of its colonial expansion towards Taiwan, at the end of the nineteenth century, they were administered until 1972 by the United States, which entered in its possession after World War II. Returned to Japan, they are nonetheless claimed both by Beijing and Taipei.

They form part of the Ryukyu Island chain, which must be passed by a hostile power on its way to the Japanese heartlands. As such, they provide territorial sea space considered of utmost importance by Japan for defensive purposes. In addition, they may contain important underwater gas and oil reserves. As a result, as Tim Marshall points out, "Tokyo intends to hold to them by all means necessary".[14]

---

[13] Tim Marshall, *op. cit.*, p. 224.
[14] *Ibid*, p. 234.

For China, this is also a highly irksome issue, because in addition to the hydrocarbon reserves that may be involved, it points out to the heart of its rising nationalist expectations. No other country has harmed China so much as Japan did in the twentieth century, and high decibels of emotions are still involved in all that relates to this country.

China's expanded "Air Defense Identification Zone" covers this area since 2013. Any plane flying through the zone must identify itself or face defensive measures. So far, Japan, together with the United States and South Korea, had been flying through it without doing so. This might change at any moment, though, if China decides to enforce its ruling. Tensions around the Senkaku–Diaoyu are always high, and can boil up as a result of any minor incident.

As in the case of South Korea, this is an area where existing defensive agreements with the United States, can drag this country into war. On February 3, 2017, US Secretary of Defense James Mattis reaffirmed Washington's commitment to defending Japan, including these islands. According to his statement: "I made clear that our long-standing policy on the Senkaku Islands stands — the US will continue to recognize Japanese administration of the islands and as such Article 5 of the US–Japan Security Treaty applies".[15]

China and India confront several sensitive issues. The first of them relates to Northeastern Indian state of Arunachal Pradesh, which China claims as "South Tibet". Until recently, China only claimed the Tawang area in the extreme west of the state. However, at the beginning of the new millennium, China began to state that the whole of Aruchanal Pradesh was Chinese. In 2017, China renamed several places within the state, which appeared with their new names in Chinese maps.

In 1962, China and India went to war over the sovereignty of the regions of Arunachal Pradesh, which were under Indian control, and over Aksain Chin under Chinese possession. On both fronts, China won, retaining the *de facto* control of Askain Chin and temporarily occupying Arunachal Pradesh. The latter, thus, is an old contention issue.

---

[15] Brad Lendon, "Mattis: US will defend Japanese islands claimed by China", CNN, 3 February 2017, https://edition.cnn.com/2017/02/03/asia/us-defense-secretary-mattis-japan-visit/index.html. Accessed 7 June 2018.

The fact that the Indians welcomed the Dalai Lama after the Chinese annexation of Tibet, and that the Tibetan independence movement is based in their Himachal Pradesh' city of Dharamshala, continually sours the relations between both countries.

But besides these confrontations, there is the more recent problem derived from the blue water navy that China plans to locate in the Indian Ocean. This is compounded by the string of deep-water ports that China is building in the Bay of Bengal, within India's sphere of influence. At the same time, Beijing has invested billions of dollars in the coastal city of Gwadar in Pakistan, where it also has built a deep-water port. China's political closeness to Pakistan, India's main rival, is another matter of much resentment in New Delhi.

Conversely, for the last quarter of a century, India has been involved in a "look east" policy, which aims to contain China's rise. As a result, India has strengthened its relations with Burma and the Philippines, who have maritime contentions with China, while it has been working with Vietnam and Japan to check China's increasing domination of the South China Sea. The interconnectedness of these different issues has the potential to ignite an armed conflict between these two Asian giants.

Mutual Assured Destruction and Gulf Rivalry

The tensions between India and Pakistan date back to their independence from Britain. Partition between them was a very nasty affair. The first of their several wars and military skirmishes began shortly after. In 1947, they fought over Kashmir, which was divided in 1948 but reclaimed in its totality by both parties. In 1965, there was another war over Kashmir, which Pakistan lost. In 1971, India and Pakistan went again to war for the independence of East Pakistan, which resulted not only in a new loss for Pakistan but in the birth of the new country of Bangladesh.

In 1984, they fought at the Siachen Glacier at 22,000 feet of altitude. New fighting in the same area followed in 1985, 1987 and 1995. In 1999, another war erupted as a result of Pakistani troop occupation of the Kargil District in India. A year before, India had detonated five atomic bombs, which were reciprocated by the explosion of another six atomic bombs by Pakistan. Hence, there was fear that the Kargil War could have escalated into a nuclear exchange.

As a result of this nuclear arms race, both countries became hostages to the mutual assured destruction principle. This limited their military options, without increasing their possibility of imposing their own will upon the other. However, in 2002, the two of them came very close to an atomic exchange. India possessed at the time 49 bombs that could be launched in their Agni-2 ballistic missiles, while Pakistan had between 22 and 43 atomic bombs that could be delivered through their Ghauri-2 missiles.[16] While border incidents and skirmishes continue, both sides have tried to undermine the other. The Pakistani Secret Service has supported several terror attacks inside India, which included the infamous Mumbai massacre of 2008. The possibility of India's brilliant economic future being suddenly turned into nuclear fumes hangs in the air.

The Iran–Saudi Arabia fault line, not only confronts the ambitions of those two countries of becoming the dominant power of their region, but also their respective versions of Islam. While Iraq was under the control of Saddam Hussein, a powerful buffer separated the two of them. Saudi Arabia and Iran continue their rivalry through proxy wars, most notably in Yemen.

In 2017, Saudi Arabia promoted an economic blockade on Qatar, of which the United Arab Emirates, Egypt and Bahrain were part. Qatar was accused of promoting terrorism; however, its political proximity to Iran was one of the reasons behind such a move. This resulted in aid from Iran, which has further increased the divisions of the Gulf States.

Saudi Arabia, which together with Israel resented the 2015 American-led deal on Iran's nuclear facilities, was instrumental, again with Israel, in pushing the Trump Administration against such a deal. The reintroduction of sanctions against Iran by the United States in August 2018, which widened the gap between Washington and Europe, added up tensions to the region and reopened the possibility of Teheran acquiring nuclear weapons. So far, Saudi Arabia and Iran have been involved in a cold war, but a direct confrontation between the two cannot be ruled out. In such a case, several other neighboring countries could be dragged into it, putting the prosperity of the Arab Gulf States in serious jeopardy.

---

[16] Alfredo Toro Hardy, *The Age of Villages: The Small Village Vs. The Global Village* (Bogotá: Villegas Editores, 2002), p. 24.

As seen, then, Asia can be a fundamental supporter of globalization, and its most promising area of economic expansion. But it is, at the same time, one of the most politically unstable regions in the world. One in which war could erupt at any time. If things go in the wrong direction, few other places could inflict so much damage to the preservation of globalization as Asia.

And then, we have populism and the Fourth Industrial Revolution as the two main forces playing against globalization. How consistent is the threat they pose?

Are Populists for Real?

The main question to be asked in relation to populism is: how much longer can its ascendancy and disruptive power last? Emmanuel Macron's remarkable victory in May 2017 seemed to be offering a message of hope to an angry and depressed country. His youth, good looks and easy charm, combined with an optimistic liberal message, looked as an alternative to the ascendant march of populism. Like Prime Minister Justin Trudeau in Canada, he presented a refreshing image, which sharply contrasted with the ugly message and the nasty overtones of a Donald Trump.

A couple of months before Macron's success, Netherlands' incumbent Prime Minister Mark Rutte defeated his populist challenger Geert Wilders, who had a very good chance of winning. Anger appeared to have been tamed, as a liberal–conservative message prevailed. Many saw the successes of Macron and Rutte as a reversal of fortunes for populism. More than one pundit, indeed, wrote about the peaking of populism. Time though proved otherwise, as other populist challengers kept winning elections or subverting the political landscape in Europe.

Nonetheless, the two above-mentioned triumphs showed that liberal governments still have an important presence in Europe, and that the fight for their principles was very much alive. Moreover, Angela Merkel, humbled by the ascendancy of populism that her intransigent policies had helped to provoke, seems ready for contrition and political change.

According to Brookings: "Angela Merkel, Germany's chancellor, has ended her long silence on the proposals for European reform made by the French president Emmanuel Macon...The chancellor is stretching out a hand not only to France, but also to Europe's economically beleaguered south…Ms. Merkel's plan is an implicit apology for past German intransigence on economic policy, and signals that Germany wants to return to its old role as a bridge-builder…Ms. Merkel accepts that Germany, Europe's richest economy, needs to contribute more than others…She wants to use the EU budget for investments in growth and innovation in Europe's more troubled economies…Ms. Merkel is much closer to Mr. Macron on immigration and asylum policy. She accepts that an earlier German-led attempt to force a mandatory quota system in member states was a failure. Instead, she sketches a system of common European asylum standards, a real European border security agency and a European refugee agency…Ms. Merkel's initiative is a genuine attempt at a positive response to a dramatic array of new internal and external threats to Europe. Its conciliatory tone holds out the promise of a big tent that could appeal to many EU member states".[17]

Clearly enough, Ms. Merkel is trying to make amendments in relation to her past excesses as a harsh creditor, a rigid deficit comptroller and a too generous but at the same time imperious voice in immigration. If that happened, and even if politically weakened, she still has a lot of influence to bear upon European matters. If she decides to join efforts with Mr. Macron's proposed revival of liberal democracy, there is much that the two largest EU economies could do together. Especially so, if they do it in a clever way.

It could be extremely helpful, as well, if other minor European figures like Prime Minister Rutte seriously reflect and amend in relation to past policies. Rutte's rigid position in relation to Southern European debt led to immense social distress and political disruption. If liberal democrats were able to develop more sensitive, pragmatic and politically astute attitudes, they could still present a good front against populism.

Enablers of Populism

The enablers of populism in Europe and Western democracies, in general, have been economic dislocation, inequality, sociocultural insecurity and

---

[17] Constanze Stelzenmuller, "Germany's Chancellor offers a unifying economic plan to mollify a divided Europe", 6 June 2018, https://www.brookings.edu/blog/order-from-chaos/2018/06/06/germanys-chancellor-offers-a-unifying-economic-plan-to-mollify-a-divided-europe/. Accessed 6 June 2018.

uncontrolled immigration. There is much that can be done in these areas, without going into the extremes. If, on the one hand, people's worries are addressed seriously, and their legitimate grievances are listened to with attention and respect, anger can be mollified. On the other hand, smart political communications are needed. Populism won at the political pulpit of Internet, unchallenged by liberal opinion makers.

Elitist arrogance, either in terms of believing that people in charge know best, or by deafness to the popular will, has to be eradicated as well. Italian President, Sergio Mattarella, is a good example of what goes wrong within liberal democracies in Europe. Ignoring the will of 50 percent of his fellow citizens (against fragmented alternatives), he attempted to appoint a caretaker government who would be responsible for summoning a fresh election. That implied going against a clear majority of the electorate, which had already chosen. As mentioned before, his was the typical establishment's policy of keeping the citizens voting, until they voted "right". That was certainly not the way to confront populism, especially so because this manipulation of the popular will was one of the main grievances that led to its emergence.

Populism, on the other hand, is usually better at winning elections than at producing results when in government. Their simplistic approach to problems works better in opposition than when confronting the complexities of ruling a country. Hence, the high expectations they were able to elicit with their simplistic formulations might well be inversely proportional to their capacity for results. If so, their political erosion in government can prove to be high.

There does not seem to be anything inevitable in relation to European populists. If liberal democrats were to join efforts, change entrenched arrogant behaviors, address the people's concerns and anguishes, listen to what they have to say and develop pragmatic and smart policies as well as good political communications, much can be done to revert the ascendancy of populism. Populist themselves could do the rest, if they prove unable to fulfill the immense expectations that they have created.

But the European Union needs to clean its act as well. According to the *Washington Post*, there are seven reasons why so many Europeans hate the EU: (a) the generous wages and special minimum taxes of their bureaucrats, (b) their wasteful travel, (c) their overreaching regulations, (d) their lack of accountability, (e) their autism in relation to the will of the voters, (f) their huge and unnecessary bureaucracy, (g) their immensely costly translations;[18] in other words, too many bureaucrats, too much spending, too many regulations, too much deafness and arrogance, and too little accountability. If the European Union does not want to be the instrument of its own destruction or irrelevance, it has to reform itself thoroughly. This could also help much in reverting the ascendancy of populism in Europe.

Change is equally imperative in the United States, if the triumphal march of populism is to be stopped. But changes within its political system are even more difficult than in Europe, as money and politics are interwoven to the extent of being symbiotic. Vested interests in the US control the political process for their own benefit and, by extension, in detriment of the needs and concerns of a majority of the citizens.

This situation represents an open invitation for demagogues to do their bidding, and an inducement for the forgotten many to willfully accept them. The US bipartisan system and the counterbalance represented by its coastal global cities and minorities' coalition can however impose limits in this regard. The former reduces the room for maneuver available to populists, as it is only through the control of the established political parties that they can become a relevant force. The latter creates a wall of contention for the expansion of the anger prevailing within white middle class inland America.

Coastal global cities, though, host many liberals and highly indebted young college graduates at odds with the current *status quo* of the country. They, too, have proven to be attracted by the populist message, in this case, the more moderate left-wing version of populism. On the same token, non-white economically excluded minorities are not exempted from being attracted by left-wing populism as well. On the contrary, there are many reasons why its message could reverberate with them.

Populism, of one kind or the other, can thus prove to be resilient if changes do not materialize. Iron triangles, lobbies, political action committees and independent political expenditures cannot run uncontrolled, at the expense of a declining middle class and a rising inequality. It should be no surprise, as aforementioned, that confidence in Congress ranks below that of any other institution, including banks or big business.

---

[18] Michael Birnbaum, "7 reasons why some Europeans hate the E.U.", 25 June 2016.

And even if there are no easy solutions to the social problems involved, especially so with major technological disruptions in sight, there is a real demand for the political system to become more sensitive to the needs of the many. If America's liberal democracy wants to confront the political dislocations in motion, it has to stop being so conniving with big business, address the people's concerns and anguishes, listen to their grievances, develop more inclusive policies and put in place smart political communications.

Populism is not inevitable, but neither should it be considered a transient vogue. Much effort will be needed to neutralize its worst excesses and stop its ascendancy. Only time will tell if the willingness for change materializes and the march of populism can be reversed. In the end, as Kishore Mahbubani has written: "If liberal ideology were to die (and I fervently hope that it doesn't), it will not be the result of murder. It will be the result of a suicide. Ideologies live and die on the basis of their performance, not on the abstract beauty of their ideas".[19]

Technological Horizons

The threat posed by the Fourth Industrial Revolution is certain. What may not be so certain is how soon disruptive technologies will materialize. Hence, what needs to be clarified is the timing involved. A team at the Imperial College London published a thought-provoking table of 100 disruptive technologies that may or may not materialize in the next 100 years.[20]

They arranged such technologies in a matrix, composed of four horizons. Horizon 1 is called "executable" and contains disruptive technologies that are already finding application. Horizon 2 is labeled "experimental" and refers to technologies that should become reality in the next or the following decade. Horizon 3 is called "exploratory" and refers to technologies beyond 2030. Horizon 4 has been named "dreamable" and comprises

---

[19] "Should the West worry about the threat to liberal values posed by China's rise?", *The Economist*, 8 June 2018.
[20] Roberto Saracco, "A wonderful table of disruptive technologies", IEEE Future Directions, 17 March 2018, http://sites.ieee.org/futuredirections/2018/03/17/disruptions-ahead-outline/. Accessed 11 June 2018.

technologies that are not impossible from a scientific point of view, but are unlikely to materialize with today's scientific knowledge.

Within horizon 1, we find technologies such as vertical farming, cultured meat, precision agriculture, microscale ambient energy harvesting, layer technology, deep ocean wind farms, smart control and appliances, robotic care companions, cryptocurrencies, concentrated solar power, autonomous vehicles, delivery robots and passenger drones, wireless energy transfers, intention decoding algorithms and so forth.

Within horizon 2, there are technologies like smart energy grids, peer-to-peer energy trading and transmission, metallic hydrogen energy storage, balloon-powered Internet, airborne wind turbines, autonomous ships and submarines, autonomous passenger aircrafts, autonomous robotic surgery, drone freight delivery, algal biofuels, programmable bacteria, human organ printing, emotionally aware machines, avatar companions, public mood monitoring, 3D printing of foods and pharmaceuticals, diagnostic toilets, force fields and on goes the list.

Within horizon 3, we find full arrival of new materials, fusion power, vacuum tube transport, broadcasting of electricity, swarm robotics, thought-control machine interfaces, conversation machine interfaces, all-advisors and decision-making machines, implantable phones, bioplastics, pollution-eating buildings, four-dimensional materials, DNA data storage, data uploading to the brain, battlefield robots, etc.

Within horizon 4, there could be zero-point energy, beam-power propulsion, self-reconfiguring modular robots, artificial consciousness, space solar power, digital footprint eraser, human cloning, asteroids mining, shape-shifting matter, among others.

The Economist, using as source a poll of more than 350 experts on Artificial Intelligence, also published its own chart. With a 50 percent of probabilities, the following robotic activities should be materializing in the years herein mentioned: winning poker tournaments (around 2026), telephone banking activities (around 2027), vocal synthesis (around 2027), explaining its own actions in the course of a game (around 2028), driving a truck (around 2030), writing a best-seller (around 2050), replacing a surgeon (around 2050), carrying mathematical research (around 2065), etc.[21]

---

[21] The Economist, "Infographic: Quand L'Intelligence Artificelle Sera Aussi Forte Que L'Human", *Le Monde en 2018*.

As we can see, then, there are current technological disruptions to globalization, employment and economic activities, as well as medium and long-term ones. Some disruptive technologies, though, might never come to fruition. While certain economic activities can thus expect to have a shorter life span in their current form, others would have a larger one. Contrary to populism, in any case, the Fourth Industrial Revolution is inevitable. The full impact of this tsunami may still take a few decades, but it will definitively arrive.

The aforementioned complexity generates a conundrum for Latin America, who — as we shall see next — will need to come to terms with and manage to the best of its abilities.

CHAPTER SEVEN

LATIN AMERICA'S ROUTE MAP

As we have seen, globalization still has many stakeholders and supporters. Among them, China's economic umbrella and Asia's middle class, whose expansion is estimated to represent 80 percent of the world's middle class increase up to 2030, remain as the fundamental forces. It is in Asia, and very particularly in the Indo-Pacific region, where globalization meets all the right opportunities.

However, the talk of China and Asia is not just about economic expansion. It is also about contending borders, expansive geopolitics, arms increase, political mistrust, and past and potential wars. Betting too much on Asia can thus be a risky business. Hedging Asia must be parallel to staking on its future.

On the other hand, populism and the displacement that disruptive technologies bring with them seem to be the defining traits of Western developed economies. While the former creates boundaries and discourages free trade, the latter advances towards a decoupling between developed and developing economies. Under such impulses, globalization is bound to lose ground. In terms of international trade opportunities, the future is not in the Western world.

Populism is not inevitable, and can yet be reversed if liberal democracies put their act together and assume ambitious political reforms. Disruptive technologies, however, cannot be stopped or reversed. Nonetheless, they will not arrive all at the same time, and, in some cases, they will take their time to do so. All in all, betting on Western developed economies is definitively a risk. Populism will not fade away easily, while disruptive technologies, even if still delaying its full impact, will be relentless in taking one economic stronghold after another.

What can Latin America do under such circumstances? Several steps seem to be in line for its countries. Among them, the following ones are discussed in this chapter.

Prioritizing the Indo-Pacific Region

In the first place, they should prioritize Asia with particular reference to the Indo-Pacific region. Within the latter, Chindia maintains the leading role, although ASEAN has a secondary but still very relevant position.

China is at the forefront of economic opportunities, as it is there where the biggest expansion markets lie. If the One Belt, One Road initiative materializes, as it seems it will, China will be leading a project that encompasses 65 percent of the world's population, about one-third of the world's gross domestic product and about a quarter of the world's trade.

It represents the most ambitious initiative to improve economic integration and connectivity on a transcontinental scale. Huge infrastructural developments would take place along six overland corridors and the twenty-first century Maritime Silk Road. At the same time, it would put in motion a financial dynamo able to enhance efficiency and facilitate economic flows around the regions involved. Trade and foreign direct investment among countless countries would be greatly enhanced as a result.

This would bring with it another booming period for commodities, as infrastructural developments of such a scale would require immense amounts of iron, steel, aluminum, cement, copper, oil, coal and the like. Latin America could play a key role within this process as a provider of much needed raw materials. However, there could be more into it than the role of commodities provider, as there is now talk of expanding these infrastructural developments to Latin America as well. Indeed, Chinese Foreign Minister Wang Yi called Latin American and Caribbean countries to join its One Belt, One Road Initiative. The invitation was made within the context of a meeting between China and the 33 members of the

Community of Latin American and Caribbean States (CELAC), held in Santiago de Chile on 22 January 2018.[1] But more than just the One Belt, One Road Initiative, it is necessary to look into China's emerging cities. James Kynge puts this in context when saying: "In China, urbanization is still an infant. There are approximately 400 million people living in big and small cities at this moment, but by 2050 it is expected this number to rise to 600 or 700 millions to reach a billion or 1.1 billion people. The investment required to accommodate so many people in an urban environment is impossible to calculate precisely, but it is clear that the global demand of steel, aluminum, copper, nickel, iron, oil, gas, carbon and many other raw materials and resources will remain strong as long as urbanization in China reaches its limits."[2]

According to the McKinsey Global Institute, it is expected that 100 new cities will emerge in China.[3] Not surprisingly, as mentioned before, earlier this decade Joseph Stiglitz proclaimed that the two main forces that would shape global prosperity in the twenty-first century were US technological innovation and urbanization in China.

In the decade between 2003 and 2013, trade between China and Latin America increased at an amazing average rate of 27 percent per year, rising to an unprecedented US$289 billion in 2013.[4] The main beneficiary of this process was South America, the principal exporter of commodities within the region, whose exports expanded threefold. Since 2013, though, the price of commodities fell. China's rebalancing towards domestic consumption and its positioning away from commodity-heavy sectors, where over-capacity exists, were responsible for it. Nonetheless, The One Belt, One Road initiative and its current urbanization process announces a new period of expansion.

---

[1] Fabian Cambero and Dave Sherwood, "China invites Latin America to take part in One Belt, One Road", Reuters, 22 January, 2018.

[2] James Kynge, *China Shakes the World* (London: Phoenix, 2006), p. 29.

[3] Richard Dobbs *et al.*, "Urban World: Mapping the Economic Power of Cities", 2011, http://www.mckinsey.com/insights/urbanization/urban_world. Accessed 12 March 2018.

[4] Robert Devlin and Theodore Kahn, "Latin American Trade with India and China" in Riordan Roett and Guadalupe Paz (eds.), *Latin America and the Asian Giants: Evolving Ties with China and India* (Washington D.C.: Brookings Institution Press), p. 151.

India could also offer a bright opportunity for Latin American exports, essentially for its commodities. According to the Inter-American Development Bank: "Any cursory analysis of the complementarity between the two economies shows that the potential for massive bilateral trade is there".[5]

Indian trade growth with Latin America is comparable to that of China, albeit from a much lower base. Bilateral trade between India and Latin America grew 22 times between 2000 and 2014, whereas that of China and Latin America grew 24 times during the same period.[6]

Even though both the pattern of trade and the trade growth between India and Latin America followed that of China and Latin America, the numbers reveal a different picture. According to Robert Devlin and Theodore Kahn: "Trade with India, by contrast has yet to reach a critical mass. Though growth has been fast...total trade reached only $43 billion in 2013, about 15 percent of the region's trade with China".[7]

On the other hand, India's trade balance with Latin America has been more beneficial to the region than that of China. In 2014, for example, India bought US$29 billion in goods from the region, while it sold at US$17.53 billion. By comparison, that same year, China bought US$95.3 billion from Latin America but its sales to it were US$190.38 billion.[8]

It seems clear that Latin America's commodities producers can highly benefit from the Indian market. And yet, the question is whether, as stated by the Inter-American Developing Bank, the "potential for massive bilateral trade is there"? This requires some analysis.

It could be argued, *prima facie*, that with 1.3 billion people and a growth rate of more than 7 percent, India could follow China's place in relation to Latin America. However, this is far from certain. On the one hand, India's development model did not follow the classic Asian strategy

---

[5]Mauricio Mesquita Moreira, Coordinator, *India: Latin America's Next Big Thing?* (Washington D.C.: Inter-American Development Bank, 2010), p. ix.

[6]Robert Devlin and Theodore Kahn, in Riordan Roett and Guadalupe Paz (eds.), *Latin America and the Asian Giants: Evolving Ties with China and India* (Washington D.C.: Brookings Institution Press), p. 11.

[7]*Ibid*, p. 153.

[8]R. Evan Ellis, *Indian and Chinese Engagement in Latin America and the Caribbean: A Comparative Assessment* (Washington D.C.: Strategic Studies Institute and U.S. Army War College Press, March 2017), p. 11.

of a labor-intensive, export-oriented economy. To the contrary, as afore-mentioned, it emphasized services over industry and high technology over low-skilled manufacturing.

As a result, it has been successful in high-end services and capital- and knowledge-intensive manufacturing, but it has not been able to create a broad industrial base. Hence, it may never become a magnet for commodities producers in China's scale. At the same time, India seems to be entering into a contraction of its high-end service exports, as a consequence of big data and the automation of knowledge work in developed economies, which could have a negative impact on its growth rates.

However, the Indian government is currently aiming at reaching China's level of investment in infrastructure, which is estimated to be of 9 percent of its GDP. The Delhi–Mumbai Industrial corridor, which has been in discussion for the last few years, would be a good example of this objective. This project envisages an infrastructural corridor larger in land size than Japan, stretching from New Delhi down to Mumbai. This US$90 billion plan envisages numerous infrastructural and industrial developments, susceptible of tripling the industrial output across the six states through which it runs.[9]

The need for infrastructural modernization is evident, as shown at the end of July 2012. On that occasion, 600 million citizens in 20 states and union territories were affected by a huge electricity blackout that plunged half of India into darkness. Moreover, McKinsey Global Institute estimates that 13 new cities will be built in India to accommodate the migration of people from the countryside.[10] If India materializes its infrastructure and urbanization ambitions, it could indeed become a second China.

ASEAN, Japan, South Korea and China Again

But more than Chiindia itself, Asia's expanding middle classes and urbanization process are immense opportunities to look into, especially so as most Asian countries lack natural resources. While 80 percent of the

---

[9] Matthias Williams and Lyndee Prickitt, "Project will 'change lives' in India", *thestar.com*, 5 November 2011, http://www.thestar.com/news/world/article/1081409--project-will-change-lives-in-india.

[10] Richard Dobbs, *et al.*, *op. cit.*

global middle class expansion will take place in Asia, with its corresponding increasing levels of consumption, Asia's rate of urbanization will be 53 percent. Under such a scenario, existing and future cities in Asia should be absorbing around 1.4 billion new people.[11]

Within this context, ASEAN plays a crucial role. This economic bloc composed of 10 South East Asian countries and is home to about 620 million people with a GDP of more than US$2.3 trillion, which is equivalent to 3.3 percent of the global GDP. ASEAN economies are also among the world's most open, with merchandise exports of US$1.2 trillion, nearly 7 percent of the global total.[12]

In 2030, ASEAN should be the fourth largest single market in the world. According to a British Foreign and Commonwealth Office Report: "But by the 2030 the ASEAN economy is predicted to eclipse Japan's and be the fourth largest market after the EU, US and China. The Asia Development Bank (ADB) predicts the size of the middle class in South East Asia will rise from 24% of the population in 2010 to 65% in 2030".[13]

Importantly, Japan and South Korea, the two oldest Latin American economic partners in Asia, will not offer the same kind of opportunities that Chindia and ASEAN would do. Latin America's trade with Japan amounted to US$44 billion in 2015, and with the Republic of Korea US$48 billion in 2013.[14] However, these two countries seem to be following the same approach as the West toward the Fourth Industrial Revolution. As a result, they shall probably decouple themselves from developing

---

[11] Sergio Bitar, *Global Trends and the Future of Latin America: Why and How Latin America Should Think About the Future* (Washington D.C.: Inter-American Dialogue, December 2013).

[12] Asian Development Bank Institute, "2030: Toward a Borderless Economic Community", 2014, https://www.adb.org/sites/default/files/publication/159312/adbi-asean-2030-borderless-economic-community.pdf. Accessed 14 June 2018.

[13] Foreign and Commonwealth Office, "ASEAN 2030: Economic opportunities and challenges", London, October 2012, https://epas.secure.europarl.europa.eu/orbis/sites/default/files/generated/document/en/ASEAN%202030.pdf. Accessed 14 June 2018.

[14] Inter-American Development Bank, *A Virtuous Cycle of Integration: The Past, Present, and Future of Japan-Latin American and the Caribbean Relations* (Washington D.C.: IADB, 2016), p. 33.; Economic Commission for Latin America and the Caribbean, "Economic Relations between Latin America and the Caribbean and the Republic of Korea: Advances and Opportunities" (Santiago de Chile: ECLAC, 2015), p. 23.

economies in the same way as the Western developed ones. And their markets would tend to decline for Latin America as a result. According to Forbes: "'Japan is looking at science, technology and innovation as a growth engine for the economy', says Yuko Harayama, an executive member of Japan's Council for Science, Technology and Innovation (CSTI)...The enabling technologies that CSTI and the ministries will promote to help bring about the fourth industrial revolution, include cyber security, AI, Big Data analysis, robotics, Internet of Things (IoT), biotech, and materials and nanotechnology".[15]

As for South Korea's path, Korea.net refers to President Moon Jae-in's drive towards the Fourth Industrial Revolution: "Emphasizing that his government aims to create a vigorous economy that leads to the creation of innovative business and new industries, President Moon said... 'Korea, too, must focus its efforts on responding to the fourth industrial revolution'. The president vowed to invest more in the Internet of Things (IoT), big data and 5G wireless communication".[16]

Of course, China too is very much involved with the Fourth Industrial Revolution. Already in 2014, China had 25 percent of the industrial robots of the planet, and it has kept investing heavily in that direction. In Guangdong province alone, Beijing is planning to invest 154 billion dollars in robotics. In Jiangsu, the Pearl Delta River and other parts of the country, similar programs are in progress. In 2015, Martin Ford wrote that in 2017 China should have attained the largest robotic manufacturing capacity of the world.[17]

Moreover, China's consumer economy is now among the world's most digitized, and its business landscape is packed with technological start-ups. China has become the largest e-commerce market in the planet, with mobile payments representing 11 times more than their equivalent

---

[15] John Boyd, "Japan Looks To Fourth Industrial Revolution to Help Reach 'Impossible' GDP Target", 24 June, 2016, https://www.forbes.com/sites/jboyd/2016/07/24/japan-looks-to-fourth-industrial-revolution-to-help-reach-impossible-gdp-target/2/#4be8e15eaea5. Accessed 15 June 2018.
[16] Sohn JiAe, "President emphasizes 'people-centered fourth industrial revolution'", 11 October 2017, https://www.korea.net/NewsFocus/policies/view?articleId=149973. Accessed 15 June 2018.
[17] Martin Ford, "China's troubling Robot Revolution", *The New York Times*, 10 June 2015.

value in the United States. China's place now is at the top ranks of venture-capital investments in virtual reality, autonomous vehicles, 3-D printing, drones and artificial intelligence.[18]

However, the sheer size of its population forces China to diversify its economic strategy more thoroughly. Indeed, Beijing has to play simultaneously in several economic grounds. As a result, its advances within the Fourth Industrial Revolution coexist side-by-side with its ambitious infrastructural and urbanization strategies. Moreover, just feeding 1.4 billion people generates a gigantic market for commodities. As a consequence, China will remain a vibrant market for Latin American goods.

At the end of the day, though, raw numbers speak for themselves. A United Nations study of June 2013, stated that world population will swell to 9.7 billion people in 2050, with Asia reaching 5.2 billion. As a consequence, it will be largely surpassing Africa, which will come number two with 2.5 billion people, and will be substantially ahead of the Americas and Europe.[19] Feeding, housing, clothing and providing energy for such a large number of people will certainly require substantial amounts of commodities.

The agreements of the Asia-Pacific Cooperation Forum (APEC), the Forum for East Asia Latin America Cooperation (FEALAC), the creation in 2012 of the Pacific Alliance among Mexico, Colombia, Peru and Chile, the 2018 signing of the Trans-Pacific Partnership (TPP) of which Chile, Mexico and Peru are members, the summits and ministerial forums of the China–CELAC, are all important and forward-reaching institutional steps toward the economic integration with Asia. Of them, the Pacific Alliance could perhaps serve Latin America as a whole, facilitating institutional links with Asia.

Regionalization vs. Localization

In the second place, and this relates specifically to Mexico, the argument of production localization in the United States should be countered with

---

[18] McKinsey & Company, The Shortlist, 13 July 2018, https://www.mckinsey.com/~/media/McKinsey/Email/Shortlist/4/2018-07-13? Accessed 14 July 2018.
[19] Steve Wilson, "World population to reach 9.7 billion by 2050 new study predicts", *The Telegraph*, 2 October 2013.

the argument of regional production. In other words, Mexico should try to convince US corporation about the convenience of aiming at regional manufacturing instead of local manufacturing.

In Finbarr Livesey words: "Companies in many countries are deciding to have their production either in their home or nearby, reshoring and nearshoring".[20] Mexico's perfect solution would be that US companies returning from Asia, decide to follow the "nearshoring" option. That is, using Mexico as a regional production hub, instead of moving into the customer's backyard in the United States itself.

Livesey explains the benefits of regionalization as follows: "The temptation is to work at the extremes — everything is global or everything is local...Regionalization will be driven by the balance of forces between the scale required to have efficiencies and the desire to reduce time to customer...".[21] If regionalization prevails over localization, the journeys would be a bit longer and the factories not so small. The longer trip would be compensated by the efficiencies of larger scale. Although supply chains will get much smaller as a result of 3D printing and will move much closer to the final production point, regionalization may still bring the benefits of "the scale required to have efficiencies".

Mexico exhibits advantages and disadvantages in relation to this dichotomy between regionalization and localization. Its main advantage is that the imperiled trade negotiations with the US seem to be in good track, after both countries announced a preliminary trade deal on August 28, 2018, and that Mexico is close and ready enough to provide the benefits of regionalization. The latter means having production facilities and distribution networks in place, which certainly would ease the reconversion process. Mexico's main disadvantages are Donald Trump's protectionism, his aim of raising Mexican wages in order to reduce the gap with American ones, US corporate tax reduction and the fact that many states and cities in the United States, dragged down by economic decay are betting on localization to resurge.

Protectionism can be a huge headache for Mexico. Speaking at the Stern School of Businesses, Jeff Immelt, then General Electric's CEO,

---

[20] Finbarr Livesey, *From Global to Local: The Making of Things and the End of Globalization* (New York: Pantheon Books)., p. 21.

[21] *Ibid*, p. 136.

talked in favor of localization. His claim was that the localization strategy would insulate the company against protectionism, as they would be within US boundaries.[22] If a company with a market capitalization of around US$300 billion worries about protectionism, what can be expected from the rest? Notwithstanding that free trade with Mexico survives, protectionism will always be a Damocles sword in the latter's head.

Trump's aim of reducing the salaries gap between his country and Mexico, as made evident by the preliminary trade deal, conspires against Mexico's main competitive advantage, propitiating automation in the United States.

Reduction of corporate taxes will also tempt companies focused on the US market to relocate there. The passage of the Tax Cut and Jobs Act in December 2017 brought a sudden infusion of cash for corporations through a massive corporate tax rate cut. This makes investing in the US much more attractive than before.

At the same time, tying up the resurgence strategy of states and cities with the localization process will definitely push investments inland. In addition to promoting the economic revival of economically distressed communities by way of technological developments, as mentioned in Chapter Five, the Tax Cuts and Jobs Act of 2017, established the so-called "Opportunity Zones".

These opportunity zones encourage, through multiple incentives, long-term investments in low-income urban and rural communities in the United States. According to the Rockefeller Foundation: "Opportunity Zones have the potential to become the largest community development program in our nation's history".[23]

Today, more than 50 million Americans live in areas that are known as "economically distressed communities", where high poverty and few opportunities for job creations exist.[24] If the idea of localization is identified with that of reversing the decline of these areas, this may become a

---

[22] *Ibid*, p. 149.

[23] Rockefeller Foundation, "Opportunity zones: Encouraging long-term investments in communities across the United States", https://www.rockefellerfoundation.org/our-work/initiatives/opportunity-zones/? Accessed 31 July 2018.

[24] Senator Cory Booker, "The American Dream Deferred", Brookings, June 2018, https://www.brookings.edu/essay/senator-booker-american-dream-deferred/? Accessed 30 June 2018.

very potent argument. Mexico will have a tough job in overcoming the combination of protectionism, reduction in the salaries gap, tax cuts and the economic revival of distressed communities.

Moreover, there is no obvious reason why the efficiencies of regionalization could not take place within US boundaries themselves, instead of in Mexico. America's seven national regions (West, South West, North West, Middle West, South East, Mid Atlantic and North East) could very well become manufacturing hubs covering their respective areas.

Although Mexico faces an uphill battle to retain the advantages of regionalization, it has no option but to keep pushing in that direction. If the US market were to decline Asia would be an insufficient option for Mexico to compensate for that loss. Though a member of TPP, the Pacific Alliance and other multilateral institutions with a Pacific Basin orientation, Mexico's labor-intensive manufacturing economy has little to offer Asia. On the other hand, its exportable commodities, even if attractive to Asia, would be insufficient to sustain the needs of its foreign trade.

Circling the Wagons

In the third place, Latin America should strengthen regional integration. During the post-World War II period, integration became a fundamental aim for Latin Americans. As a matter of fact, it was a by-product of the import substituting process. Not much thought was given during that process to the obvious fact that unequal distribution of income in Latin America engendered rather small markets, insufficient to sustain the industrialization effort. With the probable exception of larger countries with bigger domestic markets, such as Brazil or Mexico, or countries with a substantial middle class like Argentina, the rest of Latin American nations struggled with the limitations of their reduced markets. To enlarge consumer markets, economist from the Economic Commission for Latin America (ECLA), suggested economic integration.

Regional or subregional economic integration allowed for the products of each country to be sold in the others. Thus, the "inward-oriented growth", which guided the import substituting process, evolved from a national approach into a regional or a subregional one.

Unfortunately, insofar as Latin American countries were engaged in building the same type of industries, the scenario turned out to be in many cases more competitive than complementary. Integration, thus, ended up being more difficult than expected, especially so as each country showed different levels of inflation, or different costs for its manpower or different exchange rates against the dollar. However, in spite of many pitfalls, integration continued to be a fundamental goal for Latin American countries.

As a result of the Washington Consensus and the GATT Uruguay Round, Latin America opened its gates to international markets. Although regional or sub-regional integration continued, much of its relevance was lost. It couldn't be otherwise, as the true economic integration that was taking place was with the world economy. Nonetheless, a whole array of regional or subregional integration mechanisms, many of which included non-Latin Caribbean countries as well, were put in place.

The fact is that integration was not really successful, as a common report by OECD, CAF–Latin American Development Bank, the ECLA and the Caribbean, showed: "Latin American regional integration is limited: only 16% of total Latin American exports go to the regional market".[25] In other words, 84 percent of Latin American trade goes elsewhere.

Significantly, though, much of the higher value-added exports remained within the region. Let us take the example of Argentina, which in 2006 directed 69 percent of its manufacturing exports to other Latin American nations.[26] The reason for this is clear: competition from China or other Asian labor-intensive manufacturing economies is intense, deflecting Argentinian possibilities to export its manufactures outside MERCOSUR.

Indeed, in 2010, over 90 percent of Brazilian and Argentinian manufactured exports were under threat due to China's competition. But, while manufacturing exports in Mexico represented 72 percent of its total, they just amounted to 39 percent in the case of Brazil and 27

---

[25] Organización para la Cooperación y el Desarrollo Económico, CAF-Banco de Desarrollo de América Latina y Comisión Económica para la América Latina y El Caribe, *Perspectivas Económicas de América Latina 2018: Repensando las Instituciones para el Desarrollo* (París: Éditions OCDE, 2018), p. 20.

[26] Kevin P. Gallager and Roberto Porzecanski, *The Dragon in the Room* (Stanford: Stanford University Press, 2010).

percent in the case of Argentina.[27] Hence, both Brazil and Argentina exported the bulk of their commodities to China, while selling a major part of their manufactures to each other, and to their other partners within MERCOSUR.

As a result, the total amount of Latin American trade within its own region continues to be small. Nonetheless, thanks to the economic integration mechanisms in place, there exists a safe haven for products that would otherwise be difficult to export. And, it is the natural destination for higher value-added exports. Not surprisingly, faced with the need of renegotiating NAFTA with uncertain results, Mexico is in the process of increasing its exports to other Latin American countries with which it has free trade agreements.

With dark clouds in its Northern border and uncertainties in the Pacific Basin, Mexico should indeed look more carefully to the South. Latin American countries in general should pay much more attention to their own region. Not only because uncertainties are growing everywhere and circling the wagons would be advisable, but as a protection against a declining trend in US and European markets, and as a hedge against potential conflicts in Asia. Autarky, of the sort that prevailed during the import substituting process, would not make much sense when important international trade options are still open. However, much more can be done within the realm of regional integration.

Besides increasing the amount of trade between them, Latin American countries should make use of the institutional mechanisms that join them together, regionally or subregionally, to undertake common strategies and policies to cushion the impact of disruptive technologies. Through those mechanisms, Latin American governments could put in place strategic thinking teams and coordinating bodies, while linking Latin American universities, think tanks, business federations, professional associations and unions, in the common effort of preparing for the incoming tsunami of the Fourth Industrial Revolution. Economic diversification processes, the search for niches outside the boundaries of technological leaps, extensive educational reforms and the search for potential leapfrogging areas, should be included in common agendas.

---

[27] *Ibid.*

Resilience, understood as the capacity to confront big challenges and stand up again with renewed energy, becomes fundamental to face what lies ahead. A top priority shall be then to build resilience capabilities through common action and by means of the institutional integration mechanism already in place. Besides much assertiveness and creativeness, this will require great doses of coordination.

The Vanishing Upper Side of the "Smile Curve"

In the fourth place, Latin America should leave aside hopes of expanding its economic opportunities, by way of the international tradable service sector. This option, which looked as a bright light in the horizon, is vanishing away. This requires explanation.

Until not long ago, many services were difficult or impossible to supply beyond their frontiers. This changed as a result of the exponential advance in information and communication technologies. Thanks to them, distance disappeared and many hitherto domestically encapsulated services became global. Within the frame of the Information Technology Enabled Services (ITES), an immense variety of services could be provided at a distance, giving a tremendous boost to the offshoring of white-collar jobs.

This sector represented the upper side of the "smile curve", referred by Stan Shih, in the early 1990s. According to the smile-curve logic, as mentioned in Chapter Two, services related to manufacturing activities are adding more and more value, while simple manufacturing adds less and less.

The outsourcing of numerous non-core activities, traditionally performed inside the company, gave rise to the so-called "back office" phenomenon. Moreover, whenever quality could be maintained and costs reduced, the outsourcing of activities such as accounting, client management, salary payments, data processing, to mention just a few, gave way to offshoring into emerging countries.

In the words of Saurabh Mishra, Susanna Lundstrom and Rahul Anand: "The mid 1990s saw two seemingly separate but related developments. First was the revolution in information and communication technology (ICT) and, second, rapid growth in the global forces often referred to as the 3Ts — technology, transportability, and tradability — with the advent of the Internet age. Both events had a profound impact on the nature, productivity, and tradability of services. This has resulted in rapid growth of what can be called *modern impersonal progressive services...* These services differ significantly from the *traditional personal services*, which demand face-to-face interaction".[28]

In 2006, Alan Blinder, Director of the Center for Economic Policy Studies at Princeton University, asserted that impersonal services were at the brink of a gigantic revolution. These, the ones not requiring a face-to-face interaction with the customer or patient, were to be transferred in their tens of millions to emerging economies, where a gigantic pool of talent converged with lower costs.[29] In another study that Blinder co-authored with Alan B. Krueger, their conclusion was that jobs that required a high degree of education and qualification were, if anything, more offshorable than the rest.[30]

This implied a potential massive migration of impersonal services jobs to emerging economies. From accountants to software engineers, from designers to architects, from doctors to researchers, from financial consultants to lawyers, the service jobs herein involved seemed countless.

Unfortunately, when this window of opportunity was being opened for Latin America, the Fourth Industrial Revolution knocked at the door. Looking for offshored cheaper white-collar jobs no longer makes sense when algorithms can provide the same kind of services locally at even lower costs.

In their book *The Future of Professions: How Technology Will Transform the Work of Human Experts*, Richard Susskind and Daniel Susskind detail how one profession after another are being sieged by algorithms. From lawyers to doctors, from management consultants to tax and

---

[28] Saurabh Mishrah, Susanna Lundstrom and Rahul Anand, "Service sophistication and economic growth", The World Bank, South Asia Region, Policy Research Working Paper 5606 (Washington DC: March 2011), pp. 2–3.

[29] Alan S Blinder, "Offshoring: The next industrial revolution", *Foreign Affairs,* 2006, Volume 85, pp. 113–128.

[30] Alan S Blinder and Alan B Krueger, "Alternative Measures of Offshorability", National Bureau of Economic Research, Working Paper 15287, http://www.nber.org/papers/w15287. Accessed 25 July 2015.

audit experts, from architects to engineers, the list is long. Systems like "algorithmic design", "computational design", "computer aided engineering", "Public System of Digital Bookkeeping", "TurboTax", "TaxAct", "Pyramid Principle", "Kensho", "McKinsey Solutions", "Cybersettle", "Kira", "eBrevia", "ContractExpress", "Exari", "KnIT", are just a few of the emerging masters in the professional field.[31]

If the world's leader in this sector, India, is finding increasingly difficult to withstand the impact of algorithms, there is nothing for a newcomer like Latin America to look at. This window of opportunity is being shut, or to put it more bluntly, slammed in the face of the region's hopes.

Emphasizing the Fringe

In the fifth place, Latin America should emphasize the unorthodox aspects of its idiosyncrasy when dealing with the Fourth Industrial Revolution. The region excels in lateral thinking, creative approaches to difficult situations and capacity for improvisation. This will serve it well when faced to the drowning of certainties and conventional wisdom.

Latin America is an acculturated society, which by extension should entail that it has an acculturated identity. However, even if powerful influences moved in every direction as a result of its mix between Iberian, indigenous and African ethnicities, the Iberian component remained as the undisputed guiding force within the group. It was the one, indeed, that imposed upon the rest, language, religion, culture, law, family values and architectural traditions. As a result, a Roman-Christian heritage prevailed as the dominating sign of regional identity. This means that Latin Americans inhabit the Western Civilization.

Latin Americans, however, live in the periphery of the said civilization. It is clear that the dominant Roman-Christian set of values have to coexist, sometimes peacefully, sometimes wistfully and at times even belligerently, with the values of their other two cultural identities. Metaphorically speaking, even if Latin Americans are within the perimeters of Western civilization, their location lies very close to the walls that

---

[31] Richard Susskind and Daniel Susskind, *The Future of Professions: How Technology Will Transform the Work of Human Experts* (Oxford: Oxford University Press, 2015).

encapsulate this world. Their neighborhood, let us say, borders the exit gates of such civilization.

Perhaps the most outstanding feature of Latin Americans is their open mindset. This comes from their position as inhabitants of the fringe, able to move with total ease inside the perimeters of Western Civilization, while at the same time being able to cross outside and watch their walls with a critical and even surprised perspective. Few other Westerners, if any, enjoy such a flexible condition, which is a very intriguing one indeed.

As a result, Latin Americans excel in lateral thinking — not surprisingly, magical realism is a regional brand. Creativeness, imagination and improvisation come easily to them, given the variety of their roots and influences and the necessity to continuously search for a synthesis within themselves. As a result, music, literature, the movie industry, the entertainment industry or software, are among the varied niches where Latin Americans are internationally recognized.

Latin Americans equally possess adaptive and improvisational talents when confronted by rapidly evolving situations. In his classic 1962 book *The Structure of Scientific Revolutions*, Thomas Kuhn speaks of paradigms. They are a system of beliefs and assumptions that operate together to establish an integrated and unified worldview. One so convincing, that it is regarded as tantamount to reality itself. Not surprisingly, once accepted they become extremely resistant to change. Paradigm shifts are difficult, because novelty emerges only with difficulty, confronted by resistance from the *status quo* and supported by a background of expectations.[32]

Latin Americans' fluidity of mind seems particularly well suited to deal with novelty and changing landscapes. As such, they are well prepared to move ahead, improvise and adapt in the middle of traumatic changes, where paradigms are being challenged and abandoned.

Such traits should be embraced, particularly in the field of education, a fundamental area to prepare for the tsunami that the Fourth Industrial Revolution will bring with it. According to Margie Warrell, up to 40 percent of what college students learn today will become obsolete in a decade

---

[32]Thomas Kuhn, *The Structure of Scientific Revolutions* (Chicago: University of Chicago Press, 1996).

from now, when they will be working in jobs that have yet not being created.[33] Alternatively, and according to Cathy Davidson, 65 percent of the children entering into the educational system in 2011 will end up working in careers that have not been invented yet.[34]

Even if continuous education is the obvious response when confronted with such challenges, there is more to it than meets the eye. Indeed, being able to unlearn what has been learnt will turn out to be a fundamental skill. As Alvin Toffler once wrote, the illiterates of the future are going to be those that cannot learn, unlearn and relearn. As existing paradigms are going to become the bigger obstacles to speed movement, being able to leave behind which was conventional knowledge until the day before will become a necessity. Margie Warrell resorts to the example of painting a wall surface, asserting that, as painters know well, 70 percent of the work involved consists in removing the old painting.[35]

A highly advanced educational system such as that of Finland is changing its traditional educational curriculum in order to emphasize creativity and critical thinking, at the expense of the accumulation of knowledge. Knowledge, then, cannot have the same meaning as it did before, when an iPhone alone provides access to more information than can be processed in a lifetime. Critical thinking, lateral thinking, imagination, the capacity to improvise, these are the kinds of tools that are needed to learn, unlearn and relearn in rapid succession.

Always at odds with rigidity of mind, Latin Americans seem to be perfectly in tune with the triad of learning, unlearning, relearning and to have the resilience that this emerging world requires. Hence, instead of trying to adapt to conventional educational formulas, such as those represented by the OECD Program for International Students Assessment (PISA), Latin Americans should embrace its distinctiveness and shape its educational system in accordance to it. Simon Rodriguez, one of Latin America's founding fathers, whose main preoccupation was creating an educational system for the newly freed societies, always insisted on the

---

[33] Margie Warrell, "Learn, unlearn and relearn", *Forbes*, 3 February 2014.
[34] Cathy N Davidson, *Now You See It: How Technology and Brain Science will transform Schools and Business for the 21ˢᵗ Century* (London: Penguin Books, 2012).
[35] Margie Warrell, *op. cit.*

need to be original. That is, in shaping educational models in accordance to prevailing idiosyncrasy, and not importing foreign ones. The Fourth Industrial Revolution imposes upon Latin Americans the need to be original. Rodriguez' long delayed advice should be finally implemented.

Leapfrogging Around

In the sixth place, Latin America should try to take advantage of the Fourth Industrial Revolution to leapfrog in every possible area. The costs of disruptive technologies, no doubt about it, are going to be devastating for the region. Especially so in the service sector, which generates 80 percent of Latin America's urban employment.[36] The only benefit that this traumatic change could offer to the region is the possibility of jumping beyond its current limitations. Regional and national strategic thinking teams should be quick in identifying the potential areas where this can happen. Concisely, the following describes some of the options available.

Number one, localization or regionalization of factories need not be the privilege of developed economies. Latin America can also benefit from the lower costs of manufacturing and the lower entry barriers into manufacturing, brought about due to robots and 3D printing. Following the logic of localization and regionalization of factories, multinationals will want to bring their new smaller factories into the backyard of Latin American consumer markets. Why passively wait for them to do so, instead of taking advantage of this window of opportunity to reindustrialize the region in Latin America's own terms? Conversely, why let faraway Asian manufacturers inundate such markets with their products, when Latin Americans could produce locally or regionally at equally low costs?

The low costs of the new robotics, indeed, allow competing with the lowest manpower cost of labor-intensive Asian producers. This not only benefits highly developed economies, but smaller economies as well. Referring to the case of Estonia, a small country of just 1.3 million citizens which is taking full advantage of new technologies, Alec Ross

---

[36] Sistema Económico Latinoamericano (SELA), *Informe sobre el proceso de Integración Regional 2011–2012* (Caracas: Agosto, 2012).

explains: "How does a little country like Estonia compete in the same global marketplace as China, which has a labor force a little more than 1,000 times the size of its own? It takes advantage of the fact that robots enable a relatively small workforce to produce higher levels of output than would be the case in an all-human workforce. Estonia and China will never be equal competitors by sole virtue of their different size, but Estonia can compete at a level far above what its size would suggest by virtue of being cutting-edge in the field of robotics as both producer and consumer".[37]

Something similar could be said in relation to 3D printing, which substantially lowers the entry barriers into manufacturing. By collapsing design cycles, blurring the lines between prototype and product, lowering at will the volumes of production, eliminating the need to hold inventories, increasing the lifespan of products no longer limited by existing inventories and reducing the number of parts and pieces involved in manufacturing, 3D printing becomes an available manufacturing option for small companies.

The ideal situation would be the emergence, within the region, of a wide network of small and medium-sized enterprises, whereas, as direct producers, or as supply chain providers of larger producers. This would allow to bring back, under a new cover, the factories that disappeared as a result of the neoliberal ideas and the Chinese competition. With the exception of Mexico and, to a lesser extent, Brazil and Argentina, technological job displacement in the manufacturing sector will not be all that relevant, as Latin America deindustrialized a while ago.

Number two, Latin America's domain expertise in the commodities sector should take advantage of big data, in order to increase its productivity. The combination of domain expertise and algorithms can substantially improve the positioning of Latin America as a natural resource producer. While algorithms can come from many sources, domain expertise is the result of a thorough knowledge of a certain economic area.

Referring to the case of New Zealand, Alec Ross provides the context once again: "With a strong domain expertise in dairy farming, local farmers and farm-equipment manufacturers knew that if they could feed their

---

[37] Alec Ross, *op. cit.*, p. 3156/5911.

cattle more efficiently, that would increase output enough for them to export to China. What happened? Sales of beef from New Zealand to China soared 478 percent in one year (...) What happened in New Zealand can and will happen in other industries where there may not be a deep history of big data and analytics, but where there is a domain expertise in another industry that knows where and how analytics would add value. The big data applications themselves are easily scalable...".[38]

World class expertise of Brazilian beef, poultry, soya, coffee, sugar or orange producers, or of Argentinian beef and soya ones, or of Venezuelan, Mexican and Colombian oil producers or of Chile and Peru copper producers, to mention but a few, could highly benefit from access to big data analytics.

Number three, there is the possibility of benefiting from peer-to-peer networks. That is in line with what Jeremy Rifkin and other authors call the Collaborative Commons. According to Rifkin, within a capitalist economy the benefits are on the margins. Within the process of production and commercialization of a given good, each part involved obtains a benefit that justifies its participation within the process.

However, thanks to the Internet and the ubiquity of computing, the chain of participants and its cumulative profit margins can be substantially reduced and, in some areas of the economy, pushed to its minimum. This creates a drive towards the zero marginal cost and the cheapening of the final product price.

Within this context, "prosumers" (which are at the same time producers and consumers), armed with a small 3D printing machine and benefiting from descending energy costs (as solar and wind energy also tend towards zero marginal costs), are becoming able to directly market and sell their products on a global scale through the Internet. It is, as Rifkin calls it, the democratization of world economy.

In his words: "And cheap printers are being purchased by hobbyists interested in printing out their own parts and products. The consumer is beginning to give way to the prosumer as increasing numbers of people become both the producer and the consumer of their own products (...) In the Third Industrial Revolution, a small 3D printing operation anywhere

---

[38] Alec Ross, p. 2901/5911.

in the world can advertise infofactured products on the growing number of global Internet marketing sites at nearly zero marginal cost. Etsy is an eight-year-old company started by a young American social entrepreneur named Rob Kalin. Currently 900,000 small producers of goods advertise at no cost on the Etsy website. Nearly 60 million consumers per month from around the world browse the website, often interacting personally with suppliers. When the purchase is made, Etsy receives only a tiny commission from the producers. This form of laterally scaled marketing puts the small enterprise on a level playing field with the big boys, allowing to reach a worldwide user market at a fraction of the cost (...) A 3D printing process embedded in the Internet of Things infrastructure means that virtually anyone in the world can become a prosumer".[39]

As countless Latin Americans are bound to lose their jobs, as a result of the incoming disruptive technologies, it may be an option for them to become prosumers capable of taking advantage of those same technologies. It is, as Rifkin refers, the materialization of the artisanal economy once promoted by Mahatma Gandhi, made viable at a global scale, thanks to technology. Countless Latin Americans could hence become high-tech artisans.

Many other examples could follow, but what is important to outline is that Latin America will need to be pragmatic, resilient, creative and imaginative. Moreover, its members will have to close ranks and coordinate their actions. Latin Americans will have to prove to the world and to themselves that they are up to the task.

---

[39] Jeremy Riffkin, *The Zero Marginal Cost Society: The Internet of Things, The Collaborative Commons and the Eclipse of Capitalism* (New York: Pelgrave), pp. 89 and 91.

CONCLUSION

Latin America finds itself at the crossroads of the pro- and the anti-globalization forces. Having been pushed totally unprepared into globalization, by international circumstances beyond its control and mistakes of its own making, Latin America reluctantly moved into an interconnected world economy. Forced to run before it was prepared to walk, it adapted and survived.

Whatever the options might have been, Latin America found its space within the globalized economy. Were the rules of the game to change now, the region would certainly suffer. Uncertainty, however, is an even greater challenge because positioning itself and planning ahead amid conflicting signs will be extremely difficult.

Globalization emerged as a result of political intention and technological feasibility. Now, it finds itself seriously challenged for the same reasons. In both cases, political intention and technological feasibility are clearly identified with developed economies.

The political impulse to globalization came from several converging fronts, all controlled by the main Western countries. The GATT Uruguay Round, the Washington Consensus, the structural adjustment policies of the International Monetary Fund, and the birth and expansion of the World Trade Organization were some of the fundamental expressions of that political will.

Globalization, as its promoters assumed, would mainly benefit liberal democracies. In a fluid world economy, the most advanced economies — which were at the same time the most advanced liberal democracies — were supposed to become the natural winners. Fast moving nations, indeed, appeared to be the better prepared to take advantage from a rapidly moving global marketplace. Based on this conviction, Western capitals, and the trade and financial multilateral institutions under their control, built the conceptual framework of globalization, taking all the necessary steps to make it a reality.

Political intention was reinforced by technological feasibility. This feasibility was centered in the so-called supply chains and global chains of value. In accordance with the first, Western corporations went on the chase of the lowest-cost blue-collar worker, wherever she or he could be found. In pursuit of the latter, they also included the better qualified lower cost white-collar worker. The offshoring of countless manufacturing and service jobs to developing economies, particularly to China and India, was the main outcome of this process.

Supply chains are tantamount to an exponentially complex puzzle, where countless pieces, parts and components move in every possible direction. Mobilizing, monitoring and controlling this process requires huge technological advances in the fields of information, communication and transport.

Within global chains of value, services became the most valuable activity, thus introducing new technological complexities into it. Herein involved is the full range of activities required to bring a product from its conception and design to its final marketing, distribution and attached services to the buyer. Only a highly sophisticated technology is capable of integrating all these disparate elements at a global scale. Not surprisingly, the coining of the expression "death of distance" is used to describe this new reality.

However, political intention has reversed course, and it is now moving in the opposite direction. The massive contraction of employments and the dramatic shrinking of middle classes within developed economies ignited this process. Unintendedly, countries that benefited from the offshoring of economic activities were empowered and incredibly strengthened, especially China. As a consequence, Western economies became embattled fortresses.

As Charles Kupchan, clearly explains it: "A crisis of governability has beset the Western world. It is no accident that the United States, Europe and Japan are simultaneously experiencing political breakdown; globalization is producing a widening gap between what electorates are asking of their governments and what those governments can deliver... Globalization was supposed to have played to the advantage of liberal societies, which were presumably best suited to capitalize on the fast and fluid global market-place. But instead, for the better part of two decades, middle-class wages in the world's leading democracies have been stagnant and economic inequality is rising sharply. The plight of the West middle class is the consequence primarily of the integration into global markets of billions of low-wage workers from developing economies".[1]

Massive immigration into developed countries, or the perceived threat of it, compounded the above situation. Liberal democracies within the Western world are besieged by a powerful populist movement. Piece by piece, the traditional strongholds of liberal democracy, including Washington itself, are falling into the hands of populism and its extreme views. As a result, globalization is also under siege, as protectionism, economic nationalism, rejection of economic multilateralism and anti-EU attitudes express the emerging political credo.

Technological feasibility, on its side, makes possible the onshoring of economic activities to the Western world, proclaimed as an aim by political intention. The populists, though, seem unwilling to recognize or confront the fact that within developed economies, the Fourth Industrial Revolution is going to harm even further the groups already affected by globalization. However, populism and technological leaps factually converge in providing the impulse for the onshoring of economic activities.

As things stand, the convergence and feedback of digital technology and robotics, additive manufacturing, nanotechnology, bioengineering and genomics, the Internet of things and new energy technologies, among other leaps, are leading to the obsolescence of supply chains and global chains of value. Why, indeed, go manufacturing or looking for service providers afar, when technology allows for cheaper options at home?

Does this mean that the old political intention and technological feasibility have been trumped by new ones? Whatever the answer to this question, it will not be straightforward, as this is not a black and white

---

[1] Charles Kupchan, "Refunding good governance," *The New York Times*, 19 December 2011.

dichotomy, where newcomers impose their rules. Gray prevails in this picture, with forces on both sides battling over with uncertain outcome. Inconsistencies on both sides, and the need of a longer period of time for the full materialization of the Fourth Industrial Revolution, complicate things even more.

What kind of route map can Latin America follow amid this confusing situation? There seems to be no alternative to playing in both directions, with the aim of minimizing costs and maximizing opportunities. Neither closing ranks with globalization, neither choosing the opposite trend. Within this highly fluid situation, pragmatism, resilience, creativeness, imagination and the joining together of Latin American forces will have to guide the region's actions in the foreseeable future.

BIBLIOGRAPHY

Alan B Krueger, "Offshoring: The next industrial revolution", *Foreign Affairs*, 2006, Volume 85, pp. 113–128.

Alan S Blinder, "Offshoring: The next industrial revolution", *Foreign Affairs*, 2006, Volume 85, pp. 113–128.

Alan S Blinder and Alan B Krueger, "Alternative measures of offshorability", National Bureau of Economic Research, Working Paper 15287 (August 2015). http://www.nber.org/papers/w15287. Accessed 25 July 2015.

Alec Ross, *The Industries of the Future* (New York: Simon & Schuster, 2017).

Alejandro Izquierdo and Ernesto Talvi, coord., *One Region, Two Speeds?* (Washington D.C.: Inter-American Development Bank, 2011).

Alfredo Toro Hardy, *The Age of Villages: The Small Village Vs. The Global Village* (Bogotá: Villegas Editores, 2002).

Alfredo Toro Hardy, *Tiene Futuro América Latina?* (Bogotá: Villegas Editores, 2004).

Alfredo Toro Hardy, *Hegemonía e Imperio* (Bogotá: Villegas Editores, 2007).

Alfredo Toro Hardy, *The World Turned Upside Down: The Complex Partnership between China and Latin America* (New Jersey: World Scientific, 2013).

Alfredo Toro Hardy, *Understanding Latin America: A Decoding Guide* (New Jersey: World Scientific, 2017).

Alvin Toffler, *El Cambio de Poder* (Barcelona: Plaza y Janés Editores, 1991).

Andre Gunder Frank, "The world economic system in Asia before European hegemony", *The Historian*, 1994, Volume 56, Issue 2, pp. 259–276.

Anil K Gupta and Haiyan Wang, *Getting China and India Right* (San Francisco: Jossey-Bass, 2009).

Arianna Huffington, *Third World America* (New York: Crown Publishers, 2010).

Arthur W Brian, "Where is technology taking the economy", McKinsey Quarterly, October 2017, https://www.mckinsey.com/business-functions/mckinsey-analytics/our-insights/where-is-technology-taking-the-economy. Accessed 15 May 2018.

Asian Development Bank Institute, "2030: Toward a borderless economic community", 2014, https://www.adb.org/sites/default/files/publication/159312/adbi-asean-2030-borderless-economic-community.pdf. Accessed 14 June 2018.

Atif Mian and Amir Sufi, *House of Debt* (Chicago: The University of Chicago Press, 2014).

Ben Simpfendorfer, *The New Silk Road* (New York: Pelgrave Macmillan, 2011).

Bernardo Kosacoff and Sebastián Campanario, *La Revalorizacion de las Materias Primas y sus Efectos en América Latina* (Santiago de Chile: CEPAL, 2007).

Bernie Sanders, *Our Revolution: A Future to Believe In* (London: Profile Books, 2017).

Branko Milanovic, *Global Inequality: A New Approach for the Age of Globalization* (Cambridge, MA: The Belknap Press of Harvard University Press, 2016).

C. Fred Bergsten, "The dollar and the deficits", *Foreign Affairs*, 2009, Volume 88, pp. 20–38.

Carl Benedikt Frey and E. Osborne Michael, "The future of employment: How susceptible are jobs to computerization", Oxford University, 17 September 2013, http://www.oxfordmartin.ox.ac.uk/downloads/academic/The_Future_of_Employment.pdf. Accessed 25 July 2016.

Cathy Davison, *Now You See It: How Technology and Brain Science will Transform Schools and Business for the 21ˢᵗ Century* (London: Penguin Books, 2012).

Claudio Loser, *The impact of globalization on Latin America task force* (Miami: University of Miami Center for Hemispheric Policy, 2012).

Comisión Económica para América Latina y El Caribe, *La República Popular China y América Latina y el Caribe: Diálogo y Cooperación ante los Nuevos Desafíos de la Economía Mundial* (Santiago de Chile: Junio, 2012).

Dambisa Moyo, *How the West was Lost* (London: Allen Lane, 2011).

Dan Prud'homme and Max Von Zedtwitz, "The changing face of innovation in China", *MIT Sloan Management Review*, 2018, Volume 59, Issue 4, pp. 24–31.

Daniel Quinn Mills and Rosefielde Steven, *The Trump Phenomenon and the Future of US Foreign Policy* (New Jersey: World Scientific, 2016).

Daniel W Drezner, "The new new world order", *Foreign Affairs*, 2007, Volume 86, pp. 3–20.

Daniel Yergin and Joseph Stanislaw, *The Commanding Heights* (New York: Simon & Schuster, 1998).

David Forgacs, *Antonio Gramsci Reader* (London: Lawrence & Wishart, 2002).

David Held and Anthony McGrew (eds.), *The Global Transformations Reader* (Cambridge: Polity Press, 2000).

Economic Commission for Latin America and the Caribbean, *Economic Relations between Latin America and the Caribbean and the Republic of Korea: Advances and Opportunities* (Santiago de Chile: April 2015).

Edward Luce, *Time to Start Thinking: America and the Spectre of Decline* (London: Little, Brown, 2012).

Edward Luce, *The Retreat of Western Liberalism* (London: Little, Brown, 2017).

Emily Sinnot, John Nash and Augusto de la Torre, *Natural Resources in Latin America and the Caribbean: Beyond Booms and Busts?* (Washington D.C.: The World Bank, 2010).

Emir Sader, Ivana Jinkings, *et al.*, coord., *Latinoamérica: Enciclopedia Contemporánea de América Latina y El Caribe* (Madrid: Clacso-Ediciones AKAL, S.A.,2009).

Erik Brynjolfsson and Andrew McAffe, *Race against the Machines: How Digital Revolution is Accelerating Innovation, Driving Productivity, and Irreversibly Transforming Employment and the Economy* (Lexington Mass.: Digital Frontier Press, 2011).

Erik Brynjolfsson and Andrew McAffe, *The Second Machine Age* (New York: W.W. Norton & Company, 2014).

Erin Blackwell, Tony Gambell, *et al.*, "The great remake: Manufacturing for modern times", McKinsey & Company. https://www.mckinsey.com/business-functions/operations/our-insights/the-great-remake-manufacturing-for-modern-times. Accessed 19 June 2018.

Fareed Zakaria, *The Post-American World and the Rise of the Rest* (London: Penguin Books, 2009).

Ferguson Niall, *Empire: How Britain Made the Modern World* (London: Penguin Books, 2004).

Finbarr Livesey, *From Global to Local: The Making of Things and the End of Globalization* (New York: Pantheon Books, 2017).

Food and Agriculture Organization, "How to feed the world in 2050", Presentation at the World Summit of Food Security in Rome, 16–19 November, http://www.fao.org/fileadmin/templates/wsfs/docs/expert_paper/How_to_Feed_the_World_in_2050.pdf. Accessed 18 October 2012.

Foreign and Commonwealth Office, "ASEAN 2030: Economic Opportunities and Challenges". London, October 2012, https://epas.secure.europarl.europa.eu/orbis/sites/default/files/generated/document/en/ASEAN%202030.pdf. Accessed 14 June 2018.

Frances Cairncross, *The Death of Distance* (Cambridge, MA: Harvard Business School Press, 1997).

Gordon Brown, *Beyond the Crash: Overcoming the First Crisis of Globalisation* (London: Simon & Schuster, 2010).

Greg Grandin, *Empire's Workshop: Latin America, the United States and the Rise of the New Imperialism* (New York: Metropolitan Books, 2006).

Homi Kharas, "The emerging middle class in developing countries", OECD, February 2010, http://www.oecd.org/dev/44457738.pdf. Accessed 3 January 2017.

Hugh White, *The China Choice: Why America should Share Power* (Oxford: Oxford University Press, 2013).

Ian Bremmer, *Every Nation for Itself: Winners and Losers in a G-Zero World* (New York: Portfolio, 2012).

Inter-American Development Bank, *A Virtuous Cycle of Integration: The Past, Present, and Future of Japan-Latin American and the Caribbean Relations* (Washington D.C.: IADB, 2016).

International Renewable Energy Agency, "The power to change: Solar and wind cost reduction potential to 2025", http://www.irena.org/DocumentDownloads/Publications/IRENA_Power_to_Change_2016.pdf. Accessed 29 February 2018.

James Kynge, *China Shakes the World* (London: Phoenix, 2006).

James Manyika, "Technology, jobs, and the future of work", McKinsey Global Institute, Executive Briefing, May 2017. https://www.mckinsey.com/featured-insights/employment-and-growth/technology-jobs-and-the-future-of-work. Accessed 23 April 2018.

Jane Meyer, *Dark Money: How a Secretive Group of Billionaires is Trying to Buy Political Control in the US* (New York: Doubleday, 2016).

Jeremy Riffkin, *The Zero Marginal Cost Society: The Internet of Things, the Collaborative Commons, and the Eclipse of Capitalism* (New York: Pelgrave, 2014).

Joan E Spero and Jeffrey A Hart, *The Politics of International Economic Relations* (Belmont, CA: Thompson/Wadswoth, 2003).

John B Judis, *The Populist Explosion: How the Great Recession Transformed American and European Politics* (New York: Columbia Global Reports, 2016).

John Naisbitt and Doris Naisbitt, *China's Megatrends* (New York: Harper Business, 2010).

Joseph Stiglitz, *Globalization and its Discontents* (London: W.W. Norton & Company, 2002).

Joseph Stiglitz, *Making Globalization Work* (London: Allen Lane, 2006).

Joseph Stiglitz, *Freefall: Free Markets and the Sinking of the Global Economy* (London: Penguin Books, 2015).

K. Eric Drexler, *Radical Abundance: How Revolution in Nanotechnology Will Change Civilization* (New York: Public Affairs, 2013).

Kevin Kelly, *The Inevitable: Understanding the 12 Technological Forces That Will Shape our* Future (London: Penguin Books, 2016).

Kevin P Gallager and Roberto Porzecanski, *The Dragon in the Room* (Stanford: Stanford University Press, 2010).

Kishore Mahbubani, *The New Asian Hemisphere: The Irresistible Shift of Global Power to the East* (New York: Public Affairs, 2008).

Klaus Schwab, *The Fourth Industrial Revolution* (London: Portfolio Penguin, 2017).

Leia Parker, "Google, singularity university visionary Ray Kurzweil on the amazing future he sees", *Silicon Valley Business Journal*, 6 September 2016, http://www.bizjournals.com/sanjose/news/2016/09/06/exclusive-google-singularity-visionary-ray.html. Accessed 25 October 2017.

Mark Z Delucchi, Mark Z Jacobson, , Zack A F Bauer, *et al.*, "100% clean and renewable wind, water, and sunlight all-sector energy roadmaps for 139 countries of the world", Joule, 6 September 2017, https://web.stanford.edu/group/efmh/jacobson/Articles/I/CountriesWWS.pdf. Accessed 19 May 2018.

Martin Ford, *Rise of the Robots: Technology and the Threat of a Jobless Future* (New York: Basic Books, 2015).

Martin Jacques, *When China Rules the World* (London: Allen Lane, 2009).

Mauricio Mesquita Moreira, Coordinator, *India: Latin America's Next Big Thing?* (Washington D.C.: Inter-American Development Bank, 2010).

McKinsey Global Institute, "Disruptive technologies: Advances that will transform life, business, and the global economy", May 2013, https://www.mckinsey.com/business-functions/digital-mckinsey/our-insights/disruptive-technologies. Accessed 19 May 2018.

McKinsey Quarterly, "Where is technology taking the economy?", https://www.mckinsey.com/business-functions/mckinsey-analytics/our-insights/where-is-technology-taking-the-economy. Accessed 15 May 2018.

Michel Albert, *Capitalisme contre Capitalisme* (París: Editions de Seuil, 1991).

Noreena Hertz, *The Silent Takeover* (London: William Heinemann, 2011).

OECD, "Looking to 2060: Long-term global growth prospects", OECD Economic Policy Papers, No. 03, February, http://www.oecd.org/eco/outlook/2060%20policy%20paper%20final.pdf. Accessed 25 February 2017.

Organización para la Cooperación y el Desarrollo Económico, CAF-Banco de Desarrollo de América Latina y Comisión Económica para la América Latina y El Caribe, *Perspectivas Económicas de América Latina 2018: Repensando las Instituciones para el Desarrollo* (París: Éditions OCDE, 2015).

Organization of Economic Cooperation and Development, "Looking to 2060: Long-term global growth prospects". Paris: OECD Economic Policy Papers, N. 03, 2012.

R. Evan Ellis, *Indian and Chinese Engagement in Latin America and the Caribbean: A Comparative Assessment* (Washington D.C.: Strategic Studies Institute and U.S. Army War College Press, 2017).

Richard Baldwin, *The Great Convergence: Information Technology and the New Globalization* (Cambridge, Mass.: The Belknap Press of Harvard University Press, 2016).

Richard Susskind and Daniel Susskind, *The Future of Professions: How Technology Will Transform the Work of Human Experts* (Oxford: Oxford University Press, 2015).

Rick Smith and Mitch Free, *The Great Disruption: Competing and Surviving in the Second Wave of the Industrial Revolution* (New York: Thomas Dunne Books/St. Martin's Press, 2016).

Riordan Roett and Guadalupe Paz (eds.), *Latin America and the Asian Giants: Evolving Ties with China and India* (Washington D.C.: Brookings Institution Press, 2016).

Robert D Kaplan, *Asia's Cauldron: The South China Sea and the End of a Stable Pacific* (New York: Random House, 2014).

Robert Kagan, *The Jungle Grows Back: America and Our Imperiled World* (New York: Knopf Publishing Group, 2018).

Robert L Rohthstein, *Global Bargaining: UNCTAD and the Quest for a New International Economic Order* (Princeton: Princeton University Press, 1979).

Robyn Meredith, *The Elephant and the Dragon* (New York, W.W. Norton & Company, 2007).

Samuel P Hungtinton, *¿Quiénes Somos? Los Desafíos de la Identidad Nacional Estadounidense* (Barcelona: Paidós, 2004).

Saskia Sassen, "The global city: Introducing a concept", *Brown Journal of World Affairs*, 2005, Volume XI, Issue 2, pp. 27–43.

Saurabh Mishrah, Lundstrom Susanna and Rahul Anand, "Service sophistication and economic growth", The World Bank South Asia Region Policy Research, Working Paper 5606 (March 2011), Washington D.C.: The World Bank.

Senator Cory Booker, "The American dream deferred", Brookings, June 2018, https://www.brookings.edu/essay/senator-booker-american-dream-deferred/?. Accessed 30 June 2018.

Sergio Bitar, *Global Trends and the Future of Latin America: Why and How Latin America Should Think About the Future* (Washington D.C.: Inter-American Dialogue, 2013).

Shell Group of Companies, *Peoples and Connections: Global Scenarios for 2020* (London: Shell Editions, 2002).

Sistema Económico Latinoamericano, *Informe sobre el Proceso de Integración Regional 2011–2012* (Caracas: Agosto, 2012).

Sistema Económico Latinoamericano, *Las relaciones entre China y América Latina y El Caribe en la actual coyuntura económica mundial* (Caracas: Venezuela, 2012).

Stephen D King, *Grave New World: The End of Globalization and the Return to History* (New Haven: Yale University Press, 2017).

T. N. Srinivasan, *Growth, Sustainability, and India's Economic Reforms* (Oxford: Oxford University Press, 2011).

T. X. Hames, "The end of globalization? The international security implications", War on the Rocks, 2 August 2016, https://warontherocks.com/2016/08/the-end-of-globalization-the-international-security-implications/. Accessed 13 February 2017.

T. X. Hames, "Will technological convergence reverse globalization", Strategic Forum, National Defense University, July 2016, http://ndupress.ndu.edu/Portals/68/Documents/stratforum/SF-297.pdf. Accessed 18 August 2017.

The London School of Economics and Political Sciences, "Globalisation and nationalism: Squaring the circle in Chinese international relations theory", LSE Research Online, March 2009, http://eprints.lse.ac.uk/23038/1/Globalisation_and_nationalism%28LSERO%29.pdf. Accessed 18 September 2016.

Thomas Kuhn, *The Structure of Scientific Revolutions* (Chicago: University of Chicago Press, 1996).

Thomas L Friedman, *The World is Flat: A Brief History of the Twenty First Century* (London: Penguin Books, 2006).

Tim Marshall, *Prisoners of Geography: The Maps that Tell You Everything You Need to Know About Global Politics* (London: Elliot and Thompson Limited, 2016).

Tulio Halperin Donghi, *História Contemporánea de América Latina* (Buenos Aires: Alianza Editorial, 1997).

Victor Bulmer-Thomas, *The Economic History of Latin America since Independence* (Cambridge: Cambridge University Press, 2003).

Victor Bulmer-Thomas, John H Coastworth and Roberto Cortes Conde, *The Cambridge Economic History of Latin America, Volume II: The Long Twentieth Century* (Cambridge: Cambridge University Press, 2006).

Victor Mayer Schoenmberg and Kenneth Cukier, *Big Data: A Revolution That Will Transform How We Live, Work and Think* (London: John Murray, 2013).

Will Hutton and Anthony Giddens (eds.), *Global Capitalism* (New York: New York Press, 2000).

World Bank, *Latin America and the Caribbean's Long-Term Growth: Made in China?* (Washington D. C.: September 2011).

Yuval Noah Harari, *Homo Deus: A Brief History of Tomorrow* (New York: Harper Collins, 2017).

Zachary Karabell, *Superfusion: How China and America Became One Economy and Why the World's Prosperity Depends on It* (New York: Simon & Schuster, 2009).

INDEX

Printed in the United States
By Bookmasters